EMMAUS

DENIS McBRIDE

Emmaus

THE
GRACIOUS VISIT
OF GOD
ACCORDING
TO LUKE

DOMINICAN PUBLICATIONS

First published (1991)
and this edition published (2003) by
Dominican Publications
42 Parnell Square
Dublin 1

ISBN 1-871552-90-7

Cover design by
David Cooke

Printed in the Republic of Ireland by
Betaprint Ltd
Dublin 17

Acknowledgements
Scriptural quotations are from the the Jerusalem Bible
© Darton, Longman and Todd Ltd, and,
where noted RSV, from the Revised Standard Version of the Bible,
copyrighted 1946, 1952, © 1971, 1973.

The front cover painting is *Supper, 1963*, by George Tooker,
egg tempera on gesso panel, 20 x 24 inches. Private Collection.
Reproduced by courtesy of DC Moore Gallery, New York City

To the memory of
VERONICA JAMES CRIMMINS
a great companion
who died out of season

Contents

Preface

LUKE IS the only evangelist to tell the story of Emmaus: how a stranger joined two forlorn travellers on the road from Jerusalem; how he listened to them tell of the death of Jesus of Nazareth as the death of Israel's hopes; how he responded to their story by opening the Scriptures and revealing to them the mystery of the passion; how he accepted their offer of hospitality to stay with them; how he revealed himself as the risen Lord in the breaking of the bread. The story of the mysterious visitor, whose revealing word and presence gives hope to his disappointed followers, has appealed to many Christians as a moving summary of the Gospel. It takes account of how Jesus finds people and how he leaves them, how he addresses their pain and confusion with his own story of God's purpose in life and in death.

As the geographical journey moves from Jerusalem to Jerusalem, the inward journey moves from desolation to hope, from blindness to recognition, from bewilderment to understanding, from death to life. In the Emmaus account the real destination of the disciples is understanding that the death and resurrection of Jesus mark the fulfilment of the hope of Israel.

Luke writes of the way to Emmaus as a journey through Scripture to meet the risen Christ. The structure of this book follows the pattern of that story: it journeys through Scripture to understand how Luke writes the story of Jesus as a story which emerges from the story of Israel and fulfils its ancient hopes. As Emmaus stands at the turning-point of the Gospel and Acts, we will move beyond Emmaus to see how Luke writes the story of the early Church. It emerges as a corporate witness from the revealed word of the risen Jesus and the gift of the Holy Spirit, and the word of salvation is proclaimed from Jerusalem to the ends of the earth.

Throughout his writing Luke gives a sense of continuity to the revelation of salvation, from its beginnings in Israel, through its fulfilment in the mission of Jesus, to its proclamation to the Gentiles. This book aims to show how Luke gives substance to that continuity by adopting two Old Testament concepts, the visit of God and the word of God, concepts which he brings into the Gospel and Acts. These prove to be major links which fasten the story of Israel to the story of Jesus, and the story of Jesus to the life of the apostolic and post-apostolic Church.

In his visit and in his word God is seen to take the initiative in letting his presence be known and his thoughts be revealed. If the revelation of salvation celebrates what God does and says, it also says in the same breath how this is understood and interpreted in the light of human experience. The offer of God must be addressed to the world of the particular if it is to give shape to the human story; his visit and word are first experienced before their saving significance is proclaimed to others. We shall see how Luke celebrates the visit and the word of God in the person of Jesus and how the evangelist reserves the authoritative interpretation of all this to the risen Jesus himself.

For Luke it is only when the risen Jesus visits his disciples and discloses the meaning of what has happened that the beginning of an Easter faith is possible. That Easter experience is only interpreted to others as a word of salvation when the disciples are empowered to witness by the Spirit. Further, the dramatic move to accept Gentiles into the Church without demanding total obedience to the Law is recounted as an inspired decision by Peter which emerges from the visit of God and which is supported, in turn, by the word of God in Scripture. Luke roots the growth of the Gentile Church in post-apostolic times in the act of the same God who first chose Israel from among the nations. Thus he maintains the continuity of the revelation of salvation from the time of its beginning to his own era.

This book has grown out of teaching courses on Luke to priests, religious and lay people, and I would like to acknowledge their encouragement and critical support.

Introduction

DELIVERING THE GOODS

I WAS travelling on the London Underground from Charing Cross to Euston station, mid-morning. It was quieter than I expected and there was plenty room for my bulky suitcase. At Leicester Square a young couple came trundling in, carrying mountains of bags and parcels: I thought they must have been doing early Christmas shopping for their street. They were arguing.

She sits next to me in a heap of parcels, looking like an up-market bag lady. She turns to her companion and says: 'That's all very well for you to say, but you did promise.'

He says, 'Give over, you know I'll do it.'

She says, pointing to the bags: 'Yeah, look at all this stuff, we don't need half of it. And all I want is one thing from you. When do I get the wedding ring?'

He looks up and sees that they have captured the interest of everyone else in the carriage. Newspapers and books have been abandoned in favour of this real-life drama.

He says: 'Look, I promise, OK. January or February, I'll surprise you. Promise. Just trust me, you'll see.'

She says: 'Promises, promises, promises! That's all I ever get from you. I'm worn out with promises.'

He says: 'Oh, give over.'

They sit in silence. Everyone in the carriage goes back to where they left off in their newspapers and books. The couple stare down at their assembly of shopping. I look too: I don't know what's in all the bags, but I know what small article is not. Euston Station comes and my two fellow travellers are still quiet. I get out, wondering if she will be surprised by his promise in the coming year.

PROMISES

He made her a promise, so he put himself in debt, inviting his girlfriend to trust in him until the day he delivers on his word. Sometimes we promise too much too quickly and we soon learn that we cannot deliver the goods. As the Roman poet Ovid observed two thousand years ago, when it comes to promises we can all be millionaires. On the other hand, we are sometimes so doubtful of our own capacity to keep promises that we hesitate to make any.

To believe a promise is an act of trust in the person who makes it; it's to live in expectation, holding fast to someone's word. And when promises are fulfilled there is a deepening of the original trust. If people have a distinctly wobbly track record on keeping their word, however, we tend to be cautious about their sparkling new promises. We know some people will promise you anything, but their word is as valuable as Monopoly money, good only for games. These promises we tend to file under 'Long Shots' and forget them.

When the four evangelists come to write their Gospels, each of them shows the same care in connecting the new story of Jesus back to the story of Israel or beyond. They all knew Jesus was a Jew, that his first disciples were Jews, and that Christianity claimed to be the fulfilment of the Hebrew scriptures. The past of the movement was Jewish, so the new story of Jesus had somehow to be connected to the promise of that past or to a time beyond it.

Mark opens his Gospel by building a bridge back to the Jewish scriptures through the prophecy of Isaiah, eighth century BC. That prophecy is secured in the present tense in the person and ministry of John the Baptist. The breathless pace of Mark's Gospel begins in the midst of ongoing drama – as ancient promises are fulfilled, as John heralds an unknown follower, and as Jesus appears from obscurity to begin his prophetic mission.

Matthew begins his Gospel by announcing the identity of Jesus as 'son of David, son of Abraham.' He proceeds at a leisurely pace with Abraham, nineteenth century BC, and anchors the identity of Jesus in the Jewish tradition as he catalogues the names of Jesus' weird and wonderful ancestors. God's curious choices include cheats, prostitutes, thieves, adulterers, and murderers – illustrating through biography that God's salvation comes through the foolish and the fragile, the crooked and the cracked. All these people are, unknowingly, heading for one name, the promised Jesus. Five times in his infancy narrative Matthew sounds the note that what is happening is to fulfil ancient promises (1:22; 2:5; 2:15; 2:17; 2:23).

Luke builds his bridge back to the Hebrew scriptures through introducing us to four ancient characters: Zechariah, Elizabeth, Simeon, and Anna. They are people who hunger for an ancient word to be fulfilled, for a promise to be kept. While their story is focused in sacred space, in the Temple, the story of Jesus transpires in secular space, first in the village of Nazareth and then in the town of Bethlehem. Later, in his genealogy, Luke presses the ancestry of Jesus back beyond the reaches of the Jewish story to the beginning of the human story in Adam, son of God. This original human connection is grounded in the belief that Jesus is not only the kept promise of Israel but a light for all nations.

John's Gospel begins not with an adult Jesus by the River Jordan or a newborn baby in Bethlehem, but before the beginning of the world. For John, the details of Jesus' earthly beginnings are irrelevant – no mother is introduced, no time is recorded, no place is noted, no witnesses are named – because his true origin is beyond the cosmos: 'In the beginning was the Word, and the Word was with God, and the Word was God.' John goes back beyond the prophetic story and the Jewish story and the human story, to rework Genesis and anchor the beginning of the Jesus story in the originality of God. From the tenor of John's Gospel you can see that it is clearly written at a time of dispute with the synagogue: 'the Jews had already agreed to expel from the synagogue anyone who should acknowledge Jesus as the Christ.' (Jn 9:22) Thus, unlike the other evangelists, John celebrates Jesus' origin as one that is far beyond the Jewish story.

What is typical of Luke's narrative is his emphasis on the way that events unfold in accordance with the promises of God. In this Luke was not original: this interpretative technique is familiar from the Old Testament where past history is seen as disclosing God's purpose, while future history is the object of prophecy. Luke maintains this dynamic way of looking at events, setting the stage of his Gospel with the motive that his narrative will concern 'the events that have come to fulfilment among us.' (Lk 1:1) This motif is repeated, especially at key moments in his narrative. Both the birth of John the Baptist and Jesus are seen to be the fulfilment of the promises of God expressed in scripture. The opening scene of Jesus' ministry in the synagogue in Nazareth is capped by the words: 'Today this scripture has been fulfilled in your hearing.' (Luke 4:21) So too the central story of Jesus' passion, death and resurrection is seen as one which is already coded in prophecy. The risen Jesus is seen to decipher the ancient promises as he explains to the disciples of Emmaus: 'Then, beginning with Moses and all the prophets, he interpreted to them the things about himself in all the scriptures.' (Lk 24:27)

LOOKING AT THE PRESENT AS A PLACE OF NO PROMISE

The theological practice of interpreting key events as fulfilling God's promises is precisely what the two disciples cannot manage as they reflect on recent happenings on the road to Emmaus. They remain stuck inside the immediacy of what has just occurred, without appealing to a larger story, one that can enable them to interpret events in a new light. Although they have an extensive frame of reference in the scriptures to help them make sense of what has happened, they do not employ it, remaining caught in the events surrounding the violent death of Jesus.

The story of Emmaus is unique in the New Testament because it is the only narrative that allows us to listen to how disciples of Jesus interpreted his death immediately following the event. We meet two disciples heading away from Jerusalem, the place that is identified as the graveyard of their hopes. Although we cannot identify the village of Emmaus, it is the road that is important, one of the famous lost roads of history. There is no indication that Cleopas and his companion lived there – perhaps Emmaus was the first night's stop for those travelling north to Galilee – for it seems likely that the two disciples, like the others, were from Galilee. In Mark's resurrection narrative the young man's annunciation to the women at the tomb includes the instruction: 'But go, tell his disciples and Peter that he is going ahead of you to Galilee' (Mk 16:7). With such a catastrophic loss behind them, it seems likely that the two disciples are heading home to Galilee, where, no doubt, they will try to pick up the old rhythm of the lives they led before they met Jesus.

One of the disciples is identified as Cleopas. The further mention of Clopas in John 19:25 seems to indicate that it was a familiar name, also suggesting that his companion was his wife, Mary. According to Eusebius, quoting Hegesippus, (*Historia Ecclesiastica* 3, 11) Cleopas was the uncle of Jesus and his brother James. Cleopas is identified as the brother of Joseph and the father of Simeon, who succeeded James in the leadership of the Jerusalem church – thus keeping leadership within Jesus' own family. Simeon would, of course, have been Luke's contemporary.

Whatever about the identities of the two disciples, the narrative focuses on their condition as two people who are overcome by their own loss, frankly bewildered by the violent turn of events that have recently happened. They speak out of their experience of Jesus: that he proved himself a prophet mighty in deed and word in the sight of God and the people. They go on to speak of their expectation of Jesus: they had hopes that he would be the one to set Israel free.

We listen to Cleopas as he puts together both the disciples' experience of Jesus and their expectation of him. This association makes sense, since we not only have experience of people, but our positive experience of others leads us to have expectations of them. If having experience of people means that we learn about them over time, our expectations of them are deepened the more positive our experience is; our expectations are nourished by respect and familiarity, because we are given additional ground to hope through what we see in their behaviour.

Cleopas shares the sad new that he and his companion's expectation about Jesus are now well and truly ended: 'But we had hoped that he was the one to redeem Israel.' (24:21) Their hopes are in the past perfect tense: it is not only the body of Jesus that has been buried, but their hope in Jesus has been buried as well. Who they were was tied to who they believed he was; they were disciples because he was their master and teacher. Their governing self-identity as disciples of Jesus has been shattered; they are identified by what they were, now literally a 'has been'. Their situation is caught in the lines:

> All that memory loves the most
> was once our only hope to be.

>   And all that hope adored and lost
>   has melted into memory.

Experience means learning through direct personal contact with people and things, and new experiences or new information can challenge people to think again. The disciples are forced by their new experience of the death of Jesus not only to reassess Jesus but also to reassess themselves. Now they are former disciples of a dead prophet with nowhere to go but away from Jerusalem, the place where everything went wrong. And by any account, that is not a great self-identity to be carrying on any road.

The phrase, 'Oh we had great hopes for him,' is one that we hear at the funerals of those who have died out of season. Parents, relatives and friends share the sad recognition that an untimely death also means that they have to give up any hopes they cherished for the dead person. Death and hope are not good conversational partners.

Cleopas explains the reason for abandoning hope in Jesus: 'Our chief priests and leaders handed him over to be condemned to death and crucified him.' (24:20) Jesus did not die of old age or natural causes or by accident; rather, his death was an execution organised by the hierarchy and effected by the civil authority. It was not done secretly at night but in public at high noon, in full view of everyone; what happened did not take place in a corner (Acts 26:26). In fact so public that Cleopas earlier wondered about his fellow traveller: 'Are you the only stranger in Jerusalem who does not know the things that have taken place there in these days?' (24:18) The death sentence, authorized and executed by the highest authorities, seems to proclaim with finality the official legal estimation of Jesus as a criminal, the one the disciples knew as the prophet mighty in deed and word. Two contrary estimates collide: the official one seems to be the decisive one.

The disciples look on the death of Jesus, as many probably did, as the end of a promising calling, not the fulfilment of a promised one. Their hope that Jesus would prove to be the awaited messiah is now cancelled by their experience of what has happened to him. In that sense, one has to acknowledge the disciples' level-headedness: they do not hold fast to their hopes when their experience tells them otherwise. Their expectations have been reluctantly laid down in the tomb, beside the dead body Jesus.

Our expectations are always modified in the light of our experience. If expectations about others or situations mostly grow out of our experience, our experience tends to have the final say. If we know that someone is dead, why would we bother placing our hope in him? Expectations are deepened, modified or cancelled in the light of what we learn over time. Only fools or saints hold fast to their hopes when hard reality tells them the ground of their hope has collapsed. I say saints because there is another perspective. Vaclav Havel, former President of the Czech Republic and a political prisoner for years, was asked in an interview: 'Do you see a grain of hope anywhere?' He replied:

> I should probably say first that the kind of hope I often think about (especially in situations that are particularly hopeless, such as prison) I understand above all as a state of mind, not a state of the world. Either we have hope within us or we don't; it is a dimension of the soul, and it's not essentially dependant on some particular observation of the world or estimate of the situation.
>
> Hope is not prognostication. It is an orientation of the spirit, an orientation of the heart; it transcends the world that is immediately experienced, and is anchored somewhere beyond its horizons.
>
> I think the deepest and most important form of hope, the only one that can keep us above the water, and the only true source of the breathtaking dimension of the human spirit and its efforts, is something we get, as it were, from 'elsewhere'. [1]

That observation is a profound one: hope is not essentially dependent on some particular observation of the world or estimate of the situation. Hope is not prognostication; prognosis means literally 'to know before', like a doctor who forecasts a patient's future in the light of the symptoms he sees. Prognostication is based on the evidence; hope comes from elsewhere.

The disciples are stuck in the present as a place they see as profoundly hopeless. They have been abandoned by Jesus in death; he has been violently taken from them. Since they have no 'elsewhere' from which

---

1 V. Havel, *Disturbing the Peace* (New York: Vintage, 1991) p. 181

to fund their injured hope, it dies. All the signs they see point unambiguously to the double truth that not only is Jesus finished but so too is their own discipleship.

Their situation parallels a growing number of people in the church today and many who have left the church over their shoulders, as the disciples did Jerusalem. A considerable number of people leave the church not because of an argument with a priest or as a protest against official church teaching, but because what was once alive now seems dead, what was once appealing now seems wearisome. For many, the sacramental life of the church has ceased to matter in a world of competing interests. As one mother said to me: 'I ended up following the example of my children by lapsing. At first I felt guilty, but the guilt soon evaporated and I was surprised to discover that I wasn't really missing anything at all.'

Those who remain in the church in Western Europe look around and see that in the majority of parishes white hair dominates the assembly. While there are groups of young parents with children, there is a noticeable absence of youth and young people. That is why confirmation has been referred to as the last sacrament: for many young people, it is their last connection with the official church. Amidst growing scandals and falling vocations, decreasing attendance and the growth of alternative spiritualities, a diminishing respect for authority and an increasing appreciation of the individual's own experience and judgement, some people who remain in the church feel bewildered and hurt. In this new climate the church they knew and loved seems to have been rudely taken away from them and they are left feeling abandoned and betrayed. Some wonder if there will be a future for the Christian community in Western Europe, one that is in concert with its historic past, or whether it will gradually but surely diminish to the level of an eccentric sect. People look around them and hunt the horizon for signs of new hope.

There is a sense in which we can see the two disciples on the road to Emmaus as our contemporaries, fellow travellers journeying through a grey landscape of ambiguity and disappointment, where, in the uncertain light of what is seen and sensed, so many cherished hopes, now withered, have been relegated to lost causes. Yet the story of their loss is what we call Gospel, what we name as scripture. When their story is proclaimed in the assembly, the priest adds the words, 'This is the Gospel of the Lord.' What the disciples saw as hopeless we interpret as good news, not least because we interpret their story in the larger frame of scripture. And that is what the risen Jesus does in his response to his two disciples.

LOOKING AT THE PRESENT AS A PLACE OF HOPE

The risen Jesus, still a stranger, re-interprets his disciples' experience of recent events in the light of the past story contained in scripture. He offers a different interpretation of the same events the disciples have described, one that tries to make sense of pain and rejection and brokenness. In this section of the narrative Luke employs a strategy that is not peculiar to theological interpretations but is used in other disciplines, for instance in psychiatry and therapeutic counselling. Often when a client goes for counselling, what prompts the need is some sense of having lost one's way or feeling powerless when it comes to coping with everyday living and its demands or being unable to make any sense of what is happening in one's life.

While the client's conversation starts with describing the current crisis, the counsellor always tries to get a sense of the bigger picture. Who we are today is not explained by today but by the sum of our yesterdays. The key to unravelling the present lies somewhere in the past; the answer to why we are the way we are today is concealed in what has already happened. The dynamic is to stop staring at the present moment, the place of pain, and travel backwards into the old story in the hope that, seeing the new event in this larger context, one can understand not only what is happening but also what is going on. Thus associations to events in the past are sought to make sense of what is happening now.

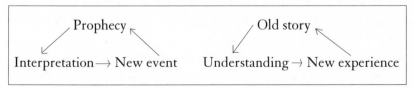

In the narrative, we watch Jesus moving away from an exclusive inspection of the details of what has happened during 'these last few days' to placing that story into the context of prophecy. This is always done in the belief that this larger context can help to understand the immediate frame of the new event. In this, as he does elsewhere, Luke is not just reflecting on what has happened, but presenting his interpretation in the perspective of faith and prophecy. It is this perspective that will be the source of new insight. The circle of association, beginning with the new experience/event, reaches back in time to ancient stories, and returns to re-interpret the new experience in the light of that journey of discernment.

In the case of Luke's interpretation there is a double dynamic: it is not only the present that is re-interpreted in the light of the past, the past is also re-evaluated in the light of recent events. In a sense the past is rewritten to catch up with new revelation. Thus, for example, nowhere in the Old Testament or in any writings of pre-Christian Judaism is it written that the Christ must suffer. While Luke does not specify any passages to support his reading of scripture, he recasts the ancient understanding of the Messiah to catch up with recent events in the story of Jesus, the one who is now recognised as 'Lord and Messiah' (Acts 2:36). Luke construes the suffering of Jesus as a necessary preface to glory (doxa), the splendour associated with the Messiah.

The practice of assessing the past afresh in the light of new events is something we do ourselves periodically, and sometimes we discover how time dramatically alters our perception of events. We can probably think of an event in our own past that at the time it happened did not register as critical or significant in our life story; only when we look back at our life from a different vantage point do we appreciate how important that event was for the course of our life. More often than not, the significance of an experience or an event is not offered at the time it happens; sometimes we have to wait months or even years before we can truly appreciate the importance that some events have exercised in our life story. The past is not dead; it lingers on as a resource for meaning or it waits for new interpretation. If life happens chronologically, its meaning does not come to us in such a linear fashion – which is why the American playwright, Arthur Miller, entitled his biography *Timebends*.[2]

2   A. Miller, *Timebends: a Life* (London: Methuen, 1987)

The teaching exercise of opening up of scripture is not an academic one, but one that is eminently practical: its purpose is to re-interpret the experience of the two disciples in such a way that a sense of divine providence is intelligible in what has happened these last few days. If the ancient maxim holds true – 'Ignorance of scripture is ignorance of Christ' – then the disciples are ignorant of their own sacred tradition, and that unawareness deprives them of making sense of their own experience. Even so, the new perceptiveness does not lead the disciples to recognise the identity of their fellow traveller.

Luke manages the story with a shrewd use of suspense: while the revelation on the road leads to burning hearts, the recognition itself is reserved for table fellowship. I would imagine another factor at play here, namely that Luke is writing for a community who will never meet the risen Lord on whatever roads they travel, but have an opportunity to meet him in the breaking of the bread. As Goulder wryly observes: 'But of course Christ's being known in the breaking of the bread, and his immediate vanishing, are a part of the weekly experience of every Christian at the Eucharist.'[3]

The structure of the Emmaus story, at the heart of which is the breaking of the bread, gives the Christian community a perfect reminder of coming to know Jesus as Lord in the Eucharist:

> the coming together
> the hearing of the story
> the gathering around the table
> the breaking of the bread
> the recognition of Jesus as Lord
> the renewal of personal discipleship
> the departure to share the new experience as good news.

In the light of their new experience, their recognition of the risen Jesus, the disciples again reassess their past: a recent past of injured hope is now healed in this fresh revelation. They are now able to understand why their hearts were burning within them. Their new experience enables them to make sense not only of the last few days but also why they

3. M. Goulder, *Luke – a New Paradigm* Vol 2 (Sheffield Academic Press: Journal for the Study of the New Testament, 1989) p.783

felt the way they did on the road when the stranger was unfolding scripture to them. The recent and the immediate past is again reappraised in the light of new awareness and insight; they are liberated from their own tragic interpretation of the last days of Jesus and their own self-image as leftover disciples of a dead prophet.

Their new experience gives them a new sense of purpose and a new authority, so they go back to the place they longed to leave over their shoulder. Jerusalem is now their chosen destination, not the city they discarded earlier in the day. Even though the day is far spent, they go back; their return is not only to a place but, more importantly, to rejoin a community, one they presumably believe to be as wretched and desolate as they were at the beginning of their journey. When they return, their new experience is recounted as an addition to the testimony that the Lord has appeared to Simon.

CONCLUSION

If the road to Emmaus is one of the great lost roads of history, it has a way of reappearing in people's lives. There are times when all of us can condense our gathered disenchantment and our withered aspirations into the phrase, 'we had hoped … '

We can all think of hopes that we once cherished that have now, however reluctantly, been discarded.

> We had hoped …
> that our loved ones would not be taken from us;
> that life would get easier;
> that every hurt would be balanced by joy;
> that God would become clearer somehow;
> that peace would be secured among peoples;
> that comedy would triumph;
> that peace and justice would be established;
> that our good health would endure;
> that people would become kinder;
> that racism would disappear;
> that every religion would be esteemed;
> that tragedy would happen only onstage;

that wrinkles would appear only on our clothing;
that we could lay down our burdens;
that we could forsake our sins;
that we would not be forgotten;
that ...
You can make you own list.

Yet the story of Emmaus counsels us not to hang around the graveyard nursing our grief and loss, but to consult the larger picture that is provided for us in the pages of scripture.

The Bible is not written in code for a select few; rather, it is offered to all of us as a living voice to guide us on our journey to God and our dealings with one another. Granted, there are lists and genealogies that seem utterly strange and far from helpful. But there are passages of matchless beauty that call out to us from a culture and time different from ours to the heart of our own experience. The great narrative thrust of the Bible is a call from a world of conflict and suffering and passion to our own world of conflict and suffering and passion; it bids us not to limit wisdom to our own generation but to learn about God and grow wise about one another from the shared insight of those who have journeyed before us. For all our real differences with our ancestors in the faith, we are not total strangers, but fellow pilgrims journeying towards our common destiny in God.

The whole Bible provides us with a vast moving picture into which our own stories can find new meaning. Our own life stories are illuminated when seen within the larger frame of the biblical narrative, so evident in the story of Emmaus. Throughout scripture we meet people at the crossroads of life: a father, without argument and without tears, walks with his son on a silent journey towards holocaust; a refugee people, tormented by years of abuse, find an unlikely liberator in Moses; wayward communities, who have become fascinated by the surrounding culture of success, are called back to their own dignity as the people of God; two bewildered disciples are put in touch with their sacred tradition as a neglected source of wisdom for their lives. We meet human beings not symbols, people not ciphers, complex individuals not cardboard cutouts. We come face to face with our ancestors in the faith when they are troubled and exultant; we are drawn into the struggle of their lives; we are moved by their mourning and loss as we are exalted by their daring and faith. It is our own story writ large, which is why it has been proclaimed and read for centuries.

Many of us, however, do not use it as the great resource it is but, like the two disciples on the road to Emmaus, stare awkwardly and impulsively at our own litany of disappointments. We should hear the echo of an older voice, 'Oh, how foolish you are and so slow of heart to believe ...' (Lk 24:25)

PART ONE | # The Offer
of Revelation

CHRISTIAN FAITH and theology begin with the necessary acknowledgement that God begins the gradual process of divine self-revelation in history. History is the natural environment of revelation; the God who reveals himself through his saving plan cannot do so out of time or out of place if this disclosure is to be recognised and acted upon within the dimensions of the human. Revelation must be situated in time and place, the field necessary for human understanding; it must enter the world of the particular if it is to give shape to the human story. We cannot predetermine what will take place by defining the nature of the event or choosing the people involved in it; we cannot select the place or arrange the time. We have to await the act of God's prevenient grace, since revelation emerges from divine initiative not from human compulsion. In the beginning, it is God who begins.

The revelation of God brings promise into history and sets the scene for a dynamic which is so important throughout the Old Testament and the Gospel of Luke: the historical relationship between the word of promise and the act of fulfilment. In the biblical narrative revelation is primarily related to a saving event rather than a word of knowledge: the word is spoken so that something will happen, which binds revelation and salvation in intimate union as the epiphany of the God who saves. Thus the focal point of God's revelation in the Old Testament is seen as God's visit which saves an enslaved people from Egypt: this is a choice which effectively creates them as the people of God and a word that summons them to fidelity. Their liberation from bondage is experienced and interpreted not as a skilled act of political management but as the saving power of God. In the act of creating and choosing, God reveals. So the story is told of the beginning.

1 | The Saving Visit of God in the Old Testament

THE HISTORY of revelation is frequently presented as a series of visits or visitations which God makes to his people in specific events and through the medium of chosen individuals. Oftentimes these visits are marked by blessing, sometimes by curse; but their purpose is always salvific, and is interpreted as such throughout the whole movement of the biblical narrative.

BEGINNINGS: BARRENNESS AND FRUITFULNESS

In the Yahwistic account of creation (Gen 2:4b-25) the earth is first described as a primitive wasteland, uncultivated and uninhabited, which can neither produce nor shelter life. God fashions man out of clay and with the breath of life makes him live to become the first creature on earth. Amidst a desert landscape God plans a garden as the proper environment of man; but alongside the exhortation to cultivate it there is the veto on eating from the tree of knowledge which yields omniscience and brings death. After seeding a barren place for man, God considers that man needs a suitable partner and for this purpose various animals are formed from the soil and paraded before him for naming; but none is called in kinship with him, none is recognised as appropriate for him. The search continues for a worthy companion: while man is in a deep sleep God is at work forming woman from one of his ribs, and when she is brought before him her presence evokes a clear affirmative response, 'At last!' (2:23)

The woman, however, is tempted by the serpent to eat the forbidden fruit with the promise that 'your eyes will be opened and you will be like gods, knowing good and evil.' (3:5) According to the temptation nothing will be hidden from them and, therefore, nothing will have to be revealed to them. The offer made, the woman makes her own decision: she takes the fruit, eats it, and gives some to her husband who does the same. Their eyes are indeed opened, but to no perceptible advantage; rather than becoming divine they experience a rude awakening in beholding their mutual nakedness. Their eyes testify to their new knowledge and lost innocence: ashamed of themselves and afraid of God, their first reaction is to hide parts of themselves from each other, and the whole of themselves from God. Cover-up becomes the new governing rubric in relationships.

In disobeying the word of God, the man and the woman put distance between themselves and the presence of God; they experience a new distance between themselves as the man feels betrayed by the woman and the woman feels tricked by the serpent; they realise as they hear the solemn judgement of God that their 'old' future is now totally out of reach. To find them God has to cover the new distance by seeking them out. So the first question of a questing God is: 'Where are you?' (3:9) And if salvation is a matter of being found (Lk 19:9-10) the first question of God is the root of all biblical questions. In the beginning it is God who seeks out his created humanity, who questions, who invites man and woman to emerge from a hiding-place sought in fear, to face God and take responsibility for failing to honour his word. (3:24)

The collapse of the original relationship between man and God and the finality of the banishment from the garden appear to inaugurate the time of the absence of God. God expels the first couple from the place associated with his presence and beneficence and impels them to live in the chaos of wasteland.[1] The first human beings are the first refugees: banished from the Garden of Eden to its refugee-camp, they are condemned to 'make do' in a world which is no longer subservient to their word, a world in which they will be at variance with each other and their environment. In the beginning, there was the exile, and it seems an irreparable break. But, as Barbotin writes:

> Yet, over and above the call to sinful man that reveals God's anxious concern, the predicted defeat of the serpent and the obscure promise of a salvation leave room for hope. But since God

1. For a comparison between the concept of chaos in the Priestly account and the Yahwistic account cf. B. Otzen, 'The Use of Myth in Genesis' in B. Otzen, H. Gottlieb, and K. Jeppe-sen, *Myths in the Old Testament* (London: SCM 1980) pp. 22-61.

has now become the Absent One, he will henceforth manifest himself to man only fleetingly and by way of exception, in the form of the visit. In addition, since God remains invisible, he will visit man through signs.[2]

In accounting for why things are the way they are in his own time, the Yahwistic writer depicts the Fall at the beginning of time as a story of radical human mismanagement which resulted in a litany of disorder. As a result of human action there is alienation between man and God, between man and his origins, and between man and true wisdom. Between the woman and the man there is attraction but the perpetual struggle for domination; between the woman and childbirth there is great pain; between the man and the natural environment of work there is enmity. There is dislocation throughout the whole of human experience. Everything is askew; nothing is as it was planned to be. Worst of all is the new distance between humanity and God. From now on humanity will have to await the visit of God.

To speak of the visit of God supposes a normal background of separation, habitual absence, and distance which must be crossed from God's side. The distance is not only an indication that God is not here, but also serves as a reminder of his transcendence and as a metaphor for the many differences which continue to keep man and God apart: 'Yes, the heavens are as high above earth as my ways are above your ways, my thoughts above your thoughts' (Is 55:9). The conventional language of visiting speaks of overcoming distance and separation by 'going to see', 'getting in touch with', 'spending time together', 'being with', and even 'showing one's face' – all of which reflect the initiative of one of the parties to make a decisive move. To visit someone can be to seek communion with them, to reunite after separation. It can also mean to check up on someone, to ensure that everything is in order. In the history of revelation it is always God who takes the initiative in visiting his people, during which time separation is overcome, distance is covered, and absence is replaced by signs of God's presence. But the visit is temporary: absence is the custom.

2. E. Barbotin, *The Humanity of God* (New York: Orbis, 1976) p. 255.

In the Hebrew Testament the words based on the Hebrew root *pqd* are usually translated in English as 'visit' or 'visitation'.[3] Whether the visit of God takes the form of a dream which enlightens a chosen individual (Sir 4:6) or an intervention seen to dramatically alter the course of history (Ex 3:17), it serves to witness to God's abiding care and effective power in the midst of history. Although the immediate context may speak of a variety of meanings, the word always retains its basic import of 'ensuring that everything is in order'. Thus, for example:

> the visit which creates new life (1 Sam 2:21)
> the visit which brings salvation (Ps 106:4)
> the visit which achieves liberation (Ex 4:31)
> the visit which calls sinners to account (Hos 9:7)
> the visit which wins victory for God's people (Zeph 2:7)
> the visit which punishes enemy nations (Jer 46:21)
> the visit of a shepherd who inspects his flock (Ezek 34).

In all its various meanings the visit of God is always a visible sign of the plan of God, one which reveals the primacy of God's love and the righteousness of God's judgement, and which has as its ultimate intention the salvation of the people. In that saving intention there is the heart of all biblical revelation.

The foundation for the salvation of the peoples is laid in the covenant which God establishes with Abraham, an agreement whereby God promises a land and posterity to Abraham if he will first uproot himself from his homeland and break the natural bonds that tie him to his host of relatives and his immediate family (Gen 12:1-3). Abraham is asked to abandon the security which comes from being rooted in the particular and to choose exile in favour of a land as yet unspecified and a posterity as yet unseen. The call to Abraham seems all the more demanding of trust since the Yahwistic genealogy has already described what appears to be an irreversible human condition: 'Sarai was barren, having no child.' (Gen 11:30)

---

3. Cf. J. Boan Hooser, 'The Meaning of the Hebrew Root pqd in the Old Testament' (Harvard dissertation 1962/3); also *Harvard Theological Review* 56 (1963) pp. 332ff. Cf. also F. T. Beyer in *Theological Dictionary of the New Testament* 11, ed. G. Kittel (Grand Rapids: Eerdmans, 1964) pp. 590-608.

In the first creation account God's first blessing of man and woman takes the form of a command to be fruitful and multiply, peopling the the whole earth (Gen 1:28). In sharp contrast to that original charge the wives of the three great ancestors of the chosen people are barren: Sarah, Rebecca (Gen 25:21), and Rachel (Gen 29:31). In a tradition where fruitfulness was regarded as a blessing from God (Ps 127:3-5) and barrenness a punishment and source of shame (Gen 30:1; Lk 1:25), a barren wife enjoyed the right derived from the Code of Hammurabi to employ one of her servants to be the host mother of the husband's child (Gen 16:2; 30:3-6). This practice served to perpetuate the family name, but naturally left unchanged the sterility of the wife: no human device or legal circumvention could render her fruitful.

In the biblical narrative barrenness can be seen as a dramatic depiction of human emptiness before God and as a continual reminder of human powerlessness before its own limitations. The barren womb speaks of a place absent of promise, an interior wasteland which can produce no fruit, a place where the future is cancelled. Nothing can be conceived or nourished there; no life can emerge from a place which seems a human miniature of that desolation before God began his work: a bare landscape, uncultivated and uninhabited which cannot by itself produce life (Gen 2:5). That comparison between the human condition and a bare land is elaborated in Hosea when God threatens to punish the unfaithful wife: 'I will make a wilderness of her, turn her into an arid land' (2:3 ff).

The barren woman is like that desert land and nothing can change her except a 'visit' from God. And it is precisely that which God promises to Abraham: 'I shall visit you again next year without fail, and your wife will then have a son.' (Gen 18:10)

Certainly it seems futile to promise a homeland if there will be no children to people and inherit it: land and posterity are inextricably linked and are recognised as such in the original call and covenant (Gen 12:1-3; 17:1-8). Thus God reveals his freedom of choice in electing to visit Sarah and unfolds his saving plan through her graced fruitfulness. The promised visit takes place (21:1) and is marked by divine comedy: a geriatric Sarah gives birth to the promise of God which enters history in the person of Isaac. Through the visit of God and the faith of Abraham the promise takes flesh in time. And that form of visit will be repeated with similar results in the lives of Rebecca, Rachel, the mother of Samson, and the mother of Samuel. Through each of them new beginnings will take place. That will be especially true at the beginning of the new age marked by the births of John and Jesus which Luke places firmly within the ancient tradition of the creative visits of God.[4]

THE EXODUS: GOD'S DECISIVE SAVING ACTION IN HISTORY

The visit of God who has not fallen in love with long distance but is near to his people through his active presence continues to be the most enduring of the biblical promises. And the visit which will mark the real birth of the people of God and form their identity is foretold by the dying Joseph in Egypt: 'At length Joseph said to his brothers, "I am about to die; but God will be sure to remember you kindly and take you back from this country to the land that he promised on oath to Abraham, Isaac and Jacob."' (Gen 50:24) As Vawter comments: 'this is the "visitation" which God makes either in judgement or salvation, his solemn intervention in human history that determines the lot of his people. The exodus is in view, when Israel will go forth to claim the land promised on oath by God to the patriarchs.' [5] The event of exodus will be a historical judgement on the Egyptians for their rule of tyranny and enslavement and a liberating experience for the Israelites who will come to know the power of God's creative and saving will.

Up to the time of Moses the visit of God has been seen primarily through his dealings with the patriarchal families and more particularly through ensuring their continuing line by rendering fruitful the barren wives. In the traditions of the Book of Exodus, however, the story suddenly shifts from the history of a family to the history of a nation, and Moses appears as the figure who dominates its turbulent beginnings. Again the story of the encounter with God begins in the wilderness (Ex 3:1), and it will be told as a journey from wilderness to a land rich in food and drink, the garden of the promise of God. As a wanted runaway who

---

4. Cf. D. McBride, *The Gospel of Luke* (Dublin, Dominican Publications, 1982/1991) pp. 21-27.

5. B. Vawter, *On Genesis: a New Reading* (London: G. Chapman, 1977) p. 475.

tends the flock of his father-in-law Moses will experience a radical change because of his meeting with God. He will be given a new purpose which will influence the destiny of a people: he will lead the Israelites out of bondage and guide them through the wilderness until they are within sight of the promised land.

The saving visit of God will take place because as he discloses to Moses: 'I have seen the miserable state of my people in Egypt. I have heard their appeal to be free of their slave-drivers. Yes, I am am well aware of their sufferings.' (Ex 3:7) The God of the patriarchs reveals himself as a God of awareness who notices the affliction of his captive people and hears their cry for freedom. The awareness of God is profoundly important to God's relationship with his elect. If awareness is an essential precondition for real love – we cannot love those we are unaware of – so too experience teaches us that love heightens awareness: because we love we pay attention. In the revelation of the awareness of God there is the assurance that God does not overlook what happens in the world of the particular: he does not go to sleep on specific human suffering which takes place in a land where merely to be present is to be part of a calculated injustice. Rather, God is awake to the plight of his people and in so doing gives them a pledge of salvation. If God sees, there is always hope. As the later exiles expectantly pray: 'Look down, Lord, from your holy dwelling place and give a thought to us, take heed of us and listen, look at us, Lord, and consider' (Bar 2:16-17; cf Is 63:15; Ps 44:23ff; Lam 5:1). And as Mary will proclaim at the beginning of the new age, the look of God marks the beginning of human transformation (Lk 1:46-55).

Of course, awareness is not enough, but its importance as a preface to resolute action cannot be underestimated. The awareness of God is not that of an almighty spectator who remains remote from what he sees: God's is a critical awareness because he not only observes what is happening but evaluates what is going on, and is moved to commit himself to change it. Seeing and hearing oblige God to act. Whether one agrees or not with the comment of Rabbi Hanokh, 'The real exile of Israel in Egypt was that they had learned to endure it',[6] what is clear from

6. In M. Buber, *Tales of the Hasidim*, Vol 2 (New York: Schocken Book, 1948) p. 315.

the Book of Exodus is that God did not learn to endure it. The enslavement of the Israelites was not regarded as their unalterable destiny, but a condition which could be changed because of God's solidarity with the afflicted. As God reveals to Moses: 'I mean to deliver them out of the hands of the Egyptians ... I have resolved to bring you up out of Egypt.' (3:8.17)

Thus God reveals himself as a God of salvation who acts on what he sees, who moves resolutely against an organised oppression which threatens to extirpate his people and destroy the divine plan. Salvation is action; saving is the verb of God. The exodus is revealed to be the decisive work of a God who cares and whose care takes the shape of historical liberation. He is determined to use his power and demonstrate his mighty hand (3:20) in favour of those who are exiled in their own powerlessness. In their present condition the Israelites cannot be the inheritors of a promise which is rooted in the possession of land and the enjoyment of posterity: they have no land of their own, and their male children are being systematically exterminated (1:22). Clearly, the present situation has to be changed radically; a new order has to be created, and, as God reveals to Moses, the beginning of that change will occur when the Israelites experience the saving visit as the answer to their appeals.

In the exodus God will create the Israelites anew and through this dominant experience establish their identity precisely as the people brought out from the land of Egypt (Ex 3:3-10), an identity that will be kept alive through memory and cherished especially in time of trial. At the same time, God's active intervention in history will reveal him precisely as 'saviour' and 'redeemer' (Ex 15:2; Ps 106:8ff; Is 63:8ff) and as the only true saviour:

> Yet I am Yahweh, your God since the days of the land of Egypt;
> you know no God but me,
> there is no other saviour. (Hos 13:4)

Consequently, God will be called on to free individuals and the people from a variety of crises and trials: oppression; injustice; danger; war; persecution; famine; exile; suffering; sickness. The experience of God as saviour becomes a message of profound consolation for others; it gives substance to people's hope. Thus God is invoked so frequently under the title 'Saviour' that the recurring invocations, 'Be my saviour again, renew my joy' (Ps 51:12), 'Save me and I shall be saved, for you are my hope' (Jer 17:14), sound like an abbreviated form of an ancient credo. Throughout the history of Israel it is above all the poor of Yahweh who can call on him for salvation (Ps 72:4); they will continue to acknowledge him as 'God my Saviour' (Lk 1:47) at the beginning of the new age when Jesus himself will be designated by that title (Lk 2:11).

The significance of God's revelation to Moses – that liberation and salvation are one in him[7] – will be confirmed in a multitude of concrete experiences as the history of Israel unfolds. But first Moses needs to know the name of the God who commissions him so that his sudden emergence as leader will have the necessary authority to persuade the Israelites of the authenticity of his encounter with God. In ancient Eastern thought the name not only distinguished the person but disclosed something of his nature; to know the name of God was a sign of a privileged relationship with him, one which enabled the person to call on God directly for help. If Moses can pronounce the name of God to the Israelites, that will be proof of God's self-disclosure and will serve as Moses' letter of accreditation. The request is granted: 'And God said to Moses, "I Am who I Am. This," he added, "is what you must say to the sons of Israel: 'I Am has sent me to you.' " ' (Ex 3:14)

In disclosing his name, 'I Am', God reveals himself as a God of constancy whose unchanging fidelity to his people is signified in his name, everlasting presence. The time of God will never come to an end; he will never be a 'has-been' God because 'This is my name for all time; by this name I shall be invoked for all generations to come' (3:15). The name 'I Am' or as Rendtorff writes, 'perhaps better still, "I shall be there as the one who will be there"',[8] affirms that the very nature of God is faithfulness to his promise of presence. The name of Yahweh is not only an assurance of his presence but a witness to the kind of presence which is not rumoured or transient, but actual and enduring. As Noth observes:

It is ... important to note that the verb *hyh* in Hebrew does not

7. For a discussion on the unity of liberation and salvation cf. G. Guttierez, *A Theology of Liberation* (New York: Orbis, 1973) pp. 149-178.
8. R. Rendtorff, *Men in the Old Testament* (London: SCM, 1968) p. 21.

express pure 'being', pure 'existing' but an 'active being' which does not take place just anywhere, but makes its appearance in the world of men and primarily in the history of Israel.[9]

Thus in this momentous revelation to Moses God speaks out of his awareness of his people's agony to pledge his saving help and promise his constant presence. The history of Israel will be the enactment of this revelation, and Moses is empowered to make history by speaking God's name and carrying his word to the elders of Israel: 'I have visited you and seen all that the Egyptians are doing to you. And so I have resolved to bring you out of Egypt where you are oppressed into the land ... where milk and honey flow'.(3:16-17)

The providential visit of God in the exodus is perceived by the biblical writers as the epitomy of the whole spiritual history of Israel; consequently, all that follows that event is interpreted by a faith which discerns the activity of the same God who formed a nation by the remarkable events in the exodus and in the wilderness. The same is true of all that preceded that event: the creation account is written in the light of the experience of the God who saves. Through the exodus Israel accounts for its own birth as a people determined not by blood or land but solely by God's election, one which is of primary significance for all nations because his revelation to Israel is a light which will one day illumine all nations (Lk 2:29-32). Because God is perceived as the one who acts, history is thereby given a unique importance as the primary sphere in which God reveals himself. As Wright has pointed out so clearly:

> Since God is known by what he has done, the Bible exists as a confessional recital of his acts, together with the teaching accompanying these acts, or inferred from them in the light of specific situations which the faithful confronted. To confess God is to tell a story and then expound its meaning.[10]

God's revelation through the historical act of liberation is told as a story of relationship rather than registered as a development of doctrine:

9. M. Noth, *Exodus* (Old Testament Library; London: SCM, 1962) p. 45.
10. G. E. Wright, *God Who Acts: Biblical Theology as Recital* (London: SCM, 1958) p. 85.

narrative language, therefore, is judged by the biblical writers to be the most appropriate for telling that story and disclosing its significance.[11]

Tho momentous salvific visit of God interpreted as a mark of solicitude and a pledge of salvation is to be hallowed in memory and told in story lest people forget, and celebrated in the ritual act of Passover (Ex 13:3-10). Through the meal, the visit happens again in the bringing to mind (*anamnesis*) of the story, 'This is the night', and in the sharing of the food and the drink (a structure which is evident in the synoptic account of the Last Supper and in Luke's account of Emmaus). However, soon after the deliverance from Egypt people begin to question the value of God's visit because their freedom from bondage is now freedom in wilderness. In the light of the present hardship their earlier interpretation is revised and the people succumb to the temptation of reviewing their past in terms of nostalgia and wondering a peculiar wonder: whether the pain that actually goes with freedom is preferable to the security that supposedly went with bondage (Ex 16:3; 17:3). God visits Moses in the form of a cloud and gives proof of his constancy by providing food which the Israelites name 'manna', and water from the rock at Horeb. And throughout the years spent in the wilderness, God continues to show himself through signs and to visit the people, visits which either favour them with his blessing or punish them for their infidelity to the covenant.

In the confessional presentation of the Deuteronomic history, which opens retrospectively with Israel on the threshold of eastern Palestine, God's gratuitous election is underlined as the only reason for Israel's privilege of being chosen as the people of God: 'If Yahweh set his heart on you and chose you, it was not because you outnumbered other peoples: you were the least of the peoples. It was for love of you and to keep the oath he swore to your fathers that Yahweh brought you out with his mighty hand and redeemed you from the house of slavery, from the power of Pharaoh king of Egypt.' (Deut 7:7-8)

To the promise of salvation through the chosen people the author of

---

11. Among many studies in the narrative language of the Bible cf. J. Licht, *Storytelling in the Bible* (Jerusalem: Magnes Press, Hebrew University, 1978) and R. Atler, *The Art of Biblical Narrative* (London: George Allen and Unwin, 1981).

Deuteronomy will add a new revelation: that in the fullness of time salvation will come through a Messiah who will emerge from the Davidic line and who will summarise in himself the hope for Israel's future. The whole pattern of history from the point of God's election of Israel is interpreted in terms of recurring rebellion of the people and the constant fidelity of God to his promises; it is a story which constantly demonstrates the curses, threats and judgements visited on the people for their infidelity, as well as the blessings and the persistent promise of salvation which come through fidelity to the law of God (Deut 30; Jos 22-23; Jg 2-3; 1 Sam 12). The Deuteronomist interprets the eventual division of the kingdom as a divine judgement on Solomon for compromising his beliefs and building pagan temples for his foreign wives, even in the city of Jerusalem (1 Kgs 11:1-13).

THE PROPHETIC TRADITION: SALVATION AND JUDGEMENT

In the last years of the northern kingdom, as the Assyrian power was expanding its reach in the east, Israel enjoyed a time of great material affluence which covered a corresponding moral destitution. The institution of the monarchy, with its aristocratic branches and state administration, had radically altered the original covenant system based on solidarity of one people: wealth was concentrated in the privileged classes who made a vocation out of manipulating the poor who in their turn had no hope of legal redress from courts which were themselves corrupt (Am 5:7). Into this situation came the first two classical prophets, Amos and Hosea.

In an age of complacency Amos preached against a banal optimism which regarded the protection of God as guaranteed because of cultic propriety, arguing that God was absent from the places of Israel's worship (5:4-6). Amos was radical in his prophetic witness, but he was no revolutionary: as Bright observed:

> Amos preached no revolution because he believed Israel beyond cure by such means: Yahweh, and Yahweh alone, would execute vengeance.[12]

12.   J. Bright, *A History of Israel* (London: SCM 1972) p. 260.

Predicting the total downfall of the northern kingdom (2:13-16) Amos speaks of the visit of God which will punish Israel for its infidelity:

> Listen, sons of Israel, to this oracle Yahweh speaks against you, against the whole family I brought out of the land of Egypt: You alone, of all the families of earth, have I acknowledged, therefore it is for all your sins that I mean to punish you. (3:1-2)

The national disintegration of Israel prophesied by Amos shows itself as clearly self-induced in the last days of Hosea. The preaching of Amos announcing the divine visit of judgement has no perceptible effect in the lives of the people who are moving inexorably through political anarchy (2 Kgs 15:8-31) and religious infidelity (Hos 4:11:14) to unmitigated disaster. Ignoring the warnings of Amos, the people are doomed to fulfil his prophecy. The message of Hosea to his people is shaped by his own tragic experience: using the story of his marriage to Gomer who left him and their three children to become a prostitute at the shrine of Baal, Hosea describes the parallel tragedy of how God is abandoned by his covenanted people for the worship of false gods (1-3). Like Amos, Hosea sees an unrepentant Israel as doomed to destruction under the divine judgement. God will visit the nation, and his visit is interpreted as a reversal of liberation: 'He is now going to remember their iniquity and punish [visit] their sins; they will have to go back to Egypt.' (8:13; cf 9:7-9)

However, still speaking through the allegory of his marriage, Hosea is confident that the inevitable disaster to befall Israel is not the last word: God will one day forgive a repentant Israel and restore her to himself (2:14-23).

Events proved Amos and Hosea all too accurate in their prophecies of destruction: Israel fell before the invading power of the Assyrians, large numbers of the population were deported to Upper Mesopotamia, and the dissident kingdom was no more. The disappearance of the northern kingdom was a disaster too for Judah: although the southern kingdom escaped total destruction, it lost its independence to Assyria and paid the price for a lingering survival by financial tribute and religious syncretism. As a sign of political subservience the Temple of Jerusalem housed

the gods of the Assyrians (2 Kgs 16:10-18), with the inevitable consequence in the diminishment of Yahwism, the breach of the covenant
law, and the widespread practice of pagan ways which called fundamen-
tally into question the nation's self-understanding as the covenanted
people of God.[13]

Like Israel, Judah suffered from a massive self-deception which was
no momentary indiscretion but a policy which generated a falsehood:
God would be the uncritical saviour of his people no matter how they
actually behaved. There was a marked discrepancy between their inherited identity as the people of God and their unjust and immoral practices:
their response to that was systematic delusion to cover up their inherited
obligations and the real consequences of their behaviour. Again it was
the prophetic voice which collided with the conventional wisdom: as
Amos and Hosea had done in the northern kingdom, their contemporaries, Isaiah and Micah, recalled the people of Judah to their true
identity and re-introduced them to their lost responsibilities.

The whole preaching of Isaiah (chapters 1 to 39) is informed by a deep
awareness of the holiness of God, an awareness which is rooted in the
religious tradition of Jerusalem and confirmed in his visionary experience in the Temple where he receives his prophetic commission (6:1-4).
To acknowledge God in his immeasurable greatness, to turn away from
injustice and obey him in faith, this forms for Isaiah the pattern of an
authentic life before the Holy One of Israel. However, Isaiah sees
nothing but the absence of that in his time. Having prophesied the
downfall of Israel and declared Assyria to be the instrument of God's
visit (10:5-9), Isaiah is persuaded that a similar fate will befall Jerusalem
and Judah (3:1-15). The theme of God's visit as punishment for unre-
lenting sinfulness is maintained throughout Isaiah's prophetic witness
(e.g. 10:3; 23:17; 24:22; 26:14-16), and near the end of his ministry his
oracle describes the imminence of that judgement on Jerusalem:

Suddenly, unexpectedly,
you shall be visited by Yahweh Sabaoth

13. Cf. D. R. Hillers, *Covenant: the History of a Bibilical Idea* (Baltimore: John Hopkins
    Press, 1969); H.H. Rowley, *The Biblical Doctrine of Election* (London: Lutterworth
    Press, 1950).

with thunder, earthquake, mighty din,
hurricane, tempest, flame of devouring fire. (29:5c-6)

However, the punishment will be a purification of the people, not their annihilation. There is a far side to dereliction; there is a saving purpose in what is now irreversible but not irredeemable. Isaiah sees the coming events as an integral part of the larger divine purpose in history: a necessary experience which rather than frustrate the plan of God will serve its ultimate design. The event of visitation will draw out from a largely unfaithful people a faithful 'remnant' that will form the basis for the future nation (4:2-6; 28:5; 37:30-32). And, above all, there will reign over the nation a Davidic king who will be filled with the spirit of God and who, in contrast to the present time, will not judge by appearances but establish the rights of the good; he will judge in favour of 'the poor of the land' so that there will be through him a return to the reign of peace that existed in paradise (11:1-9).

Like Isaiah, Micah scathingly denounces his own country which he sees to be under judgement for reasons similar to those of Israel where injustice, dishonesty and oppression go unreproved, and wealth flourishes at the cost of a helpless poverty – a situation which is rendered all the more hopeless by judges who are not serious about justice, priests whose concern is fixed on financial security, and prophets whose divinations are related only to their stipends (3:1-11). In a dramatic passage (6:1-8) Micah imagines God coming as the accuser with an incontestable case against his people whom he liberated from Egypt. He will not be placated by hollow cultic gestures, however expressive of official theology, but only by his people doing the good. Granted the behaviour of the people of Judah, Micah is in no doubt about the 'today' of the visit of God (7:4) when 'Zion will become a ploughland, Jerusalem a heap of rubble' (3:12). However, Micah looks beyond the visit of punishment to the day of the saving visit when the expected Messiah will come and rule not only Judah but all nations (4-5). Again the prophetic vision points through national destruction to the ultimate plan of God seeing a Davidic prince emerging from Bethlehem of Judah:

Yahweh is therefore going to abandon them

till the time when she who is to give birth gives birth.
Then the remnant of his brothers will come back to the sons of
    Israel.
He will stand and feed his flock
with the power of Yahweh,
with the majesty of the name of his God.
They will live secure, for from then on he will extend his power
to the ends of the land.
He himself will be peace. (5:3-4)

Although difficult to assess precisely, the prophetic preaching of
Isaiah and Micah can be seen to have some immediate effect in the
reform movement of Hezekiah. However, it is not until the decline of
Assyria and the resurgent nationalism in Judah that the southern
kingdom under the leadership of Josiah begins a more vigorous and
widespread movement of reform (2 Kgs 22:3-23:25). That reform, given
shape and impetus by the discovery of the Deuteronomic code in the
Temple, is rooted in a new appreciation of the national identity emerging from the Mosaic covenant and has effect in the centralization of
worship in Jerusalem, the destruction of the pagan shrines, and the
abolition of pagan practices.[14] Josiah's reformation was no doubt encour-
aged by the resounding proclamation of Zephaniah that 'the day of
Yahweh' was at hand for Judah (1:4-6; 3:1-4). That Zephaniah's preaching was ultimately ineffective is proved in the last years of Jeremiah
when the visit of God takes place with the coming of the Babylonians,
    The reform of Josiah was certainly a significant improvement on the
political and religious past of Judah, but it produced no profound change
in the behaviour of the people. Speaking of Jeremiah's evaluation of the
reform, Bright comments:

> There is evidence that he had, even before Josiah's death, become
> deeply disillusioned with the whole thing. More than once he
> complained that no real repentance had come of it, but only an even
> more elaborate cultus (e.g. 6:16-21), and that the wealthy and
> powerful, confident that the presence of Yahweh's temple was the

14. Cf. G. Von Rad, *Studies in Deuteronomy* (London: SCM, 1953).

nation's sufficient defence, were using the cultus as a cloak for the most egregious violations of covenant law. It seemed to him that the very possession of the law book had helped to create a climate in which the prophetic word could no longer be heard and that, because of this, the nation remained obdurate in its sins (8:4-9).[15]

Rather than focusing on external reforms which can be merely so much commotion masking religious complacency, Josiah asks for nothing less than a circumcision of the heart (4:14), for God is the one who searches the heart of each person (17:10).

After the death of Josiah and the collapse of the reform movement Jeremiah becomes wholly persuaded that 'the foe from the North' (4-6), identified as the Babylonians, will be God's appointed agents of judgement. In effect the Babylonians will mark the time of the visit of God. Among all the prophets Jeremiah speaks most powerfully of the visit of God's judgement, a constant theme arising from his premonition of the inevitable doom to befall an unrepentant Judah (e.g. 5:9; 6:15; 9:9; 10:15; 14:10; 23:2; 32-5; 50:27). Jeremiah lives in personal agony under the impact of such an unalterable conviction; however, he continues to preach against a groundless optimism which regards God as bound to Jerusalem and to the Davidic kings, proclaiming that God would destroy the Temple (7:14) and pursue his plan without the kings (21:12-22:30). Announcing the fall of both the state and the Temple Jeremiah is accused of treason and blasphemy; he is ostracized and nearly killed for the word of judgement he is compelled to proclaim. But he still continues to prophesy the visit of God, dramatically symbolising the destruction of Jerusalem in the smashed potter's flask (19:1-13). After the first deportations in 597 B.C., Jeremiah gives the remaining people no cause for hope, and wearing the yoke of an ox around his neck declares that it is God's doing to yoke the people with Babylon (chapter 27).

With the Babylonians encircling Jerusalem, Zedekiah calls Jeremiah from imprisonment in the royal palace in the misplaced hope that the prophet will exercise his prophetic imagination and speak words of

---

15. J. Bright, *Jeremiah* (Anchor Bible; New York: Doubleday, 1965) p. xlv.

encouragement. Jeremiah, however, is unyielding in his declared position: Zedekiah himself will be taken into exile in Babylon 'and he will stay there until I visit him – it is Yahweh who speaks' (32:5). Never to be accused of diplomacy, Jeremiah reinforces his view with apocalyptic imagery when, during a temporary respite in 588 B.C., he informs Zedekiah that even if the Babylonians were cut to pieces leaving only the walking wounded, they would still discharge their divine mission by burning Jerusalem to the ground (37:3-10).

In proclaiming the destruction of Jerusalem as a result of the visit of God rather than the consequence of political mismanagement or the unfortunate effect of colonial expansion, Jeremiah places the event firmly within the saving plan of God. It is a religious act. Jeremiah's message of judgement rather then destroying faith in the future of God's promises actually lays the ground for a future without king and without Temple and without land.

Thus Jeremiah could do what the national religion could never do: imagine a future with God in which the people are alienated from the historical signs of the continued favour of God. Jeremiah offers an interpretation of tragedy specifically in terms of the faithfulness of God to his promises, an interpretation which is essential if Israel's faith is to survive. The other side of Jeremiah's prophecy of destruction is the saving visit of God, one which is elaborated in his letter to the first exiles:

> For Yahweh says this: only when the seventy years granted to Babylon are over, will I visit you and fulfil my promise in your favour by bringing you back to this place. I know the plans I have in mind for you – it is Yahweh who speaks – plans for peace, not disaster, reserving a future full of hope for you. (29:10-11)

Jeremiah's sustained witness against Judah and his promise of the new covenant (31: 31-33) are both confirmed from Babylon by Ezekiel, who announces the destruction of Jerusalem as the sovereign judgement of God while looking to a time of restoration when God will visit his people in a new way, implanting a new heart in them. Among the Temple priests deported in 597 B.C., Ezekiel preaches to the exiles and, like Jeremiah, refuses to assuage the people with false hopes comparing those who do to fools trying to save a collapsing wall by plastering over it (13:1-16). In a prophetic vision Ezekiel is present at the future fall of Jerusalem when the divine presence of its own accord leaves the profaned Temple (chapters 8 to 11). The unfaithful say: 'Yahweh cannot see us; Yahweh has abandoned the country' (8:12; 9:9), a reversal of God's revelation to Moses, 'I have seen ... mean to deliver' (Ex 3:7-8). The ending of the divine presence in the Temple does not signify the absence of God but is interpreted by Ezekiel as making way for a much more intimate and enduring presence, a presence among the remnant at the heart of the exile, one which is to purify and prepare it to become the people of God again.[16] The promise of the presence of God originally made to Moses is repeated in the form of a new covenant:

> Yes, I have sent them far away among the nations and I have dispersed them to foreign countries; and for a while I have been a sanctuary for them in the country to which they have gone ... I will bring you all back from the countries where you have been scattered and I will give you the land of Israel ... I will give them a single heart and I will put a new spirit in them; I will remove the heart of stone from their bodies and give them a heart of flesh instead, so that they will keep my laws and respect my observances and put them into practice. Then they shall be my people and I will be their God. (11:16-20; cf 36:23-28)

The events of 587 B.C. vindicate the prophetic work of Jeremiah and Ezekiel and make for a profound need: the prophetic ability to make sense of this disconsolate experience if the faith of the people is not to go the way of the Temple. Like Jeremiah, Ezekiel interprets the destruction as the decreed punishment of God for the sins of a recalcitrant people, and situates God's visit within the larger framework of his saving plan. The exile is not an absurd accident of history but a purposeful act by a God who continually reveals through his prophets that what happens takes place because of who he is, 'I am Yahweh', and nothing, not king, not Temple, not state, can form or save the people but God alone. The unity of the name and nature of God demands recognition by

16. Cf. R. E. Clements, *God and Temple: the Idea of Divine Presence in Ancient Israel* (Oxford University Press, 1965) pp. 102 ff.

all the nations: that is why God is going to display his holiness before them.

Thus there is a negative theophany in the experience of exile which reveals the holiness of God and his uncompromising hatred of wrong-doing. Taking up the theme from Jeremiah of God's visit which calls the shepherds of Israel to account (Jer 23:1-6), Ezekiel announces God's judgement on the shepherds and the sheep and goes on to portray the figure of the shepherd-saviour: 'I myself will pasture my sheep, I myself will show them how to rest – it is the Lord Yahweh who speaks. I shall look for the lost one, bring back the stray, bandage the wounded and make the weak strong.' (34:15-15; cf Lk 15 4-7). Later, Ezekiel, using the allegory of two sticks representing the northern and southern king-doms, describes the reunion of the two kingdoms under the Messiah, and the everlasting new covenant that the faithful God will make with his people (37:15-28).

Although Jeremiah and Ezekiel speak of the exile as a provisional period of necessary discipline and an opportunity for repentance, the longer the exile continues the more difficult it is for an uprooted Israel to keep alive a faith which can imagine an eventual restoration to the home-land. If hope is always hope from a concrete situation, the circumstances of the exiles, even though not oppressively severe, do not make for a ready hope in a future centred in Jerusalem. Through the insistent wit-ness of the prophets the exiles cannot shelter under the convenient con-solations of the unconditional promises to David; moreover, since the official theology has all but collapsed there is the real temptation to turn away from the ancestral faith in a God who seems to have abandoned his already alienated people and trust the Babylonian gods who preside over an expansive empire. The suffering of the exiles is given eloquent ex-pression in the prayer of lamentation (cf. Ps 74:9; 137; Lam 2:9 etc.) which captures the experience of loss and the fear of abandonment. It is from that situation that a new voice of authority rings out through another great prophet who is referred to as Second Isaiah and whose prophecies are contained in Isaiah 40-55.[17]

17. Cf. Introduction of J. L. McKenzie, *Second Isaiah* (Anchor Bible; New York, Doubleday, 1968); C. Westerman, *Isaiah 40-66* (Old Testament Library; London: SCM, 1969).

The opening message of Second Isaiah (40:1-11) sounds the notes that dominate his poetic work: the word which consoles the people that their time of punishment is ended (vv. 1-2); the word which calls the people to a ministry of preparing the way for God so that his glory can be revealed to all humankind (vv. 3-5; cf. Lk 3:4-5); the word which cries of the constancy of the word of God (vv. 6-8); the word which announces the saving visit of the Lord who comes in power (vv. 9-11). There is no need for the exiles to look to pagan gods who can accomplish no purpose in history for the simple reason that they cannot actually do anything (41:21-24). Yahweh alone is the redeemer, active from the beginning to the end, and there is no other God beside him (44:6-8). In scorning the powerlessness of the pagan gods, Second Isaiah testifies to the ancient monotheism of Israel by underlining the power of Yahweh precisely as the only one who will come to liberate the exiles from Babylon (41:8-20). He alone is the God who saves: 'Israel will be saved by Yahweh, saved everlastingly.' (45:17)

The impending liberation of the exiles is not due to fortuitous political developments but to the sole initiative of God: for Second Isaiah there is no better reason for liberation than that contained in the recurring affirmation of the name, 'I am Yahweh', the name revealed to Moses before the exodus event (Ex 3:14). In the name of God, now as then, is the true source of liberation. In this understanding Cyrus is reckoned as the servant of God's purpose, not the architect of Israel's freedom and restoration (44:24-45:7); and Babylon, previously seen as the medium of God's visit, is now to be subjected to judgement itself. Thus this 'new thing' that is about to take place (42:9; 43:19) is the saving work of God alone who sustains Israel throughout her time of trial.

As other prophets had understood the affliction of the people in terms of the governing experience of Egyptian bondage and wilderness (Hos 2:14-20; Is 10:24-27; Jer 31:2-6; Ezek 20:30-38), Second Isaiah follows in their tradition and expectantly looks to a new exodus for the people (43:16-21; 52:11f), and further understands this redemptive act reaching back to creation itself. Commenting on the passage which enshrines this, 51:9-11, Ackroyd writes: 'What God does here and now is both what he did in creation – the mythology of creation conflict expresses that – and what he did in the bringing of Israel out of Egypt. The future event is contained in this, for the return of the exiles to Zion in rejoicing is the counterpart of the ransoming of the enslaved Israel and of the overthrow of the hostile forces of primeval chaos. The whole range of the future hope is here drawn together, and from the point of view of our understanding of Deutero-Isaiah's place in the religious tradition it is of very great significance that the expression of the hope is so bound into the historical and creative concepts of the nature of Yahweh.'[18] The creative and saving action is being accomplished again in this new beginning for the people: as it will be from exile, so it was from the visit of God in the exodus, as it was from the beginning when God turned 'wasteland into the garden of Yahweh.' (51:3) So all this is now.

Second Isaiah is certain that the God whom Israel has experienced in history is the same God who has directed the destinies of mankind since creation: as his power extends through all time so his rule is universal in scope. In the light of Israel's historical election by God its primacy of place is secure; however, the prophet does not see the vocation of Israel as exclusive but looks beyond the boundaries of his own people to the time when the nations yet unknown will be drawn to share the new covenant relationship (55:1-5). Thus, just as 'the God of Israel, the saviour' (45:15) is he who says 'Turn to me and be saved, all the ends of the earth' (45:22), so his chosen Israel is called to reflect that universal dimension to her mission by being a 'witness to all the peoples' (55:4).

The high point of prophetic promise is clearly the mysterious figure whose vocation is to save, not by visible success but through iniquitous suffering and death: he is the Servant of Yahweh, the subject of four songs (42:1-4; 49:1-6; 50:4-9; 52:13-53:12). Among other suggestions, the Servant has been identified with Jeremiah, Second Isaiah, Israel, the faithful remnant, the ideal people of God, and the future Messiah. Outside the four poems, the Servant is identified with Israel (43:9); however, there is no unanimity among scholars about the precise identification of the Servant within the poems.[19] There is general agreement

---

18. P. Ackroyd, *Exile and Restoration* (London: SCM, 1972) pp. 129-130.
19. For a review of the question: C. R. North, *The Suffering Servant in Deutero-Isaiah* (London: Oxford University Press, 1956); H. H. Rowley, *The Servant of the Lord and Other Essays* (Oxford: Blackwell, 1965) pp. 1-60.

about the messianic character of the Servant and the pattern of his mission: that he is in an unparalleled way the instrument of God's saving purpose who in obedience to his calling undergoes persecution and suffering to such an extent that he lays down his life for many and accomplishes in his death God's plan for salvation. And that plan is not limited to the people of Israel:

> It is not enough for you to be my servant,
> to restore the tribes of Jacob and bring back the survivors of Israel;
> I will make you the light of the nations
> so that my salvation may reach to the ends of the earth. (49:6)

If Second Isaiah presents the role of the Servant with a view to final salvation, unveiling at the same time the redemptive value of suffering, it would seem that the figure finds its ultimate embodiment in the Messiah, an opinion which is supported by pre-Christian Jewish tradition.[20] Certainly the interpretation which sees the Servant as the future chosen one endowed by God's spirit to sum up in himself the hope of Israel and fulfil Israel's divinely appointed mission, would honour the pattern of Second Isaiah's prophecies. That the Servant Songs find fulfilment in the passion, death and resurrection of Christ is understood by the New Testament authors and especially Luke (cf. Mt 8:17; 12:17-21; Mk 8:31; 9:12; 14:21.49; Lk 18:31; 22:18.37; 24:13-35, 44-47; Acts 2:23; 3:18; 4:28; 7:52; 8:26-35; 13:27-29; 26:22; 1 Cor 15:3; 1 Pet 2:21-25). And as Tiede proposes:

> The explicit citations of Isaiah 53 (Lk 22:37; Acts 8:32-33), the frequent references to the servant roles, and the pronouncement of Jesus' innocence may even suggest that this mode of speaking about Jesus provided the locus around which the specifically royal and prophetic vocabulary could cluster. Thus, it is as the chosen one, the servant of God, that this Jesus the messiah suffers and fulfils all the scriptures.[21]

20. Cf. W. Zimmerli and J. Jeremias, *The Servant of God* (Illinois: Allenson, 1957) pp. 53-78.
21. D. Tiede, *Prophecy and History in Luke-Acts* (Philadelphia: Fortress, 1980) pp. 124-125; cf. J. M. Derrett, 'Midrash in the New Testament: the Origin of Lk 22:67-68' in *Studia Theologica* 29 (1975) pp. 147-156; D. Juel, 'The Image of the Servant Christ in the New Testament' in *Southwestern Journal of Theology* 21 (1979) pp. 7-22.

That the promises of Second Isaiah are not for immediate fulfilment becomes acutely clear very soon. With Cyrus' edict of restoration (Ezra 1:24; 6:3-5) the Jews are permitted to return to their homeland, but to the minority who make the journey a bleak prospect awaits them: a poor, devastated land, an ambiguous political status, a depressing economic outlook, and the persistent hostility of the Samaritans. The inspiring promises by Second Isaiah of the universal triumph of Yahweh's rule seem a world away, and the initial enthusiasm of the repatriated community gives way to profound discouragement and frustration, a situation which is addressed by Haggai, Zechariah (chapters 1 to 8), and Third Isaiah (chapters 56 to 66). As Haggai interprets times past as a divine punishment for the indifference of the community, exhorting them to rebuild the Temple now without delay, Zechariah assures them of the constancy of God's favour, 'Yahweh will again take pity on Zion, again make Jerusalem his very own' (1:17), and points to the imminence of divine intervention and the prospect of messianic salvation. Stirred by the prophetic summons the new community manages out of meagre resources to finish the Temple, which serves anew as the focal point for their lingering identity as the people of God.

After the visit of judgement suffered in the exile, the post-exilic prophets speak of a new age dawning when the living fellowship with God will be restored, a renewal of life linked to a change of fortune in the political climate. What Ezekiel announced as lying in the future and Second Isaiah proclaimed to be close at hand; what Haggai and Zechariah believed would be accomplished before their very eyes (Hag 2:21ff; Zech 2:1ff) – that time when the visit of salvation would take place – continues to form the basis of faith by which the restored community live their lives. Although that time will come only by a new act of God, the prophets are concerned lest the unreadiness of the community makes for an indefinite delay frustrating God's universal saving purpose (cf. 'But when the Son of Man comes, will he find any faith on earth?' Lk 18:8).

Showing a frank realism about post-exilic misfortune while maintaining hope in the deferred fulfilment of divine promises is a feat of balance displayed by Third Isaiah and Malachi in their prophetic writings. Both prophets are aware of the radical changes which need to take place before the divine promises can be accomplished in time. For Third Isaiah, Israel's messianic future is assured; but, for the moment, the time of trial has to be endured with a confident faith and sincere holiness of life. The rebuilding of the Temple and Jerusalem itself will be a sure sign of the presence of the glory of God (59:19). The prophet displays a profound confidence in the effectiveness of divine action; at the same time, he shows pastoral care for the poor, the broken, the captives, and all those who mourn (62:1ff). In his turn, Malachi addresses the practical problems experienced by the community after the rebuilding of the Temple, listing the sins of the priests and the people (1:1-2:16), and exhorting everyone to be worthy of the great act of divine deliverance, the coming of God to judge, to punish, and to reward (2:17-3:24).

Throughout the post-exilic period the people's hope, no longer rooted in the national cult or dynastic theology, has to be reinterpreted and given new impetus if Judaism is to keep faith with the divine purpose in history. The hope of the people becomes closely linked to the Day of Yahweh, a definitive visit by God which will effectively defeat his enemies and establish his people in a new age of peace.[22]

THE DAY OF YAHWEH AND THE POOR OF YAHWEH

The transition from seeing the Day of Yahweh as a particular historical event to interpreting it as the consummation of God's purpose in history can be seen in the prophecy of Joel. If the plague of locusts is a description of the visit of God in judgement (chapters 1 to 2), the writing is transposed to an eschatalogical level (chapters 3 to 4), since the Day of Yahweh is described as the final day of judgement, a cosmic event which affects all nations. The purpose of the first part is to call people to repentance and exhort them to liturgical prayer; in the second part Joel encourages a disillusioned people to look to a future time when the ancient messianic prophecies will be fulfilled in the outpouring of the spirit of God, the victory of God over his enemies, and the streams of blessings from the Temple (cf. Acts 2:17-21).

---

22. Cf G. Von Rad, 'The Origin of the Concept of the Day of Yahweh' in *Journal of Semitic Studies* 4 (1959) pp. 97-108.

As the end of the Old Testament period approaches, the hope of
Judaism is sustained by anticipation of the climactic Day of Yahweh and
expresses itself through the new form of apocalypse. Although apocalyptic writing has precedent among the prophets, it takes its definitive
form in the last two centuries before Christ and is represented among the
canonical writings in the book of Daniel (chapters 7 to 12). Writing at a
time when the Jews are in great anguish through renewed persecution,
the author is concerned to impress upon his hearers that the movement
of history is controlled by God; that the destinies of nations and individuals are shaped by his hand; that the messianic kingdom foretold by the
prophets will indeed come and supplant earthly power; that their
eschatological hopes will be fulfilled in the final visit of salvation. More
particularly, we are introduced to the one who will make the visit, the
figure of the Son of Man:

> I gazed into the visions of the night.
> And I saw, coming on the clouds of heaven,
> one like a son of man.
> He came to the one of great age
> and was led into his presence.
> On him was conferred sovereignty,
> glory and kingship,
> and men of all peoples, nations and languages
> became his servants.
> His sovereignty is an eternal sovereignty
> which shall never pass away,
> nor will his empire ever be destroyed. (7:13-14)

As the figures like four great beasts seen earlier in the vision symbol-
ize four pagan kingdoms (v. 17), so the 'one like a son of man' represents
in the symbolism of the vision 'the saints of the most High' (7:18,22,25,27).
That the Son of Man refers to an individual is attested by Jewish
apocalyptic writing (Enoch; 2 Esd), by its use as a messianic title among
the Jews of Jesus' time, and by the witness of the Gospels where no one
uses the title but Jesus himself. And in Luke's Gospel, Jesus uses the title
when speaking of his own saving mission (19:10), his death and resurrec-

tion (9:22), his future glory (17:26.30), his coming again (18:8), the final judgement (21:36), and the apocalyptic end of history when the Son of Man will come to mark the time of final liberation (21:25-27).

In the midst of a situation where Judaism appears to have lost everything, the apocalyptic vision affirms God as the sovereign Lord of history and the Day of Yahweh as the consummation of God's saving purpose at history's end. In the meantime the people must struggle to keep their faith and hope alive by rooting them firmly in the reality of the divine promises. In keeping sacred the memory of the exodus, the exile and the restoration, along with the prophetic interpretation of those events, the remnant of Israel can ground their hope in the historical reality of the visit of God, evidence of his constant care and liberating love. The actuality of the visit of God serves in turn to nourish religious confidence that God will indeed come again to vindicate his faithful. And before the Old Testament's story comes to an end the author of Wisdom assures the persecuted Jews that even death cannot harm the one who is faithful to God as he encourages them to look to the final day of visitation:

> When the time comes for his visitation they will shine out ... and the Lord will be their king forever. They who trust in him will understand the truth, those who are faithful will live with him in love; for grace and mercy await those he has chosen. (Wis 3:7-9)

When the national catastrophe that has overtaken Israel and the Day of Yahweh that will justify the faithful are both interpreted as visits of God, that interpretation gives an unprecedented importance to those who have been preserved from the catastrophe and who look to the ultimate consolation of Israel: *anawim*, the poor of Yahweh. They are the lowly ones who put their trust in God alone, and whose religious dependence on God is closely associated with Temple piety. A faithful remnant has been preserved from an Israel that has been deprived of all worldly security and discernible means of support; but in this experience there is a teaching which educates the faithful to trust in nothing but the one who has power to save. Judaism has become profoundly poor, a condition which is described eloquently in Daniel:

Lord, now we are the least of all the nations,
now we are despised throughout the world, today, because of our sin.
We have at this time no leader, no prophet, no prince,
no holocaust, no sacrifice, no oblation, no incense,
no place where we can offer you the first-fruits
and win your favour.
But may the contrite soul, the humbled spirit be as acceptable to you
as holocausts of rams and bullocks,
as thousands of fattened lambs:
such let our sacrifice be to you today,
and may it be your will that we follow you wholeheartedly,
since those who put their trust in you will not be disappointed.
And now we put our whole heart into following you,
into fearing you and seeking your face once more.
Do not disappoint us;
treat us gently, as you yourself are gentle
and very merciful.
Grant us deliverance worthy of your wonderful deeds,
let your name win glory, Lord. (Dan 3:37-43)

A contrite soul and a humbled spirit, a renewed wholeheartedness in
following God, a longing for deliverance from a God who has acted
before in history – this forms the basis for the spirituality of the poor of
Yahweh. The poverty of the faithful becomes a force for good; it
nourishes a spirituality of fidelity to the law and surrender to the purpose
of God: in this is found salvation. As Gelin has written: 'The poor of
Yahweh lived in God's presence, totally committed, fully surrendered,
blindly confident'.[23] They are the praying, waiting, expectant remnant
of Israel. And the Gospel will introduce us to representative figures of
the poor of Yahweh whose fidelity to the Law is unquestioned, whose
Temple piety is evident, whose messianic longing finds a specific answer, and who express for a measureless number of people that the long-
awaited visit of God has taken place. Such are the people found in the
first two chapters of the Gospel of Luke.

---

23. A. Gelin, *The Poor of Yahweh* (Minnesota: Liturgical Press, 1964) p. 11.

2 | The Saving Visit of God in the Gospel of Luke

THE INFANCY NARRATIVE: THE VISIT OF GOD IN JESUS

IN THE CAREFUL DESIGN of his infancy narrative Luke takes pains to link the new age of fulfilment to the old age of promise, and not surprisingly he uses old people in Zechariah, Elizabeth, Simeon, and Anna to bridge the two Israels. The venerable ancients are connected through memory and fidelity to the old dispensation and to the new dispensation through a lively expectancy. Their age does not make them long on memory and short on expectation: their hopes are ahead of them not behind them. They are chosen as agents of God's revelation, and filled with the Spirit they recognise the time they inhabit as the time of the salvific visit of God – not out of an inspired guess but from the evidence of their experience. Something happens to them, and they interpret that something as the visit of God. Thus the beginnings of Christian history are linked to the whole salvific history of God's people.

Luke establishes an immediate connection with the Old Testament in opening his story with Zechariah, representing the ancient priesthood of Israel, and his wife Elizabeth, herself of priestly descent. Both uphold the will of God expressed through the revealed Law. However, the couple relive the seemingly hopeless condition of Abraham and Sarah who stand at the beginning of the sacred writings of Israel: measuring their hope for a child with the natural capacity to realize that their shortcomings are impressive as we learn that both couples are advanced in years and both women are barren. The empty womb stands at the beginning of both Testaments.

The motif of sterility connects the story to Hannah, the mother of Samuel (1 Sam 1-2), the mother of Samson (Jg 3:2); and Rachel, Rebecca, and Sarah, the wives of the great patriarchs. But the image of barrenness recalls not only the beginnings of the patriarchal period but also the beginning of creation when there was nothing but wasteland (Gen 2:5). In all this there is the constant image of the unseeded place where

nothing can grow unless God intervenes to act. God's creative intervention which makes the beginning is the most distinguishing mark of the
Lucan infancy narrative.

Appropriately, the setting for the first revelation is the Temple, the
centre of the traditional Jewish world, where Zechariah is the first to
hear of the messianic visitation. The apocalyptic character of the annunciation narratives is well known,[1] and their literary parallels with
Daniel, one of the last books of Israel's sacred writings, seem to suggest
that Luke is deliberately evoking the atmosphere appropriate to the last
times. If this is true, it could be argued that Luke portrays Zechariah and
Elizabeth in such a way that they recall not only the beginning but the
end of the sacred history of Israel. Certainly, Daniel 9-10 serves as a
classic back-drop for the annunciation to Zechariah, even to the point of
Daniel being struck dumb (10:15). Gabriel appears to Daniel while he is
praying in some distress during the time of the evening sacrifice. Daniel
reacts with fear, and after counselling him not to fear Gabriel voices his
concern that Daniel understand the meaning of the vision which speaks
of the time

for your people and your holy city,
for putting an end to transgression,
for placing the seals on sin,
for expiating crime,
for introducing everlasting integrity,
for setting the seal on vision and on prophecy,
for anointing the Holy of Holies. (9:24)

The Old Testament literary pattern of revelation embracing annunciation and call is adopted by Luke and can be tabulated in the following
way:

1. Revelation is marked by the presence of an angel
2. Reaction of fear by the visionary
3. Angel identifies himself and counsels visionary not to fear
4. Annunciation that woman will conceive and give birth

1. Cf. especially F. Neirynck, *L'Evangile de Noël selon S. Luc* (Paris: Pensée Catholique,
   1960).

5. The name to be given the child
6. The future accomplishments of the child
7. Objection by the visionary
8. Objection overruled by giving of a sign.

It is not simply that a literary form popular in the old dispensation proves useful to Luke; the rhythmic repetition binds what is happening to what has already happened so that it can be understood as integral to the grand scheme of God. The familiar pattern not only establishes clear links with Israel but the new revelation sets the scene for raising expectation of some unprecedented event in history. Through this studied technique Luke shows the old and the new as inseparable and demonstrates in the new revelation the central place of the long-awaited visit of God.

There is a clear structural parallel between the annunciation to Zechariah and the annunciation to Mary, but if the form of the revelation is similar the content is wholly different. The second annunciation narrative is not to an old priest but to a young virgin, and unlike the promised birth to an old and barren couple the promised birth through a virgin has no biblical precedent. Commenting on the parallelism between the two stories Fitzmeyer observes:

> The Jesus-side always comes off better. For instance, John's parents are 'upright in God's sight' (1:6), but Mary is the favoured one (1:28). John's mother, though aged and barren, eventually bears him naturally, but Jesus' mother bears him wondrously. John will be great before the Lord (1:15), but Jesus will be Great (1:32). John will walk before the Kyrios (1:16-17), but Jesus will be called Kyrios (2:11) (in a different sense, of course), as well as Saviour and Messiah. John's father queries the angel and is struck dumb (1:19-22), but Jesus' mother queries the angel and is reassured, declaring herself the handmaid of the Lord (1:34-38).[2]

In the light of Christian tradition Luke defines John's role in the Gospel as the precursor of the Messiah, and although 1:14-17 does not

---

2. J. Fitzmyer, *The Gospel According to Luke I-IX* (Anchor Bible; New York: Doubleday, 1983) p. 315.

designate John as the forerunner of the Messiah but as the messenger of the Lord, Luke's overall intention seems hardly in doubt. Against the background of Malachi which speaks of the Day of Yahweh when 'I mean to visit you for the judgement' (Mal 3:5), a time when the Lord expects to find people made ready by the prophet Elijah, Luke introduces John whose similar task it is to prepare for the coming of the Lord.

I am going to send you Elijah the prophet
before my day comes, that great and terrible day.
He shall turn the hearts of fathers towards their children
and the hearts of children towards their fathers,
lest I come and strike the land with a curse. (Mal 3:23-24)

With the spirit and power of Elijah
he will go before him
to turn the hearts of fathers towards their children
and the disobedient back to the wisdom that the virtuous have
preparing for the Lord a people fit for him. (Lk 1:17)

In contrast to the identification of John and his prophetic role, Gabriel's two-part declaration to Mary asserts the unrivalled primacy of the son she will bear. Mary must name him Jesus: the original meaning of the Hebrew name was 'Yahweh helps', but popular etymology interpreted the name to mean 'God saves' (cf Mt 1:21). Jesus will be great without qualification, will be acknowledged Son of the Most High, and will take his place on the Davidic throne forever. The textual link between messianic expectation and fulfilment can be seen when comparing Nathan's promise to David and the now of its accomplishment in Luke:

2 Samuel 7 (RSV)
9: I will make for you a great name ...
13: I will establish the throne of his kingdom forever.
14: I will be his father, and he shall be my son.
16: And your house and your kingdom shall be made sure forever

Luke 1 (RSV)
32a: He will be great, and will be called the Son of the Most High;

32b: And the Lord God will give to him the throne of his father David,
33a: and he will reign over the house of Jacob forever;
33b: and of his kingdom there will be no end.

In response to this first declaration, the 'how' question of Mary – in keeping with the pattern of biblical annunciation narratives – allows for the second stage of Gabriel's revelation about Jesus' identity. Mary will become mother of the Messiah through God's creative and active presence: the Holy Spirit will come upon her and the power of the Most High will overshadow her. The verbs 'come upon' (*eperchesthai*) and 'overshadow' (*episkiazein*) both point to the effective power of God's intervention in Mary's life. Because of this intervention the child will be called holy, Son of God. The 'therefore' (*dio kai*) makes a causal connection between conception through the power of the Holy Spirit and the existence of the Son of God: clearly, Luke has no notion of a pre-existence Christology. What Luke seems concerned to say, however, is that Jesus did not become Son of God at some later time, but through the act of divine creation he was God's Son from conception. Thus in this two-stage revelation Luke shows that Jesus is not only the Davidic Messiah but the Son of God.

Luke's christological affirmation about Jesus in 1:32,33 and 1:35 which moves from identifying him as the Davidic Messiah to acknowledging him as the Son of God can be seen in an earlier testimony of faith which first identifies Jesus as a Davidic descendant and then as the Son of God:

This news is about the Son of God who, according to the human nature he took, was a descendant of David: it is about Jesus Christ our Lord who, in the order of the spirit, the spirit of holiness that was in him, was proclaimed Son of God in all his power through his resurrection from the dead. (Rom 1:3-4)

As this formula suggests it would seem that Jesus was first acknowledged as Son of God because of what happened in the resurrection. As can be seen from Acts and the writings of Paul the testimony about Jesus' full identity is linked to the resurrection (e.g. Acts 2:32,36; 13:33; Rom 1:3-4). Only in the light of the completed mission of Jesus is his full

identity revealed and his universal significance realised, and that awareness is reached only under the guidance of the Spirit of truth and
understanding. Thus the coming of the Spirit in Pentecost makes the
beginning of the full witness to Christ, one which has central to its
proclamation the resurrection of Jesus who was crucified (cf. Acts 2:22-
39; 3;12-26; 4:8-12). In the tradition of that witness and from their own
enlightened awareness the evangelists testify and ask their readers to
believe that Jesus was the Son of God not only in the light of the
resurrection but during his life in Palestine. What Luke does in company with the other evangelists is assert that Jesus is the Son of God
before the resurrection: Mark places his declaration at Jesus' baptism,
Matthew and Luke make their declaration at Jesus' conception, while
John refers his to the beginning of time.

   Luke first identifies Jesus as the Son of God in the annunciation to
Mary, a christological affirmation which follows the statement about the
coming of the Holy Spirit (cf Acts 1:8) and the overshadowing by the
power of the Most High (cf 9:34) This is given as an answer to Mary's
question: 'But how can this come about since I am a virgin?' (1:34) The
virginity of Mary is affirmed not principally to tell us something about
Mary but to tell us something about the child: 'And so the child will be
holy and called Son of God' (v. 35d). The focus is on the fact that the child
will be conceived in her through the creative act of God. Unlike the
biblical pattern of barrenness in which the couples expectantly yearned
for a child of their own, there is no suggestion that Mary is longing for
a child; rather the objection clause which repeats the mention of her
virginity makes it clear that Mary who has not yet lived with her
husband has no expectation of a child. The revelation comes to her not
as a response to prayerful longing but as the disclosure of the total
initiative of God. The child is God's idea and the virginity of Mary
underscores this.

   If the old people in Luke's infancy narrative are a sign of continuity
with the old dispensation centering on the Jerusalem Temple, the young
Mary is a sign of what is totally new about God's plan. As the barrenness
of the old women can be seen to reflect the desolate landscape at the
beginning of time (Gen 2:5) so the virginity of Mary can be seen to reflect

the formless void at the beginning of creation (Gen 1:2). Until the coming of the Spirit the earth remained void; so until the coming of the Spirit Mary's womb is empty. In the power of that Spirit there is creation and life. In Mary the new creation begins to take flesh, the mysterious plan of God unfolds, and the visit of God happens in the person of his Son.

In the course of his infancy narrative Luke presents us with three substantial canticles, the *Magnificat*, the *Benedictus*, and the *Nunc Dimittis*, which he ascribes to Mary, Zechariah, and Simeon, respectively, Luke portrays the three speakers as representative figures of the *anawim*, the poor of Yahweh, those whose spiritual attitude of lowliness combined with their Temple piety survived the persecution of the post-exilic remnant of Israel. Their spirituality is formed from a total dependence on God and a readiness to do his will; they live in hopeful expectation of his visit which will bring the consolation promised to Israel (cf Ps 149:4; Is 49:13; 66:2).

Like the annunciation narratives, the canticles are a literary mosaic of Old Testament texts and serve the double purpose of evoking the hopes of Israel while at the same time placing those hopes within the framework of fulfilment. It would appear that Luke has adapted various compositions of Hebrew poetry which proclaimed the saving action of God and by setting them in the context of the infancy narrative applied their general sentiments to the specific occasion of the speakers. In composition and in outlook the canticles appear Jewish rather than Christian, and closely parallel the psalms and hymns written in the first and second century B.C. [3] Fitzmeyer argues to a pre-Lucan Jewish Christian source [4] while Brown attempts to identify that source further as hymns emerging from Jewish *anawim* who have been converted to Christianity.[5] Whatever the exact origin of the canticles, Luke adapts them to serve his purpose of further revealing the theological significance of what is taking place.

---

3. Cf. D. R. Jones, 'The Background and Character of the Lukan Psalms' in *Journal of Theological Studies* 19 (1968) pp. 19-50.
4. J. Fitzmyer, *op. cit.*, pp. 309-313.
5. R. Brown, *The Birth of the Messiah* (London: Geoffrey Chapman, 1977) pp. 350-355.

The *Magnificat* can be divided into four parts:

Introduction (vv. 46b-47) – Mary's whole self praises God and rejoices in the knowledge that he is her Saviour (l Sam 2:1-2; Ps 35:9; Hab 3:18). In the framework of fulfilment Jesus himself is identified as the Saviour (1:69; 2:11).

First Stanza (vv. 48-50) – In the tradition of the *anawim*, Mary compares her lowly and blessed state to the greatness of God, and praises him for his attributes of might (Deut 10:21), holiness (Ps 111:9), and mercy (Ps 103:9). In the framework of fulfilment Mary has already been told that the child 'will be great ' (v 32), has already experienced the might of the Most High (v 35), and has heard that the child would 'be called holy' (v 35). Although God's mercy 'which reaches from age to age' has not been mentioned in Mary's story, she has heard of the everlasting rule of his Kingdom (1:33), one which Luke will associate so clearly with mercy (e.g. 23:40-43).

Second Stanza (vv. 51-53) – Again from the perspective of the *anawim* these verses speak of God's preference for the 'lowly' and 'hungry', and focus on the deeds of God accomplished through his saving intervention (l Sam 2:5-8; Sir 10:14; Ps 34:11, 107:9). In the context of fulfilment the details can be interpreted to speak of the accomplished mission of Jesus. The six verbs are in the past tense and therefore speak of what has already been achieved: given that Luke is writing after the resurrection in the light of the completed mission of Jesus, these verses can be applied to the salvation through Jesus's death, resurrection, and exaltation (Acts 2:33; 5:31).

Conclusion (vv. 54-55) – The sense of fulfilment dominates these verses which recognise that what has been accomplished is intimately related to what was promised to Abraham and his descendants (Is 41:8-9; Ps 98:3; Mic 7:20). Again the past tense is used, but in the light of the post-resurrection community this serves to testify to the belief that Jesus' mission is the fulfilling of God's covenant with Abraham and his descendants.

According to one's thesis about the origin of the *Magnificat* and the other two canticles their context and content yield a variety of meanings. Although the *Magnificat* picks up themes previously mentioned in the infancy narrative its substance does not presuppose the annunciation of the birth of the Messiah; clearly, therefore, one has to look to a wider frame of reference for understanding. The fact that Luke is writing out of a resurrection faith, one which educates the way he sees the significance of Jesus and his mission, will necessarily shape the way he presents his material: we cannot expect Luke to suspend his faith and insight. Alongside that there is Luke's concern to show Christianity as a movement emerging from Judaism, a concern that can be traced throughout the Gospel and Acts, and his allied theme of the historical fulfilment of the ancient promises of God. All this would seem to indicate a layer of theological meaning, a layer which can be detected in the *Benedictus*.

Treated as a composite whole the *Benedictus* can be divided as follows:

Introduction (v 68a) – The canticle opens with Zechariah using a traditional form of blessing God, one which identifies God in his relationship with Israel. The form recalls a familiar psalmic blessing (Ps 41:14; 72:18; 106:48; also 1 Kgs 1:48).

First Stanza (vv 68b-71) – The primary reason for praising God is because 'he has visited his people'. As with 1:51ff the verb is in the past tense denoting accomplishment. The visit of God has brought salvation because he 'has raised up' a 'horn of salvation' (v. 69a) in the House of David. (1 Sam 2:10; 3::9; Ps 132:16-17; Ezek 29:21). The power of salvation is Jesus who is the Christ (John the Baptist has no links with the House of David). What God has accomplished is what he promised to do by the mouth of his holy prophets (Acts 3:21).

Second Stanza (vv 72-75) – The saving work of God is also a fulfilment of the covenant made with Abraham and his descendants (Ex 2:24; Ps 106:45; Mic 7:20). The purpose of God's liberating his people was to enable them to serve him in holiness all their days (1 Kgs 9:4-5; Jos 24:14)

Third Stanza (vv 76-77) – This Lucan insert into a tapestry of Old Testament texts answers the question, 'What will this child turn out to be?' (v 66) In conscious contrast to Jesus who has been designated 'Son of the Most High' (v 32) John will be called 'Prophet of the Most High' (v 76). He will go before the Lord (1:15,17) and enable people to experience salvation through the forgiveness of their sins (3:3).

Conclusion (vv 78-79) – Previous themes are gathered together in the concluding verses of the canticle. (Manuscripts and therefore scholars are divided on whether the tense of the verb 'visit' is past or future: given the recapitulation form of the conclusion it would seem appropriate translated in the past tense.) In his mercy God has visited his people as *anatole ex hypsou*s – literally, 'a rising from on high' (Is 60:1; Mal 3:20). Zechariah refers to Jesus as the Messiah, the 'Dawn from on High' who will appear to those in darkness (Is 42:6-7) to guide us into the way of peace (Is 59:8).

Central to the proclamation of the *Benedictus* is the revelation that God 'has visited his people' in the person of Jesus: in v. 68 the action refers to God while in v. 78 it is directly related to the coming of the Messiah. In the *Benedictus* the visit of God is a messianic concept, and since Jesus has already been identified as the Davidic Messiah (1:32,33) he summarises in his person the visit of God.

The Greek verb which Luke uses in 1:68.78 is *episkeptesthai*. In secular Greek the verb means 'to look upon, to consider, to have regard to, something or someone', and when referring to the gods means 'graciously to look upon, to care for, to watch over'.[6] In the Greek Old Testament the verb is used often to describe what God is doing and has a variety of connotations which we have already seen: in most cases it denotes the active intervention of God in history for the purpose of revealing his will and saving his people. And that action is generally linked to the most important visit of God in the experience of Israel, his saving intervention in Egypt (Ex 4:31). Luke's use of *episkeptesthai* capitalizes on its constant use in the Greek Old Testament to refer to the *action* of God visiting his people, rather than on the secular usage which speaks more of an *attitude* of mind. Among the Gospels the use of the verb to describe the action of God is peculiar to Luke and occurs elsewhere in the New Testament only in Hebrews 2:6. Luke uses it again in 7:16 and Acts 15:14, and the substantive 'visitation' in Jesus' lamentation over Jerusalem (19:44).

The visit of God proclaimed by Zechariah takes place in the city of David, which is called Bethlehem (2:4). Scholars have unresolved ques-

---

6. Cf H. W. Beyer, *Theological Dictionary of the New Testament* 11, p. 600.

tions about the historical accuracy of the events surrounding Luke's birth narrative: there is no historical record of a universal census at the time specified by Luke; the Roman custom of taxation was based on the individual's place of residence, not his place of ancestry; Quirinius was governor of Syria during the years A.D. 6-9, some ten years after the birth of Jesus. Ingenious attempts have been made to resolve the historical difficulties, but the important question which can be answered concerns Luke's theological intentions: the census places the birth of Jesus within the frame of world history; it also situates the birth in Joseph's ancestral city, Bethlehem, the place prophesied to mark the beginning of the messianic visit.

In his birth narrative (2:1-20) Luke gives more attention to the interpretation of Jesus' birth by the angels and the shepherds' visitation than he does to the birth itself. His account of the birth of Jesus is spare and simple: while the couple are in Bethlehem, Mary's time comes; she delivers her first-born, warms him in swaddling clothes and lays him in a manger because there is no room at the inn.

The first thing we are told about the new-born child is that he is wrapped in swaddling clothes, a description that will be given to the shepherds for its value as a sign to bear out the angel's message of the birth of a saviour in David's city (v. 12). The detail is not insignificant but has a purpose beyond itself: it recalls King Solomon's description of his birth:

> I was nurtured in swaddling clothes, with every care. No king has known any other beginning of existence; for all there is one way only into life, as out of it. (Wis 7:4-6)

Solomon's description of birth astride death focusing on the detail of the swaddling clothes is an important one because of who he is: he is a royal child, the son of David. The swaddling clothes, therefore, have the function of a sign because they point not to the poverty of the parents but to the royalty of the child.

The second point Luke tells us about the child is that he is laid in a manger because there is no room at the inn. Again the detail is important, not least because Luke mentions it three times: in the first instance as the place where Mary lays the child (v. 7); secondly, as a sign to the shepherds (v. 12); thirdly, as a sign which works its purpose (v. 16). The manger as a sign recalls the text from Isaiah:

> The ox knows its owner
> and the ass its master's crib (*phatne*)
> but Israel does not know [me];
> my people does not understand [me]. (1:3 RSV)

In the Septuagint the comparison between Israel and God is highlighted by the addition of 'me' in the last two lines. (Both the Septuagint and Luke use *phatne*, manger or crib.) In the text from Isaiah the dumb animals are better at recognising their owner, the source of their nourishment, than the people of Israel are at recognising the visitation of their Lord. The manger, a feeding trough for animals, becomes a symbol for the recognition of the Lord by his people. The fact that the shepherds recognise the manger as a sign of the birth of the saviour is an indication that, unlike the Israel of the past, they do know the manger of their Lord.

The manger stands in deliberate contrast to the inn, and Giblin suggests that the comparison yields more meaning in the light of Jeremiah 14:8 which he literally translates from the Septuagint:

> Why are you like one in the land of an alien, like a traveller (or inhabitant) who lodges in an inn? [7]

Jeremiah's appeal is followed immediately by an oracle of punishment: God states that he accepts his people no longer but will visit them with punishment (14:10), and reveals that the prophets who announce 'unbroken peace' are not sent by divine command (14:13-14). Jeremiah's plea, addressed to the Lord and saviour of Israel, is answered in Luke's narrative: the saviour does not stay in an inn like an alien who cannot depend on the kindness of relatives or friends, but is laid in a manger where he is recognised by his own people in the shepherds – whose location is given as 'the countryside close by' the city of David (cf Mic 5:1-5). And after the manger is given as a sign to the shepherds there is a proclamation of peace made not by false prophets but by divine messen-

---

7. C. H. Giblin, 'Reflections on the Sign of the Manger' in *Catholic Biblical Quarterly* 29 (1967) p. 99.

gers commissioned to bring God's revelation as good news.

The good news announced to the shepherds is central to Luke's birth narrative: the annunciation describes Jesus by three christological titles: Saviour, Messiah, and Lord (2:11). These titles, unlike those describing the royal child in Isaiah 9:5(6), are born of a resurrection faith which recognizes the full significance of Jesus in the light of his exaltation (cf Acts 2:36; 5:31). In the same way the canticle of the heavenly host proclaims glory to God in heaven and peace on earth to those whom God favours (2:14), while later in the Gospel narrative the whole group of disciples joyfully praise God:

> Blessings on the King who comes
> in the name of the Lord!
> Peace in heaven
> and glory in the highest heavens. (19:38)

As Brown comments: 'The same kind of poetry used to hail Jesus as the Messiah at the end of his ministry is applicable to the birth of the Messiah. But in the present Gospel sequence, Luke is telling us that the angels of heaven recognized at the beginning of Jesus' life what the disciples came to know only at the end, namely, the presence of the Messiah King who comes in the name of the Lord.'[8]

The story of the recognition of Jesus continues in the presentation account. Still within the Old Testament frame of reference Luke continues his infancy narrative with the circumcision, naming, and manifestation of Jesus (2:21-40) which parallels the account of John's beginnings (1:19-80). As the narrative opened in Jerusalem so now the action returns there (2:22,25,38) with the first appearance of Jesus in the Temple (cf Mal 3:1-2). When the day comes for them to be purified by the Law they take Jesus up to Jerusalem. Jerusalem is the place where Jesus' saving mission is accomplished, and when the days draw near for him to be taken up he resolutely takes the road to Jerusalem (9:51). Luke will use the pull of Jerusalem to give shape to Jesus' ministry, just as he will give it pride of place in the resurrection narrative and the beginning of Acts. Not surprisingly, therefore, the link between Jesus and Jerusa-

8. R. Brown, *op. cit.*, p. 427.

lem is an important motif in the infancy narrative.

The Law (mentioned five times in this section) provides the occasion
and the setting for moving the action from Bethlehem to the Jerusalem
Temple. Luke's condensed account of the presentation and purification
conflates two ceremonies: the purification of the mother and the presentation of the first-born male. In the Mosaic Law a woman was regarded
as ritually unclean for forty days after the birth of a male child. At the end
of that time she was required to present herself for the rite of purification
by a priest; she was to make her offering to the priest at the door of the
sanctuary (Lev 12:6ff). Although Luke speaks of 'their' purification, the
Law required only the mother's (Lev 12:1) Mary is shown to be obedient
to the Law, and in its fulfilment makes the offering of the poor, two
turtle-doves or two pigeons.

Alongside this account Luke writes of the presentation of Jesus. The
Mosaic Law held that the first-born male, both animal and human,
belonged to God (Ex 13:2). However, after the tribe of Levi dedicated
themselves to the service of God, parents of the first-born were released
from the requirement of the Law by an act of redemption in which they
paid a ransom to the priest (Num 18:16). While the Law obliged the
parents to pay the sum in the Temple it did not oblige them to present
the child there. In Luke's account there is no mention of a ransom –
perhaps because it would be inappropriate to his model of Samuel who
was consecrated to the service of the Lord (1 Sam 24-28).

In the story of Samuel's presentation, Elkanah and Hannah take their
child to the sanctuary in Shiloh to offer him in the service of the Lord;
there they are met by an aged priest, Eli, who blesses the parents of the
child. Luke has already introduced us to an old couple, Elizabeth and
Zechariah, whom he presented as representative figures of the *anawim*;
now the aged Simeon and Anna are portrayed in similar vein, as upright
and devout people who live in expectation of the consolation of Israel (cf
Is 40:1; 66 12-13). In describing them both as prophets in a narrative with
so many references to the Law, Luke might be bringing into focus the
Law and the prophets – his description of the time prior to the coming
of the kingdom (16:16) to set the scene for the manifestation of Jesus.
However, as is clear from the sermons in Acts and the writings of Paul,

it is the Spirit not the Law which enables people to recognise the salvation which has been brought through Jesus. So, it is that same Spirit which Luke associates with Simeon three times – which empowers the old prophet to see salvation through Jesus.

As with the *Magnificat* and the *Benedictus*, the *Nunc Dimittis* is a mosaic of Old Testament texts which are recalled and set in the new context of their accomplishment in the messianic era. As Israel was ready to die when he had looked on the face of his lost son, Joseph, (Gen 46:30) so Simeon is now prepared to die because he has seen the fulfilment of the Lord's promise in Jesus. There is no reason for Simeon to wait longer, any more than there is for a watchman to stay at his post after the arrival of the one expected: the visit that was promised by God and expected by the faithful of Israel has taken place in history. Simeon's mission is completed when he can see in Jesus the Anointed of God. His own fulfilment is bound to the fulfilment of God's plan, and that mutual fulfilment is something which Jesus expresses to his chosen: 'Happy the eyes that see what you see, for I tell you that many prophets and kings wanted to see what you see, and never saw it' (10:23-24). Simeon sees 'it' in the person of Jesus.

In his canticle Zechariah blessed God because he had visited and redeemed his people; now the canticle of Simeon widens the sphere of Jesus' influence to include not only the people of Israel, but the Gentile world. Luke recounts that Mary and Joseph are astonished at what Simeon says. This might appear surprising since Mary has already been told of the stature of the child in the annunciation, and both she and Joseph have been told of the angel's annunciation to the shepherds. Why then the surprise? This has led some scholars to argue that the annunciation, the nativity, and the presentation are separate traditions, none of which supposes the existence of the others. But it is possible to see the surprise of Mary and Joseph as a Lucan device to underline something of supreme importance: a prophet guided by the Spirit has just revealed to Mary and Joseph something which has not been contained in the previous revelations: the significance of Jesus for the Gentile world.

Simeon's canticle recognises the fulfilment of Isaiah's prophecy which speaks of the day when the watchmen of the city of Jerusalem will rejoice when they see God face to face; for God is not only consoling his people but all the nations will see the salvation of God:

> Listen! Your watchmen raise their voices,
> they shout for joy together,
> for they see Yahweh face to face,
> as he returns to Zion.

> Break into shouts of joy together,
> you ruins of Jerusalem;
> for Yahweh is consoling his people,
> redeeming Jerusalem.

> Yahweh bares his holy arm
> in the sight of all the nations,
> and all the ends of the earth shall see
> the salvation of our God. (Is 52:8-10)

Luke does not ascribe to Jesus any missionary activity to the Gentiles; and as Jeremias argues, all the evangelists limit Jesus' activity to Israel and impose similar limitations on the disciples even though Jesus expressly promises the Gentiles a share in his kingdom. [9] For Luke, the mission to the Gentiles begins only after the resurrection when the new message will 'be preached to all the nations, beginning in Jerusalem' (24:47), a message preached in the power of the Holy Spirit (Acts 1:8). In Acts 15:14, the only occasion outside the Gospel where Luke uses the verb *episkeptesthai* of God, James gives an account of Simon Peter's address to the Jerusalem meeting referring to him by his semitic name, Simeon:

> Simeon has related how God first visited the Gentiles, to take out
> of them a people for his name. (RSV)

In the old dispensation Israel was the one people chosen from all the nations (Ex 19:5); in the new dispensation the Gentile nations are the elected source for the new people of God. And that new choice, revealed through the visit of God, is recognised by Simeon in the Temple of Jerusalem.

---

9. J. Jeremias, *Jesus' Promise to the Nations* (London: SCM, 1967).

As the visit of God in the Old Testament is often associated with Israel's judgement, so in the second part of Simeon's oracle the coming of Jesus will be a critical experience for the people of Israel.

Entering a more specific note to the oracle, Simeon addresses Mary and foretells how the child will be a source of division in Israel, something which Jesus voices in his own preaching when he refers to the division he is sent to cause in families (12:51-53). He will be the occasion of the fall of many people (cf Is 8:14-15) and the rise of many (cf Ps 118:22), and a sign destined to be rejected by Israel (Acts 2:2). As part of Israel, Mary will be part of Israel's test, and a sword will pierce her own soul (2:35).

Since being part of Jesus' family does not automatically make for discipleship, Mary will have to meet Jesus' criterion of membership of his eschatological family which is constituted by faithfulness to the word of God: 'My mother and my brothers are those who hear the word of God and put it into practice' (8:21; cf 11:28). Luke, however, does not finish this episode on the negative aspect of Jesus' mission but concludes with Anna's praise of God and her role of spreading the word about this child whose significance has just been acknowledged and whose destiny has just been foretold.

Throughout the infancy narrative Luke absorbs a wealth of Old Testament references and subtle allusions, evidence of his conviction that the new age emerges from the old, that Christian history is intimately connected with the whole course of salvation history. As a tight summary of God's revelation the infancy narrative is the meeting place for prophecy and fulfilment, expectation and consummation; but it also has a perspective on the future in its pronouncements on the unique significance of Christ. That double perspective on the Old Testament and the Gospel is artistically maintained throughout the narrative, keeping the dramatic tension alive.

For the reader, the infancy narrative serves as a finale to the sacred history of Israel and as an overture to the Gospel: the promised visit of God has taken place in the birth of Jesus, who has been identified as the Davidic Messiah and the Son of God, the gift of God to all peoples.

THE VISIT REGISTERED IN TIME AND PLACE

The salvific visit of God is no dream or vision, but a person: Jesus of
Nazareth is the kept promise of God. All the moments of previous
revelation have been preparation for him: he is the definitive visit of
God, one made no longer in the guise of sign or symbol but in person.
Jesus is the absence of God overcome, the difference from God covered.
And that in the midst of history, the discernible movement of the human
story.

So it is that Luke opens his narrative by anchoring the truth of the
Gospel in the midst of history, 'the events that have taken place among
us'(1:1), and goes further by locating and dating those events by reference to local and world history (1:5; 2:1-2; 3:1-2). Luke's historical
perspective is important as a way of situating the Christ event in a
specific time and place. Although Luke is more concerned with theological proclamation than historical recollection, it does not follow that
he is uninterested in the historical basis of Christian proclamation.
Perrin's position appears extreme when he writes: 'The gospel form was
created to serve the purpose of the early Church, but historical reminiscence was not one of those purposes ... So far as we can tell today, there
is no single periscope anywhere in the gospels, the present purpose of
which is to preserve a historical reminiscence of the earthly Jesus.'[10]
Luke's historical perspective avoids severing his proclamation from the
events surrounding the historical Jesus and can be seen in the story of
Emmaus when Cleopas says: 'You must be the only person staying in
Jerusalem who does not know the things that have been happening there
these last few days' (24:18). That perspective is also reflected near the end
of Acts when Paul says: 'The king understands these matters, and to him
I now speak with assurance, confident that nothing of all this is lost on
him; after all, these things were not done in a corner.' (26:26)

If revelation emerges from 'a mystery kept secret for endless ages'
(Rom 16:25) then it meets the particular of history. Not all history is
revelation, and not all experience is encounter with God. So, there are
times not chosen, places not named, visits not made, and people not

10. N. Perrin, *Rediscovering the Teaching of Jesus* (New York: Harper and Row, 1967) pp.
     15f.

elected to mediate God's self-expression. That particularity has been the occasion for scandal and offence, as Celsus expressed in his ancient caricature of the Christians: 'It is to us that God reveals and proclaims all things. He does not bother about the rest of the world; we are the only beings with whom he deals.' [11] And that outlook is not limited to ancient writers.[12] To say that revelation is particular is not to say that it is exclusive since it expresses the salvific will of God for all people (2:30-32); rather it is to recognise the necessary historical limit of any revelation. The scandal of particularity has its focus in the person of Jesus who was born at a certain time and place, and who is the unique one who is recognised as Son of God (3:22) and a man whose roots go back to Adam (3:23-38).

The genealogy of Jesus is a litany of particularity which serves to show, among other things, that Jesus does not arrive in history as a traveller without baggage, who must choose a name, a family, a past, and a whole identity for himself. He is not rootless, but is born a member of a specific lineage; he does not begin from zero, but enters an unfolding history between a yesterday and a tomorrow; he does not invent himself, but discovers himself as a link in a long family line. He is a Palestinian Jew born in the reign of Herod and Augustus. He is in time and, therefore, in between times. And for Luke the time of Jesus marks the fulness of time itself because who Jesus is cannot be understood apart from the historical purposes of God.

Thus the saving visit of God in the person of Jesus is located in space and time which form the natural boundaries of the human life-story. To be human is always to be somewhere, never nowhere; it is always to exist sometime, never no time. Once upon a time is mythic time; the time of Caesar Augustus is historical time. Luke 'registers' the birth and death of Jesus of Nazareth, an index of the historical reality of the visit of God, and a witness to the fulfilment of the plan of God in history. So, on the road to Emmaus when the risen Christ reflects on the purpose of his life and death, he speaks of its essential place in the plan of God: 'Was it not

---

11. Origen, *Contra Celsum*, IV, 23.
12. For a modern critique of seeing Christ as the Centre, Model and Norm, cf. T. Driver, *Christ in a Changing World* (London: SCM, 1981) pp. 32-56.

ordained that the Christ should suffer and so enter into his glory?'
(24:26)

THE MINISTRY AND EXODUS OF JESUS

On the road to Emmaus the risen Christ opens the scriptures by speaking
of himself as the focal point in the plan of God: so Luke portrays Jesus
at the beginning of his ministry as the fulfilment of the ancient prophecy
of Isaiah (61:1-2). Jesus does not merely prophesy that God will visit his
people with salvation but brings that salvation to the people in his
ministry which is inseparable from himself. Now is the time of messianic
fulfilment when the poor, the *anawim* Yahweh, will hear good news
because their time of waiting is over; when those who are handicapped
because they are deprived of sight or because they are immobilized in
captivity will know the experience of liberation. The Lord's time of
favour is at hand, and his visit will tell a story of transfiguration in the
lives of the people who welcome him. The visit of God, like any visit,
looks to a welcome reception; and just as John speaks in his prologue of
the absence of welcome Jesus experiences from his own people (1:11), so
Luke illustrates the hostility which Jesus receives from his own people
at Nazareth (4:29-30), a hostility which is a foretaste of things to come.

Luke does not identify the whole course of history with salvation but
through adopting the Old Testament concept of the visit of God speaks
of the inbreaking of God's salvation into history through the person of
Jesus. I would agree with Conzelmann in holding that 'the meaning of
Jesus' life is that it is an account of salvation'[13] and with Marshall that 'the
idea of salvation supplies the key to the theology of Luke.'[14] Among the
Synoptists Luke is alone in calling Jesus 'Saviour' and in using the
abstract noun 'salvation' (*soteria* and *soterion*). The word salvation has a
range of meaning but in general denotes the experience of liberation and
restoration which people enjoy through the power of God's action
working in Jesus. If the infancy narrative serves to illustrate anything it
is surely that the time of Jesus is specifically marked as a visit of salvation,

13. H. Conzelmann, *The Theology of Saint Luke* (London: Faber and Faber, 1969) p. 187.
14. I. H. Marshall, *Luke: Historian and Theologian* (Exeter: Paternoster Press, 1979) p. 92.

an insight which Luke repeats at the close of Jesus' mission to Galilee and Judaea when, in telling Zacchaeus that salvation has come to his house today, Jesus sums up his mission: 'for the Son of Man has come to seek out and save what was lost.' (19:10)

The long-awaited visit is heralded by John the Baptist, who opens his ministry by announcing a prophecy of Isaiah (40:3-5). This visit must be prepared for by a baptism of repentance: its purpose is salvific as its scope is universal, 'And all mankind shall see the salvation of God.' (3:6) The question remains open in Luke's Gospel whether John himself 'saw' God's visit of salvation in the person of Jesus, whether he was able to identify the promised visit in the actual visitor (7:18-28); but certainly Luke presents Jesus as the one whose visit of salvation makes a marked difference in the lives of those who welcome it. In the following examples the range of the Lucan concept of salvation in Jesus can be seen:

The visit of Jesus …

brings healing:	'Receive your sight. Your faith has saved you.' (18:42)
saves life:	'Is it against the law on the sabbath … to save life or destroy it?' (6:9)
brings teaching:	'Anyone who loses his life for my sake, that man will save it' (9:24)
brings forgiveness:	'He said to the woman: "Your faith has saved you; go in peace."' (9:50)
delivers from possession:	'The man who had been possessed came to be healed' (8:36)
delivers from death:	'Only have faith and she will be safe.' (8:50)

Following the exorcism of the Gerasene demoniac, Jesus commands the healed man to proclaim what God has done for him: so he spreads throughout the town what Jesus has done for him (8:39). In the same way the ministry of Jesus receives recognition and welcome when the people see its saving power as God's mighty work: 'A great prophet has appeared among us; God has visited his people.' (7:16)

In witnessing to the nature of Jesus' mission Luke shows how Jesus is involved in delivering people from the captivity of death, an action which will serve as a concrete example of Jesus' saying to John's disciples that the dead are raised to life (7:22). The raising of the widow's son to life elicits from the people the praise of God and an important acclamation which develops Zechariah's praise and proclamation (1:68.78): in the mighty work of Jesus the saving visit of God is seen.

The salvation which Jesus brings is often associated in Luke's Gospel with meals, table fellowship, and hospitality – a sign of the messianic fulfilment of Jesus' mission (Is 25:6; 34:6; 55:1; 65:11) and an anticipation of the messianic banquet when people from the four reaches of the earth 'will come to take their places at the feast in the kingdom of God.' (13:29) The ministry of Jesus, unlike that of John, is frequently set in the context of a meal, which gives rise to the accusation: 'For John the Baptist comes, not eating bread, not drinking wine, and you say, "He is possessed". The Son of Man comes, eating and drinking, and you say, "Look, a glutton and a drunkard, a friend of tax collectors and sinners".' (7:34) The complaint does not induce Jesus to change his way of reaching out to those in need. Earlier in the Gospel Luke gives Jesus' answer to why he eats with sinners, an answer which situates his table fellowship within the larger context of why he has come: 'I have not come to call the virtuous, but sinners to repentance.' (5:32)

Table fellowship has an essential place in a saving ministry which frankly associates with sinners, not least because the sharing of food and the proximity to others form a natural setting for the visit of Jesus. The shared meal can create an atmosphere of community in which people are drawn to communion and revelation: as Barbotin has observed, 'the table has a power of epiphany.' [15] Throughout his ministry Jesus hallows the meal as an occasion of fellowship and forgiveness and as an image which reveals something of the unseen reality of the kingdom of God. In offering table fellowship to outcasts and sinners Jesus incurs the anger of his opponents, whose complaints reflect the belief that only the righteous should eat with the righteous; but Jesus uses the meal as a way of coming to righteousness. In the context of the meal Jesus announces the good news; he brings sinners to an understanding of their worth

15. E. Barbotin, *The Humanity of Man* (New York: Orbis, 1975) p. 331.

before God and offers them salvation through the forgiveness of their sins. In that understanding the meal is an education and an opportunity for commitment: it is a time of discovery and a challenge to change, both of which take place in the social setting of the human community.

If the meal is an opportunity for fellowship with Jesus, Luke also shows how the presence of Jesus does not automatically make peace in the gathering. Where Jesus is, there is conflict:

> at the house of Levi (5:29-32),
> at the house of Simon the Pharisee (7:36-50),
> at the house of Martha (10:38-42),
> at the house of the unnamed Pharisee (11:37-54),
> at the house of a leading Pharisee (14:1-24),
> in the room of the Last Supper (22:14-38).

Jesus' saving presence is never uncritical: who he is, why he has come, what he stands for always raise questions among his contemporaries, challenging them to a radical newness of life. When Luke repeats the complaint of the Pharisees and scribes, 'This man ... welcomes sinners and eats with them' (15:2) the response is three parables which have their climax in the the joy that makes for hospitality, one which reflects the joy in heaven over sinners who repent. In the third parable the joy takes the form of a shared meal, and the conflict is preserved when the elder brother remains immobile outside the house, failing to do what the servants have no trouble in doing: complete a family gathering by sharing table fellowship with his brother. The experience of hospitality transforms the younger son from the one who was lost to the one who is found, from the one who was dead to to the one who is alive: in the Lucan vocabulary he is saved (cf 19:10).

In the Emmaus account the conflict between the two disciples and their unrecognised companion is confined to the journey itself; that conflict involving contrary interpretations of recent events is resolved by the time hospitality is offered by the two disciples. It is in the context of the shared meal that Jesus reveals himself and the disciples are trans-formed. And that table fellowship with the risen Lord serves to accredit the early witnesses to those in need of salvation:

Now we are those witnesses – we have eaten and drunk with him after his resurrection from the dead – and he has ordered us to proclaim this to his people and to tell them that God has appointed him to judge everyone, alive or dead. It is to him that all the prophets bear this witness: that all who believe in Jesus will have their sins forgiven through his name. (Acts 10:41-43)

The inability of the two disciples in the Emmaus account to make sense of the recent happenings in Jerusalem underscores the Lucan point that it is precisely Jerusalem where the great salvation event takes place. Throughout his narrative Luke is preoccupied with Jerusalem as the city of destiny since it is there that the passion, death, resurrection, and ascension of Jesus occur; it is also the starting-point for the witness of the Church in the descent of the Holy Spirit and the proclamation of salvation 'beginning from Jerusalem' (24:47). Because of the central salvific importance ascribed to Jerusalem Luke depicts Jesus' whole ministry as a way destined by God's purpose to lead to the place of his exaltation:

9:31   they were speaking of his passing (*exodos*) which he was to accomplish at Jerusalem

9:51   as the time drew near for him to be taken up to heaven (*analempsis*), he resolutely took the road for Jerusalem

13:33   But for today and tomorrow and the next day I must (*dei*) go on, since it would not be right for a prophet to die ouside Jerusalem.

The 'passing' of Jesus is incomplete if it is not understood in the light of his being 'taken up': thus the salvific plan of God expressed through 'I must go on' governs the whole range of Jesus' passion, death, resurrection, and ascension. And as Stanley has noted, in using the terms *exodos* and *analempsis* Luke has 'made a lasting contribution to the expression of New Testament soteriology by providing the technical terms for the doctrine of salvation, found in no other Gospel'.[16]

---

16. D. Stanley, 'The Conception of Salvation in the Synoptic Gospels' in *Catholic Biblical Quarterly* 18 (1956) p. 361.

JUDGEMENT: 'THE TIME OF YOUR VISITATION'

As Jerusalem is the place of salvation so it is the place of judgement because in the rejection of Jesus it refuses the visit of the one who comes in the name of the Lord. Midway through the travel narrative Luke sets the stage for the impending conflict in Jesus' reply to 'some Pharisees' who advise him to 'Go away ... Leave this place' (13:31): Jesus refuses to be diverted from his commitment to finish his decreed course in Jerusalem, and concludes the exchange by saying, 'you shall not see me till the time comes when you say: "Blessings on him who comes in the name of the Lord ".' (13:35). So when the time comes for 'going up to Jerusalem' (19:28), Luke shows the disciples praising God for all the miracles they 'had seen' by crying out: 'Blessings on the king who comes, in the name of the Lord!' (19:38; cf Ps 118:26). By contrast, 'some Pharisees' ask Jesus to rebuke the disciples but again Jesus rejects their advice. The sight of Jerusalem moves Jesus to tears and evokes the second lamentation over Jerusalem because it did not recognise the time of its visitation:

> Would that even today you knew the things that make for peace! But now they are hid from your eyes. For the days shall come upon you, when your enemies will cast up a bank about you and surround you, and hem you in on every side, and dash you to the ground, you and your children within you, and they will not leave one stone upon another in you; because you did not know the time of your visitation. (19:42-44 RSV)

The visit of God now means judgement and the destruction of the city, an understanding which we have already seen to be prevalent in the prophetic and Wisdom literature and which Luke now adopts to describe the rejection of the prophet-king. The lamentation is so rich in Old Testament language and imagery that, as Dodd suggested, it would seem to refer more to the destruction of Jerusalem in 587 B.C. than in 70 A.D. [17] Whatever its source, it is certainly in the prophetic tradition of Jewish literature, particularly the prophecies of Jeremiah. [18]

---

17. C.H. Dodd, 'The Fall of Jerusalem and the "Abomination of Desolation"' in *Journal of Roman Studies* 37 (1947) pp. 47-54.
18. For a comparison between the language of the Lucan oracle and the Septuagint translation of Jeremiah cf. D. Tiede, op. cit. pp. 81-84.

In its uncompromising rejection of the visit of God Jerusalem must assume responsibility for setting itself on a course that will surely lead to disaster and destruction. As Manson has written:

> The prime cause of the material disaster is a moral failure; and the moral failure is essentially a failure of religious insight. Inability to recognise the 'time of visitation' is the same thing as inability to 'interpret this time'(Lk 12:56).[19]

However, Luke matches the ignorance of Jerusalem with the understanding that 'it is hidden from your eyes' (19:42) just as he matches the ignorance of Jesus' own disciples with the hiddenness of meaning. Before the passion the disciples do not 'see the meaning' of Jesus' prophetic word interpreting the time ahead because 'it was hidden from them' (9:45; 18:34); after the resurrection the two disciples of Emmaus display their inability to 'see' the risen Christ and interpret the time, and again Luke balances the lack of discernment with the explanation that 'something prevented them from recognising him' (24:16). And when the two disciples join the eleven assembled in Jerusalem they all think they are 'seeing a ghost' and are entreated 'see for yourselves': in this instance the meaning is not hidden from them, but Luke states that they are prevented from believing because of their joy (24 37-41).

Luke seems careful to balance the failure to recognise the time of the visit of God in Jesus with how the truth of this meaning is concealed from both Jerusalem and the disciples – in which case one could ask, in what sense is there culpable ignorance? It appears that Luke is using the manifest ignorance of people alongside the unavailability of meaning as a dramatic way of reinforcing the revelation of salvation in Jesus. This literary-theological emphasis on the saving plan of God does not exempt people from the charge of elected blindness or leaden belief as is clear from the judgement over Jerusalem and the designation of the Emmaus disciples as 'foolish men' (24:25). Jerusalem's rejection of the one who comes in the name of the Lord is intimately linked to the fulfilment of Jesus' mission: 'Now we are going up to Jerusalem and everything that is written by the prophets about the Son of Man is to come true.' (18:31)

---

19. T. W. Manson, *The Sayings of Jesus* (London: SCM, 1977) p. 321.

In the very rejection of Jerusalem the divine purpose is being accomplished, just as through the suffering of the Messiah God's plan comes to fulfilment (24:26,47).

Following the judgement of Jerusalem, Luke shows Jesus to be in possession of the Temple after he has displaced the traders from the 'house of prayer' (19:46). In the context of proclaiming Good News Jesus tells the parable of the wicked vinedressers which elaborates the accountability of Israel in refusing the visit of accredited messengers and finally the visit of the beloved son of the owner (20:9-15). The son, who is heir, is thrown out and killed; and Jesus tells his hearers that the landowner will come himself to make an end of the tenants and give the vineyard to others. In addition to the parable, which has clear allegorical features. [20]

Luke has two further sayings of Jesus, one which speaks of the rejected keystone and the other which speaks of the judgement which will befall those who reject the stone (20:17-18). Only after he recapitulates his themes of rejection and judgement does Luke recount the reaction of the scribes and the chief priests to the parable: they want to lay hands on Jesus 'that very moment' and so dramatically underscore the truth of the parable: in rejecting the visit of the beloved son they are seen to fulfil the prophetic word while at the same time writing the script for their own fateful judgement.

THE DAY OF THE SON OF MAN

The judgement of Jerusalem and the final visit of the Son of Man form the major themes in the last proclamation of Jesus' public ministry (21:6-36). Luke has already given the reader apocalyptic teaching by Jesus: in 12:35-48 the disciples are warned to be alert and prepared for the return of the Son of Man in judgement, and in 17:20-37 they are cautioned against false prophets who wrongly interpret the time as the end age, and told that 'when the day comes for the Son of Man to be revealed' it will be a visit of judgement for all. The last discourse of Jesus is a complex interweaving of two strands of thought which speak of the destruction

---

20. Cf. J. Jeremias, *The Parables of Jesus* (London: SCM, 1978) pp. 70-76.

of Jerusalem and the end of world history, although Luke makes clear
that between the two events there will be an indefinite period of time.
The discourse is not so much a summary of apocalyptic signs as a
warning preparing its hearers for the events which are to come: the fall
of Jerusalem and the end age, which are related in that they are both the
fulfilment of prophecy and take place in the last days, but unrelated
chronologically. Most scholars would agree that Luke's account is akin
to the parallel discourse in Mark 13, but there is disagreement over
whether that relationship is one of sole dependency or not. The dispute
remains unresolved.

The divine judgement upon Jerusalem (21:20-24) resonates with
classical prophetic language, not least the phrase 'days of vengeance'
which is often used to define further the visit of God in judgement (e.g.
Jer 46:21; 50:27; Hos 9:7). Between the destruction of Jerusalem and the
end age there will be the unspecified time of the Gentiles (21:24). In
disclosing the cosmic signs that herald the end age and the coming of the
Son of Man (21:25-28) Luke employs the apocalyptic imagery of Daniel
7:13-14. In Daniel's vision the Son of Man will appear at the final
consummation in a cloud. Luke's singular use of cloud recalls the cloud
of the transfiguration in which Jesus was seen as glorified by those who
beheld him (9:34). The coming of the Son of Man in glory will be
something which all people can see; it is a sign of hope for the true
disciple because it announces the moment of deliverance and liberation.
The old age will have collapsed to give way to the new age: in the end is
the beginning.

Thus the dramatic shift can be be seen in the Lucan imagery

from	*to*
the present time	the end time
of visitation/judgement	of the final visit/redemption
at Jerusalem	on earth
for those who reject Jesus	for the elect ready for the Son of Man.

So it is that Luke concludes the public ministry of Jesus. The judgement for not knowing the time of visitation is severe and irrevocable; but

that judgement, as in the prophetic tradition, does not constitute the last word. As Zechariah blessed God because he had visited and redeemed his people, as Simeon prophesied that Jesus was destined for the fall and rising of many is Israel, and as Anna spoke of Jesus to all who looked forward to the deliverance of Jerusalem, so the visit of God in Jesus is seen to be both salvation and judgement. And the final coming of the Son of Man is a redemptive one.

Thus the visit as salvation which fulfils the purposes of God has the first and last word in Luke. In the Old Testament the central revelation of God's salvific purpose was made to Moses in the disclosure that God would visit his people and free them through exodus (Ex 3:16-17). In the New Testament it is Luke who shows Jesus in the presence of Moses as the new exodus (9:31). For Luke, Jesus is the supreme visit of God in history. In his exodus he will release a new Spirit which will give a new heart to those who welcome him; they will grow in fellowship by hearing the word and breaking bread together. And the story of that new beginning is told when a stranger from Jerusalem speaks a life-giving word to two forlorn disciples on the road to Emmaus and reveals himself to them in the breaking of the bread.

3 | The Living Word of God in the Old Testament

IN THE ANCIENT Semitic world where little was ever committed to writing, the spoken word enjoyed a place of unique importance in the social and religious life of the people. The early tribes used distinguishable signs for marking cattle and private property,[1] and in the absence of an alphabet to give permanence to writing they supplied the spoken word with a persistent reality. Customs, observances and prohibitions were passed on to new generations through the act of storytelling which was the principal method of education, one which situated the hearers within their own special tradition, formed their awareness of their place in history, and educated them in the wisdom that comes from reflection on experience.

The spoken word was regarded as having a dynamism of its own, an inherent power which could effect what it affirmed, especially in solemn moments such as the blessing and the curse. For the Hebrew people a blessing was the gift of a word which had power to bring comfort and peace and life; it reflected the benevolence of God and possessed such efficacy that it could not be revoked. Thus when Isaac conferred his blessing on Jacob and realized that he had been tricked, he could not recall the blessing which had its own independent power; instead, he had to give his first-born, Esau, an inferior one (Gen 27). So too with the curse: when the mother of Micah pronounced a curse on the man who stole her silver, her own son on hearing the curse identified himself as the thief because he was afraid of its certain effect. However, the mother could not withdraw the curse visited on the culprit; she could only try to render it harmless by following it with her blessing (Jgs 17:1-2).

That dynamic power of the word is summed up in the Hebrew, *dabar*, which means both spoken word and actual event, a fullness of meaning which is reflected in the revelation of God perceived as both word and

---

1. Cf. L. Köhler, *Hebrew Man* (London: SCM, 1973) pp. 75-77.

event. And the fullness of that Hebraic meaning will have its clearest expression in the New Testament in the writings of Luke.

THE CREATIVE WORD OF GOD

If our promissory word is itself a human act, we know from experience that it comes between the intention it articulates and the event itself; but the human word does not possess the power to readily effect what it promises. Auden's poetic insight stands true: 'Words are for those with promises to keep.' People described as those whose 'word is their bond' regard the word as an act of commitment which makes them account-able to others for what they say, but the movement which closes the gap between promise and fulfilment is never an automatic one. In sharp contrast to the fragility of the human word, the divine word is seen to be inherently effective because of who God is:

> God is no man that he should lie,
> no son of Adam to draw back.
> Is it his to say and not to do,
> to speak and not to fulfil? (Num 23:19)

The word of God's revelation has effect since it is itself a concrete event and sets in motion a chain of events. For God, to say is to do, to promise is to fulfil, to speak is to accomplish. The word of God is the work of God. In Second Isaiah God reveals that he alone is king and redeemer of Israel and challenges any to gainsay his primacy: 'Who is like me? Let him stand up and speak, let him show himself and argue it out before me.' (44:7) Those who can neither stand up nor speak are the pagan idols, whose silence is silver and golden and perpetual, and whose total senselessness is satirised in Psalm 115:

> Their idols, in silver and gold,
> products of human skill,
> have mouths, but never speak,
> eyes, but never see,
> ears, but never hear,
> noses, but never smell,
> hands, but never touch,

feet, but never walk,
and not a sound comes from their throats.
Their makers will end up like them,
and so will anyone who relies on them. (vv. 4-8)

The pagan idols are incapable of revelation because they are manufactured silence; they are incapable of salvation because they are powerless, unable either to move or be moved. The fact that the idols are
wordless means that nothing can actually happen through them. And
the psalmist warns that the makers of gods are doomed to repeat their
image of God: their reliance on false gods will deform their real lives
until they are indistinguishable from the lifeless images they have made.

In contrast to the pagan gods, the one living God speaks and his
creatures hear his voice. If God's presence is reflected in the vast spread
of nature it is not through the medium of nature that Israel comes to
know God; it is through his saving visit in history which demonstrates
the power of his word and his election of a particular people. As the
religion of Israel is more concerned with word and hearing than with
vision and seeing, [2] it is understandable that throughout the biblical
narrative priority is given to the word rather than the image. No one can
see the face of God and live; but everyone must hear the word of God in
order to live. Even the purpose of the vision is that the word of God can
be heard (cf Deut 4:35-36). When God reveals himself he must also
conceal himself; to communicate his word he must also hide his face
because revelation emerges from the mystery of God, and no one
survives seeing him (Ex 33:20).

The felt presence of the God who speaks in history is reflected in
Elijah's encounter with him: 'And behold, the LORD passed by, and a
great and strong wind rent the mountains, and broke in pieces the rocks
before the LORD, but the LORD was not in the wind; and after the wind
an earthquake, but the LORD was not in the earthquake; and after the
earthquake a fire, but the LORD was not in the fire; and after the fire a
still small voice.' (1 Kgs 19:11-12 RSV) This graphic account affirms the
priority of seeing God as the one who reveals himself in 'a still small

---

2. T. Boman, *Hebrew Thought Compared with Greek* (London: SCM, 1960) pp. 206-207.

voice' over the traditional view of popular religions that saw divine manifestation in the wind, the earthquake, and the fire.

The effectiveness of God's creative word in history is poetically described in Second Isaiah:

> For as the rain and the snow come
>   down from heaven,
>   and return not thither but water the earth,
>   making it bring forth and sprout,
>   giving seed to the sower and bread
>   to the eater,
> so shall my word be that goes forth
>   from my mouth;
>   it shall not return to me empty,
>   but it shall accomplish that which I purpose,
>   and prosper in the thing for which
>   I sent it. (55:10-11 RSV)

The word which goes forth not only enters history with creative power, it actually creates history. As Schmauss writes:

> It [the word] produces history out of its own dynamism. It is always conditioned by a historical situation, and it advances history ... Only when the time is ripe, that is, when men are capable of being spoken to by him, and insofar as they are capable, does God speak to them. Then, however, he leads them to a new level of existence and a new understanding of God and of themselves. God's word produces history insofar as it moves man to definite actions. [3]

And it is precisely Israel's experience of being created as a people by God's mastery over history that forms their faith in God as Saviour (Ez 16:1-9), a faith which expresses itself through story-telling the acts/ words of God and in the ritual recital of his saving work (Deut 26:5-9; Ps 44:1). Thus Israel comes to know God not through reflection on the wonders of nature but through being formed by his creative word.

The mastery of God's word over history and the forces of nature,

---

3. M. Schmauss, *Dogma 1: God in Revelation* (New York: Sheed and Ward, 1968) p. 115.

which emerges so clearly from the narrative accounts and recitals of the
exodus event, eventually make way for the conviction that ascribes the
origin of the world itself to God's word. The beginnings of that belief can
be traced in Second Isaiah who encourages God's people exiled in
Babylon to have hope through remembering how God intervened on
their behalf in Egypt. God's saving function is given a universal dimension in the understanding that as the one true God he saved creation
from chaos in the beginning through the power of his word. The creative
power of God's word is addressed to the beginning of time to show that
God began history itself through summoning it into existence:

> 44:24   Thus says Yahweh, your redeemer,
>   he who formed you in the womb:
>   I, myself, Yahweh, made all things,
>   I alone spread out the heavens.
>   When I gave the earth shape, did anyone help me?

> 48:13   My hand laid the foundation of earth
>   and my right hand spread out the heavens.
>   I summon them
>   and they all come forward together.

The power of God's salvific word to summon creation into existence
gives the Priestly account of creation its distinct verbal stress (Gen 1-
2:4a). Von Rad's warning against treating the creation account as a
'doctrine' central to Old Testament faith is worth quoting: 'Faith in
creation is neither the basis nor the goal of the declarations in Genesis,
chapters 1 and 2. Rather, the position of both the Yahwist and the
Priestly document is basically faith in salvation and election. They
undergird this faith by the testimony that this Yahweh, who made a
covenant with Abraham and at Sinai, is also the creator of the world.'[4]
If faith in God's saving power inspires the creation narratives, it is no
surprise that the Priestly document underlines dramatically the primacy
of God's word and the coincidence between saving and enacting. God
brings form out of a shapeless void; he separates and thus brings order

---

4. G. von Rad, *Genesis* (Old Testament Library; London: SCM, 1963) p. 44.

in the midst of chaos, and he accomplishes all this through the creative power of his word. This is illustrated throughout the creation narrative in the rhythmic repetition, 'God said and there was' (Gen 1). God's word is first: it is not only at the beginning, but it creates the beginning and inaugurates the world of being, as is echoed in the 'new song' of Psalm 33:

> By the word of Yahweh the heavens were made ...
> let all who live on earth revere him!
> He spoke and it was created;
> he commanded and there it stood. (vv. 6-9).

And just as that word had power to create the beginning, so Luke will assert its effective power at the beginning of the new age: 'For no word from God shall be void of power' (1:37 RSV).

As the creation of the world is accomplished through the divine word so the creation of man is highlighted as the deliberative word of God which enacts his interior word, 'Let us make man in our image, in the likeness of ourselves' (1:26). God calls male and female into existence, and the beginning of the new relationship between Creator and creatures is marked by God's word of blessing which empowers both man and woman to share in his continuing creation by enjoying dominion over the world of harmony which he has made. That created order, even after it has been disrupted, will always be a testimonial to God, a cosmic sign which invites people to interpret it as the work of the creator, a public utterance which refers back to the original speaker (Ps 19:1-4) – a view which Luke echoes in his account of Paul's speech at Lystra (Acts 14:16-17) and which Paul expresses in his own writing (Rom 1:19-21).

That biblical view of the world as the word of God has its parallel in secular writing – for example, in Plato's thought which interprets creation as a proof of divinity and sees the plan and order of the surrounding world as testimony to the divine power.[5] That way of 'seeing' the world is in sharp contrast to the view articulated by Plotinus six hundred years later: 'If a man were to inquire of Nature, "Wherefore do you bring forth creatures?" and she were willing to give ear and

---

5. Plato, *Laws*, X, 886a, 2-5.

answer, she would say "Ask me not, but understand in silence, even as I am silent".' [6] In this view there can be no dialogue with nature because she is mute; there is only resignation to a silence which is absent of the promise of meaning and which is thereby perpetually insignificant. And it is that view which the psalmist ascribes to the pagan idols, not to God's spoken creation (Ps 115).

The power of God's word which is illustrated so effectively in the Priestly document serves to give substance to the conviction that the God of Israel who saves is the same God who enjoys dominion over the world. Since he is the one who spoke creation into existence there is ground to hope that he can re-create by speaking again, that the power of his covenant word is still active, that his word to the prophets which holds out the promise of change will reach actual fulfilment. It is in the hope of change and re-creation that God is recalled as creator:

> Who has only to speak to make things exist?
> Who commands if not the Lord? (Lam 3:37)

And it is the power of God to change history that is seen through his word of covenant and his word to the prophets.

THE WORD OF THE COVENANT

Although there is no parallel in the ancient world for the covenant relationship between God and Israel, the covenant (*berith*) itself follows the form of bilateral agreements in societies which depend not on written contracts but on the spoken word. Like the word of blessing and curse, the word of covenant was invested with an inherent power and a persistent reality that could not be cancelled. In the presence of witnesses the parties to the covenant bound themselves in voluntary agreement through their solemn word, an agreement which was usually set in the context of ritual and one which included penalties for violation. After the ceremony a memorial was often set up to witness the pact (Gen 21:33; 31:48) or a meal was shared to confirm the new fellowship (Gen 26:30; 2 Sam 3:20). The covenants between Abraham and Abimelech (Gen

---

6. Plotinus, *Enneads*, III, 8.4.

21:22-32), between Jacob and Laban (Gen 31:43-54), and between David and Jonathan (1 Sam 18:3-4) illustrate the binding quality of the covenant word: in pledging their oath they commit themselves irrevocably to the solemn agreement. And although the contracting parties do not have to enjoy equal standing, once the alliance is spoken the stronger party cannot annul the indissoluble bond at will.

At the heart of the Old Testament stands the covenant between God and Israel which took place at Sinai. The revelation of God's name and plan to Moses (Ex 3) and the confirmation of that revelation in the divine visit form the reason for Israel's belief in God's election and the ground of Israel's sense of destiny within the plan of God. The liberation from Egypt is interpreted as the fulfilment of God's promises to the patriarchs (Deut 7:7-8) and a further witness to the covenant he made with Abraham (Gen 15 and 17). Thus the patriarchs are incorporated into the covenant tradition.

Earlier in the Old Testament narrative God is shown to be the one who initiates a covenant with Noah 'on behalf of everything that lives on earth.' (Gen 9:10) The universal dimension of God's blessing on Noah and his descendants is also present in God's choice of Abraham:

Yahwist: Gen 12:3   All the tribes of the earth
                               shall bless themselves by you.

Elohist: Gen 22:18   All the nations of the earth
                               shall bless themselves by your descendants.

Wright has commented: 'The thought is that God has chosen Israel in order that all people of the earth may use her name in the formula by which they seek blessing for themselves. Through the ancient conception of blessing the writers are saying that God's purpose is to use Israel for a universal blessing.'[7]

And it is Second Isaiah who gives voice to the understanding that the God who created the earth and everything in it has made a covenant with the people for the sake of the nations, a covenant made through the servant of Yahweh:

---

7. G. E. Wright, *The Old Testament against Its Environment* (London: SCM, 1957) p. 51.

Thus says God, Yahweh,
he who created the heavens and spread them out,
who gave shape to the earth and what comes from it,
who gave breath to its people
and life to the creatures that move in it:

I, Yahweh, have called you to serve the cause of right;
I have taken you by the hand and formed you;
I have appointed you as covenant of the people
and light of the nations,
to open the eyes of the blind,
to free captives from prison,
and those who live in darkness from the dungeon. (42:5-7)

The appointment of Israel as covenant partner of God (Ex 19-24) is clearly an act of God's initiative; however, this new relationship which will forever condition the historical destiny of Israel is presented as a covenant form adapted from those in common use in the ancient world. The work of G. E. Mendenhall is well noted for pointing out the remarkable similarities that exist between the Sinaitic covenant and the suzerainty pacts used by the Hittites from the fifteenth to the thirteenth centuries B.C. [8] The securing of this point does not diminish the unique importance of the content of the covenant at Sinai: the gratuitousness of God in electing a people, pledging his continued love and protection, and promising a land where blessings would bring life and peace (Ex 23:20-31).

The six formal elements of the Hittite suzerainty pact can be identified from documentary evidence, and the parallels seen in the Sinaitic covenant and in the renewal of the covenant at Shechem in Joshua 24:

1. Preamble which identifies the covenanting king by a recital of his titles and attributes (Ex 20:2; Jos 24:2).
2. A historical prologue which lists the benefits the king has extended to his vassals obliging them in gratitude to obey his commands (Ex 20:2; Jos 24: 2:13).

8. G. Mendenhall, 'Law and Covenant in Israel and the Ancient Near East' in *The Biblical Archeologist* 17 (1954) pp. 26-46; 49-76.

3. A list of stipulations which number the obligations of the vassals (Ex 20:3-17; Jos 24:14) and the command to pay tribute to him once a year (Ex 23:17).

4. The provision is made for the deposit of the pact in the temple and for its periodic reading (Jos 24:26). The tablets of the commandments are deposited in the ark of the covenant (Deut 10:5) and the priests are required to read the law to the people on the feast of Booths (Deut 31:9-13).

5. A list of gods is given as witnesses of the contracts. In the case of the Sinaitic covenant the people themselves are the witnesses (Jos 24:22) while the heavens and the earth are invoked as witnesses to what has taken place (Deut 32:1; Is 1:2).

6. Formulas which list blessings following on the observance of the covenant and curses following on non-observance. In Deuteronomy 27-28 there are long lists of blessing and curses related to fidelity and infidelity to the covenant (cf Jos 8:30-35).

Although there is no single biblical text which reflects the unified structure of the Hittite pact, the literary parallels are clearly identifiable through a mosaic of passages. Thus Moses can be seen to describe God's relations with his elected people through the analogy of international covenant.

The language that describes how God sets up, establishes, gives the covenant makes clear that it is a divine institution. After the liberation from bondage is secured, God judges that the time is right to reveal his plan for an alliance which he does 'in the words of the Covenant – the Ten Words'. (Ex 34:28) The proposed alliance is conditional: the people must live their lives in allegiance to the revealed word of God and worship no other God but Yahweh. In return for that commitment God promises fidelity to his elected people whom he has chosen from among all the nations not because of their intrinsic merit but because of his love and his promise to their fathers (Deut 7:8). The response of the people is one of wholehearted commitment: 'All that Yahweh has said, we will do.' (Ex 19:7) So the covenanted people are a people with promises to keep; in their response they allow the word of God to give a new direction and meaning to their lives. In the covenant they aim themselves at the kind of people God wants them to be; they dedicate not a thing but their freedom in the professed love of a God who first loved them.

Two different accounts tell how the covenant is ratified in ritual. In the Yahwistic narrative (Ex 24:1-2.9-11) the covenant is confirmed in a sacrificial meal which Moses, Aaron, and seventy of the elders of Israel eat in the presence of God. Thus the word of God and the word of man come together in a solemn moment marked by the sharing of food and drink. In the Elohistic account (Ex 24:3-8) Moses brings the word of God to the people and they respond 'with one voice, "We will observe all the commands that Yahweh has decreed".' An altar is built with twelve pillars, representing the twelve tribes of Israel and bullocks are offered as a 'communion sacrifice'. Some of the blood of the sacrificial victim is poured on the altar, which represents Yahweh, and after the people have again professed their obedience to the covenant, Moses sprinkles them with 'the blood of the Covenant' (Cf Lk 22:20; 1 Cor 11:23-25). Thus God and the people are symbolically one blood, one family – a relationship which will be summed up later in the formula 'You shall be my people and I will be your God' (cf Jer 7:23). Thus ratified, the covenant forms the foundation of Israelite religion.

The solemn commitment of Israel to the Ten Words and the Book of the Covenant will govern her life and condition her religious and political future. And since people do not remain dedicated simply by continuing to exist, Israel's commitment to the word of God has to be renewed throughout her history (e.g. Jos 8:30-35; 2 Kgs 23:2ff; Ne 8:12ff; Ps 89:20-38) as it is recalled by the presence of the ark of the covenant containing the two tablets of stone which is eventually brought into the Temple built by Solomon. At that public ceremony Solomon addresses the people: 'I have built the house for the name of Yahweh, the God of Israel, and have made a place in it for the ark containing the covenant that Yahweh made with our fathers when he brought them out of the land of Egypt.' (1 Kgs 8:20-21)

But above all, it will be the prophets who will press the people to keep alive their commitment to the word of God and prepare them for the day of the new covenant.

THE PROPHETIC WORD

We have already focused on the preaching and witness of the classical prophets as that had a bearing on the salvation and judgement of God's visit; it is now time to reflect on the prophet's call as that is understood to be authorized by the word of God, and the prophetic witness interpreted as the offer of God's revelation to the people.

The Hebrew word *nabi* is usually rendered in English by 'prophet', but scholars are uncertain about its precise terminology – whether it derives from an Arabian root with the sense 'to bubble' or 'to seeth' indicating the ecstatic character of the prophetic art, or from an Akkadian root meaning 'to call' or 'to proclaim' indicating the prophetic function. The prophet is referred to as *ro'eh* (1 Sam 9:9) or *hozeh* (Am 7:12), synonyms which mean 'one who sees', the meaning of which can be seen in Balaam's self description:

> The oracle of Balaam, son of Beor,
> the oracle of the man with far-seeing eyes,
> the oracle of the one who hears the word of God.
> He sees what Shaddai makes him see,
> receives the divine answer,
> and his eyes are opened. (Num 24:3-4)

Sometimes the prophet is called 'a man of God', a title particularly popular in the books of Kings (1 Kgs 12:22; 13:1; 2 Kgs 1:9-13; 4:38ff). Southwell suggests:

> The title 'man of God' was one used primarily, though not solely, of the period between the heyday of the seers and the era of the preaching prophets, as the Israelites were becoming accustomed to the new phenomenon of prophecy. ... The phrase is used especially of Elijah and Elisha at precisely that stage, and Elijah is a classic example of a seer who began to exercise the ministry of a prophet. In this transitional period, 'man of God' conveyed no precise functional connotations, and could safely and accurately be used of anyone who, be he seer or prophet, was speaking or acting in God's name. [9]

9. P. Southwell, *Prophecy* (London: Hodder and Stoughton, 1982) pp. 24,25.

The actual origins of Hebrew prophecy are obscure, and although
Moses is referred to as the prophet without equal (Deut 34:10) most
scholars would begin their study of prophecy with the seer Samuel. [10]
Prior to classical prophetism and dating from the eleventh century B.C.
the corporate character of ancient prophecy is witnessed by roving bands
of ecstatics whose prayer, music, dancing, and singing seem to generate
an infectious enthusiasm (1 Sam 10:10), although they are sometimes
dismissed as madmen because of their eccentric ways and their culti-
vated shabbiness of dress.

However, in two hundred years the itinerant style of the prophetic life
seems to have given way to residential community living as a group of
prophets would be attached to a well known shrine and be available for
consultation, especially on feast days. Through their guilds the traditions and techniques of prophecy are taught, and it is interesting to note
that no text suggests that a call from God was a necessary requirement
for entry into such groups. As Samuel presided over a group cf ecstatic
prophets (1 Sam 19:20) so Elisha, after the conclusion of Elijah's ministry, presides over 'the sons of the prophets' (2 Kgs 2:4-6). It is not until the
middle of the eighth century B.C., when we encounter the classical
prophets from Amos onwards, that we meet the independent prophet
whose authority for his ministry is not his professional training or his
court or cultic connections, but solely the commanding word of God:

> The lion roars: who can help feeling afraid?
> The Lord Yahweh speaks: who can refuse to prophesy? (Am 3:8)

It is difficult to decide the precise differences between the ecstatic and
cultic prophets on one hand and the classical prophets on the other:
Ringgren concludes, 'Perhaps we can approach a solution to the problem
by saying that in reality no sharp distinction can be drawn.' [11] Certainly
Amos, who disclaims any connection with the professional prophetic
guilds, saying that he was a shepherd before Yahweh spoke to him (7:14-

---

10. Among many studies in the prophetic movement cf. T. H. Robinson, *Prophecy and the
     Prophets in Ancient Israel* (London: Duckworth, 1953); G. Widengren, *Literary and
     Eschological Aspects of the Hebrew Prophets* (Uppsala: Lundeqvist, 1948); J. Lindblom,
     Prophecy in Ancient Israel (Oxford: Blackwell, 1965).
11. H. Ringgren, *Israelite Religion* (London: SPCK, 1976) p. 250.

15), reflects the absolute moral compulsion to speak the word. It is not a possible career or an interesting option: it is his inescapable duty. That prophetic 'must' is reflected throughout the classical prophets, and even when Jeremiah tries for early retirement by attempting neither to think of God nor speak in his name, the effort to overcome the seductive power of God proves too much: 'the effort to restrain it wearied me, I could not bear it.' (20:8) Perhaps it is true to say that the prophets' feeling of constraint to preach the received word may reflect the inherent power of the word as event:

> I will do whatever I choose.
> I call a bird of prey from the east,
> my man of destiny from a far country.
> No sooner is it said than done,
> no sooner planned than performed. (Is 46:11)

The word of God is rooted in the prophetical writings and its primacy is shown in the vocation of the prophet. In relating their inaugural experiences and trying to find a language to name the something that happened to them, the prophets speak of the coming of the word of God (Is 6:1ff; Jer 1:9; Ez 2:8f; Hos 11f; Joel 1:1) a recurring formula which Luke uses himself: 'the word of God came to John, son of Zechariah in the wilderness.' (3:2) Although the experience may take the form of a vision as in the case of Isaiah and Ezekiel, the determining factor for the prophet is that he is called. We will look more closely at the term 'experience' in the next chapter; at the moment it is sufficient to note that the stereotyped description of the prophetic call serves to underscore the point that the word of God induces the inaugural experience, not the individual. The word of God is first. Thus if people can make judges and kings they cannot create a prophet: he is elected by divine call which gives him a mandate and graces him with power to communicate God's revelation in word, symbol, and psycho-drama.

The word which God speaks comes to nourish the prophet and is sent to nourish the people since 'man does not live on bread alone but on everything which comes from the mouth of Yahweh' (Deut 8:3; cf Lk 4:4). Jeremiah 'devours' the word (15:16); Ezekiel eats the scroll and makes the word of God his own before preaching it (3:3); Amos warns of the day when there will be famine throughout the land, a famine not of food but 'of hearing the word of Yahweh' (8:11). And for Micah the false prophets prophesy according to whether their patrons feed them or not:

> So long as they have something to eat
> they cry 'Peace'.
> But on anyone who puts nothing into their mouths
> they declare war. (3:5)

The priority of the word of God is reckoned to be an essential condition for authentic prophecy, and the prophets refer their hearers to two fundamental truths about their ministry: they are not self-appointed, but approached and commissioned by God; the words they speak are not the result of human wisdom but emerge from the wisdom of God. In contrast, the false prophets are neither called nor sent, and the words that they speak, however sincere or wise, reflect only the workings of their own minds or the drama of their dreams (Jer 23:16-28). As McKenzie has written:

> Because he lacks the prophetic insight into the moral will of Yahweh and the reality of sin, the false prophet sees no evil where it is and prophesies that all is well when it is not. He easily identifies Israel and its cause with Yahweh and His will and predicts victory; he has no conception of the sweeping and rigourous justice with which Yahweh governs. He speaks less than the truth and perverts sound religious belief to merely national and personal good.[12]

For Jeremiah, who reflects often on the origin of the prophetic mission, the fact that he is not speaking out of his own initiative is an identifiable pointer to authentic prophecy. And the messenger formula adopted by the prophets expresses this conviction: 'Thus says Yahweh', for the preached message is not primarily the creative utterance of the prophet addressed to the people but the creative utterance of God addressed to the prophet.

---

12. J. L. McKenzie, *Dictionary of the Bible* (London: Geoffrey Chapman, 1965) p. 697.

Since it is the word of God that inspires and moves the prophet, that word, in contrast to the words of the false prophets, is invested with power and has authority to shape events in history; it has the force of a hammer which can shatter the rocks (Jer 23:29), and it gives the prophet authority setting him

> over nations and over kingdoms,
> to tear up and to knock down,
> to destroy and to overthrow,
> to build and to plant. (Jer 1:10)

The authority of that prophetic word is often related to the power of God's Spirit. When Micah compares his steadfast witness to the fickleness of the false prophets he speaks of the origin of his strength as the spirit of God (3:8). Even the early *nabi'im* name the sovereign power which grasps and empowers them as the spirit of God (Num 11:25; 1 Sam 10:6; 2 Sam 23:2). The prophet is a man of the spirit (Hos 9:7), an understanding which is common to the post-exilic writers (Is 61:1; Ez 2:2, 11:5; Zech 7:12) and which is shared by Luke as he marks the beginning of Jesus' ministry (4:18ff) and the beginning of the apostolic preaching (Acts 1:8) with the power of the Spirit.

In proclaiming the word of God the prophets are offering God's revelation and counsel to the people. As Heschel has reflected:

> The words the prophet utters are not offered as souvenirs. His speech to the people is not a reminiscence, a report, hearsay. The prophet not only conveys; he reveals. He almost does unto others what God does unto him. In speaking, the prophet reveals God. This is the marvel of a prophet's work: in his words, the invisible God becomes audible. He does not prove or argue. The thought he has to convey is more than language can contain. Divine power bursts into the words. The authority of the prophet is in the Presence his words reveal.[13]

In the offer of that revelation there is always a challenge to everyone – kings, priests, prophets, and people. The prophets do not try to seduce

13. A. Heschel, *The Prophets* (New York: Harper and Row, 1969) p. 22.

people by sweet reasonableness any more than they were seduced by such; their insight and care always seem to be under the pressure of time so that they embrace whole groups and nations in their accusations. If anger is not known as a tool of precision, the prophetic anger is not so much focused on accuracy as repentance. Long after everyone else has settled for compromise, the prophet still mourns the loss of fidelity; long after everyone else has forgotten to lament, the prophet still hurts from the community's loss (Jer 9). And it is that unyielding challenge which refuses to go elsewhere, which refuses to compromise, which refuses to decrease its intensity on demand, that is the word of God among the people. Because of that prophetic constancy at least one thing is certain: 'Whether they listen or not, this set of rebels shall know that there is a prophet among them.' (Ez 2:5)

The word that God speaks through the prophet brings alive the memory of commitment to the covenant. If the Sinaitic covenant first appeared as a pact between God and his people, the prophets elevate that juridical analogy to the level of encounter in love seeing Israel as the spouse and Yahweh as the bridegroom (Hosea; Ez 6:6-14), Israel as the son and God as the Father (Jer 3:19), a relationship of love that is so constantly represented throughout the Deuteronomic writing. That relationship is underscored by the understanding throughout the biblical narrative that there is an intimate connection between the revelation of God's word and the response of man's heart, since God speaks to the heart (Hos 2:16) and man hears and welcomes that word not so much with his ears as with his heart. And whether he welcomes that word or rejects it depends on his heart condition. Fidelity to God is 'to set your heart on Yahweh and serve him alone' (1 Sam 7:3), being wholehearted in the search for him (Deut 4:2); infidelity is having an 'uncircumcised heart' (1 Lev 26:41). The heart is the inward place to which God turns and where religious experience and understanding have their roots, just as hardness of heart is always an indication of unwillingness and stubbornness to let the word of God come close (Ps 95: 7-8).

The Ten Words of the covenant are near if they are inscribed on the heart (Deut 6:6), just as the words of the new covenant will be written on the heart (Jer 31:32); and that will be made possible because God will initiate a movement of regeneration which will be marked by a change of heart (Ez 36:26). Thus the heart is the proper keep of the word of God; it is the most intimate place where the word-event of the new age will be stored (Lk 2:51). So the heart tells its own story of the word: for Jeremiah the word is like 'a fire burning in my heart, imprisoned in my bones' (20:9); so too with the disciples of Emmaus who reflect on the inside story of the word: 'did our hearts not burn within us as he talked to us on the road and explained the scriptures to us?' (Lk 24:32)

The interaction between God's word and the human heart, between the offer and the response, is what forms the shape of future events. The future is not predetermined by a God who is not in consultation with history or one who is incapable of 'repenting' in the light of the people's change of heart (cf Jonah); rather, the future is determined by those who share the responsibility in shaping it. As men immersed in the movement of their own time, the prophets interpret what will happen in the future in such a way that aims to influence what is happening in the present: their announcements have a declared pastoral purpose. Thus the purpose of interpreting the future time as a visit of judgement is to move people to repentance, as the purpose of announcing the future visit of salvation is to generate hope in the midst of despair. Both interpretations are aimed at a change in attitude and behaviour in the present tense. As DeVries points out in his study of the Hebraic concept of time:

> The revelatory interpretation concerning the past and the revelatory interpretation concerning the future have a paranetic concern. In other words, their intent is to motivate the present. Israel is anxious to understand its past and to anticipate its future in order to make a right choice in its present moment of responsible decision. 'That day', past and future, has no other function than to illuminate 'today'.[14]

Notwithstanding the service of historical criticism in situating the prophets as people of their time who struggle to influence the course of events by 'forthtelling' the word of God, it is still important to appreciate

14. S. DeVries, *Yesterday, Today and Tomorrow: Time and History in the Old Testament* (London: SPCK, 1975) p. 340.

the place of prophetic 'foretelling'. If it is true to say that the prophet is the chosen interpreter of the signs of the times, it must also be admitted with Vriezen that 'prophetism had more influence over the future than upon its own times'.[15] There is little evidence to suggest that the prophets manage to bring about any dramatic social or religious changes among their contemporaries; rather, their interpretation of events has more influence on future generations who from their retrospective stance can discern a harmony in the prophetic preaching that discloses the saving purposes of God. The effect of the prophet's utterance cannot be limited to a specific time for, as H. Robinson points out, we cannot help but notice 'a different kind of detachment of the prophetic word from its original environment. This is seen in the subsequent interpretations that may be given to it, beyond the historical meaning.'[16] In remembering the declarations of the prophets later generations can see how their word came to be true, how its inherent power had effect far beyond the limited range of the prophet's historical activity, how the prophetic word had its own history as an independent event precisely because it was the word of God: 'I too watch over my word to see it fulfilled.' (Jer 1:12)

As the prophets grow in their own understanding of the purposes of God their prophecy leans towards a future time which will see the fulness of what is now partially revealed, an eschatological tendency which is given clearer witness in the apocalyptic writers. There is a part of prophecy which struggles through the trials and pressures of the present to point in hope to the climax of Israel's history when there will appear a prophet like Moses (Deut 18:15) who will deliver his people from oppression and make a new covenant with them (Jer 31:31). This is not to reduce the prophetical writings to proof-texts to be plundered by apologists; rather, it is to see what the New Testament writers wish us to see: that the whole pattern of the Old Testament is a gradual revelation of God's purpose which does have its time of fulfilment in history. It was Jeremiah who proffered the criterion for the truth of prophecy: the prophet 'can only be recognised as one truly sent by

---

15. Th. C. Vriezen, *The Religion of Ancient Israel* (London: Lutterworth, 1969) p. 198.
16. H. W. Robinson, *Inspiration and Revelation in the Old Testament* (Oxford: Clarendon, 1967) p. 171.

Yahweh when his word comes true.' (28:9) In the New Testament that word is seen to come true when the whole sweep of the Old Testament, when all the scriptures are seen to be fulfilled in Jesus the Christ. And the pattern and purpose of the scriptures will be first uncovered and interpreted in that light by the risen Christ on the road to Emmaus (Lk 24:27).

4 | The Living Word of God in the Gospel of Luke

IN MOVING from the Old Testament to the Gospel of Luke there is no great stylistic or theological divide to be crossed since there are so many links which connect the ancient hopes expressed through the prophets and their fulfilment in the Gospel. Luke adopts those hopes as the ancestors to his Gospel and integrates them into the narrative while at the same time announcing the time of their issue in history. For Luke the Gospel is not utterly new but the accomplishment of God's saving plan in history. Drury points out:

> To turn from Luke to Old Testament narrative ... is to cross no boundaries but to remain in the same country, to hear the same language in the same forms describing similar events. Why? The answer is simple and takes us deeper still: because the same God, who as Lord of history works his purpose out by prophecy and fulfilment as year succeeds to year, is working all in all. There is no interruption.[1]

That uninterrupted flow can be traced in the influence which the Septuagint clearly has on Luke's writing,[2] on Luke's presentation of Jesus as the great prophet like Moses, and through Luke's demonstration of the creative power of the word of Jesus.

PROPHECY AND FULFILMENT

Luke grounds his whole narrative of Gospel-Acts on the promises and the plan of God and constantly refers to the events that take place as the kept promise of God and the fulfilment of his plan. This is illustrated poetically and movingly in the prophetic-apocalyptic character of the

1. J. Drury, *Tradition and Design in Luke's Gospel* (London: Darton, Longman and Todd, 1976) pp. 7-8.
2. Cf. *ibid*. pp. 44-66.

infancy narrative where the outpouring of the prophetic spirit plays such a significant part in attesting the significance of what is said and done. The work of the Spirit in the infancy narrative clearly resembles the pentecostal outpouring of the Spirit in Acts:

> I will pour out my spirit on all mankind.
> Their sons and daughters shall prophesy,
> your young men shall see visions,
> your old men shall dream dreams. (2:17)

In setting the stage for Jesus' appearance with a series of prophetic utterances Luke is carefully conditioning the way we should interpret the arrival of Jesus – as the fulfilment of spirited prophecy. This stratagem enables Luke to root his story in the past of Israel and give a history of expectation to the new event of 'today' (2:11); it also signals the unique importance of the one who will be proclaimed as *Christos Kyrios* (2:11; cf Acts 2:36).

We have already discussed in the first and second chapters many of the links between the infancy narrative and the Old Testament; it will be sufficient to mention here how Luke illustrates the role of the prophetic word and the prophetic spirit in the last times. Gabriel who stands in the presence of God (1:19) is the first to reveal the word of God. He prophesies the birth of John the Baptist, how he will be filled with the Holy Spirit from his mother's womb (cf 2 Kgs 2:9-16; Is 61:1; Ez 11:5), and how his future mission will be conducted in 'the Spirit and power of Elijah' (1:17). Because Zechariah fails to believe 'my words, which will come true at the appointed time' (1:20) he is silenced. In Elizabeth's conception the word of God is seen to happen, and that word-event will serve as the sign revealed to Mary

In revealing the word of God to Mary, Gabriel further unfolds the saving plan of God and prophesies that Mary will conceive a son who will be 'Son of the Most High' (1:32). In answer to Mary's 'how' question, Gabriel announces the intervention of the Holy Spirit and the overshadowing by the power of the Most High which designates Jesus as Son of God. Mary's acceptance of the word of God is not only consistent with the Lucan portrait of discipleship (8:19-21) but shows the creative power of God's word: 'let what you have said be done'. In Mary the word of God becomes event, for nothing said by God is impossible.

That close relationship in revelation between word and event, between promise and fulfilment, is elaborated further in the story of the visitation. As Mary has received a revelation about Elizabeth so the aged mother receives a revelation about the mother of her Lord: the already busy prophet is seen to verify the prophecy that he would be filled with the Holy Spirit from his mother's womb (1:15). Inspired by the prophetic Spirit, Elizabeth speaks as a prophetess in a canticle which blesses Mary among women (cf Jdt 13:18-18) and blesses the fruit of her womb (cf Deut 28:1.4). Rather than limit the blessing to physical motherhood like the woman in the crowd who 'raised her voice and said, "Happy the womb that bore you and the breasts you sucked!"' (11:27), Elizabeth continues in the spirit of the Gospel to bless Mary because she 'believed that the promise made her by the Lord would be fulfilled' (1:45), thus anticipating Jesus' maxim to the woman in the crowd, 'Still happier those who hear the word of God and keep it!' (11:28) So Luke depicts two responses to the revealed word of God: the old priest who is punished because he does not believe in the inherent power of the word of God; the young virgin who is blessed because she believes that God's word will indeed be accomplished in her.

If Zechariah and Mary differ in their response to the revealed word of God, Luke shows how in their respective canticles they are united in praising God for the fulfilment of his prophetic promises. Because of what God has done, Mary prophesies that future generations will call her blessed (1:48), and in the conclusion of the Magnificat she praises God for keeping his covenant with Israel in this new act which brings salvation in Jesus

> – according to the promise he made to our ancestors –
> of his mercy to Abraham and to his descendants for ever.(1:55)

In his turn, Zechariah is filled with the Holy Spirit and praises God for fidelity to his prophetic word and covenant word

> even as he proclaimed,
> by the mouth of his holy prophets from ancient times (1:70)

thus he remembers his holy covenant,
the oath he swore
to our father Abraham (1:72b-73)

After listing these reasons to bless God, Zechariah goes on to prophesy how his son will be called 'Prophet of the Most High' (1:76). Thus, at the heart of both hymns there is celebration in recognition of the power of God's word, a word that is not empty of power or destiny but which achieves its purpose at the appointed time.

The appointed time is 'today' (2:11) and this good news is revealed by another angel to shepherds caring for their flocks. The annunciation to the shepherds is accompanied by a sign (v. 12) and a brief hymn of praise by the heavenly host (v. 14). The shepherds respond to the revealed word of God by travelling to discover its truth: literally, they go to see 'the word' (*rema* which is usually translated as 'word' is used here as a Semitism by Luke like the Hebrew *dabar* translated as both word and event.) When the shepherds verify the revealed message they in their turn praise God 'for all they had heard and seen; it was exactly as they had been told.' (v. 20) Mary's response to 'all these things' (translating the plural of *rema*) is to keep these word-events and interpret them in her heart. Thus as the annunciation to Mary concluded with Gabriel's maxim that with God no *rema* is impossible (1:37) and with Mary's response that it should be 'according to your *rema*' (1:38), so the actual birth is narrated as the word-event of God. In effect Luke states that the beginning of the new age is marked by the word of God becoming event.

The word of God in the Law and in the prophets forms the setting for the presentation of Jesus in the Temple: the obedience to the Law of the Lord brings Jesus into contact with two prophets who are connected to Israel by their expectancy of its restoration and to the new age by their prediction of the future greatness of Jesus. Luke mentions the influence of the Holy Spirit on Simeon three times before the old prophet is seen to recognise that his time of waiting is over because God has kept his word. Simeon sees the fulfilment of God's promise in the bundle in his arms which moves him to hymn a blessing and to utter prophecy.

The aged prophetess, Anna, is presented in terms reminiscent of Judith, the personification of Judaism (cf Jdt 15:5-16:17). Portrayed as a

waiting figure of patience and fidelity, Anna is a summary of the poor
of Yahweh whose devotion opens her to the word of God (cf Acts 2:17).
In her turn she is moved to praise God and proclaim Jesus to all who are
looking for the the redemption of Jerusalem.

Thus throughout the infancy narrative, which is an intricate theological tapestry of Old Testament motifs, the time of fulfilment is
recognised in the word-event; the recognition moves to testimony as the
prophetic Spirit is seen at work in praise and prophecy, as poetry
becomes the appropriate medium, and rejoicing the only conceivable
response for those who witness the word-event taking place in their
midst.

If the coming of Jesus is interpreted as the fulfilment of ancient
prophecy, it also provides the occasion for new prophecy especially in the
person of John the Baptist. The word of God comes to John not in the
precincts of the Temple but in the wilderness; in the tradition of the
exodus it is the place for new beginnings. John is destined to be the new
Elijah of popular expectation (1:17f; cf 7:27 citing Mal 3:1 and Is 40:6), the
forerunner who will prepare the people with a prophetic word. John
announces the imminent judgement of God and calls everyone to
submit to its scrutiny: being a child of Abraham does not exonerate
anyone from its claim (3:9). He calls people to a change of heart and
baptises them with a baptism which prefigures the baptism of Jesus'
passion (12:50). When the one who is to come appears, John must give
way to the other's pre-eminence: 'Up to the time of John it was the Law
and the Prophets; since then the kingdom of God has been preached'
(16:16).

Conzelmann interprets 16:16 theologically to mean that John is not
the forerunner of Jesus but a prophet who is excluded from the new time
of salvation.[3] However, *apo tote*, 'since then', can be read to include John,
and since Luke has already marked the inauguration of the time of
fulfilment with the announcements of the births of John and Jesus, and
referred to the 'Good News' preached by John (3:18), it seems hardly
likely that he wants to exclude him from the message which Jesus will
preach (cf 7:26f). Further, when Peter offers guide-lines in the choice of

3. H. Conzelmann, *The Theology of Saint Luke*, pp. 22 ff.

a candidate to replace Judas Iscariot, the principal requirement is 'someone who has been with us the whole time that the Lord Jesus was travelling round with us, someone who was with us right from the time when John was baptising' (Acts 1:21-22). This reading would seem to support including John the Baptist in 'the period of Jesus'. Certainly Luke has John in prison when Jesus is baptised, but this seems a literary device to give undivided attention to Jesus' own prophetic ministry.

In discussing the diversity of the evangelists' treatment of John the Baptist, Wink has noted their unity on one point:

> Each continues to make him the 'beginning of the Gospel'. Jesus himself appears to have been the source of this estimate of John's role in God's saving activity. The conviction that John is the beginning of the gospel is the theological expression of a historical fact, that through John's mediation Jesus perceived the nearness of the Kingdom of God and his own relation to its coming.[4]

John the Baptist does appear as the occasion of Jesus' emergence from obscurity and stands, therefore, not only at the turning-point of two ages but at the turning-point of Jesus' life. Jesus may have been a disciple of John, accepting his baptism and associating with him until the time came to embark on his own ministry, John's Gospel reports that Jesus' first disciples were disciples first of John the Baptist (1:35-39; cf Acts 1:21f), and that Jesus baptised alongside John in the Jordan so that they were soon considered rivals (3:22-27). Although there are many affinities between John and Jesus, the people are able to discern clear differences (Lk 7:33-35). Jesus is seen to recognise the unique importance of John (7:7:26ff) setting his baptism within the framework of God's plan: 'All the people who heard him, and the tax-collectors too, acknowledged God's plan by accepting baptism from John' (7:29). And when Jesus accepts John's baptism with 'all the people' (3:21) the plan of God for him is revealed in the descent of the Holy Spirit preparing him for his ministry, and in his identification as 'my son'.

---

4. W. Wink in *The Interpreter's Dictionary of the Bible*, Supplementary Volume (New York: Abingdon, 1976) p.488; cf. also his study, *John the Baptist in the Gospel Tradition* (Cambridge: Cambridge University Press, 1968.

THE PROPHETIC MINISTRY OF JESUS

In Mark's account of the baptism of Jesus it is after Jesus undergoes immersion that the heavens are rent, the Spirit descends on him, and the heavenly voice identifies him as 'my Son, the Beloved' (1:9-11): in Luke 's account it is while Jesus is at prayer that this happens to him. Luke has already told us who Jesus is (1:32, 35; 2:11) and how he is begotten Son of God by the Holy Spirit (1:35): the descent of the Holy Spirit at his baptism is not, therefore, Jesus' being begotten Son of God – that is the meaning of the birth narrative. Rather, the descent of the Spirit marks the beginning of Jesus' prophetic ministry. Jeremias has commented:

> In the Judaism of the time, the importance of the spirit almost always means prophetic inspiration: a man is grasped by God, who authorizes him to be his messenger and preacher and speaks through him. Thus when it is said that the spirit descends on Jesus, the meaning is that Jesus is called in this way to be God's messenger.[5]

The significance of the descent of the Spirit is conveyed further by a proclamation of the God who speaks, and in the prayer experience of Jesus, Luke shows by way of composite quotation the unique relationship between Jesus and his Father:

Ps 2:7   *You are my son,*
         today I have become your father

Is 42:1 Here is my servant whom I uphold,
         my chosen one in whom my soul delights.
         I have endowed him with my spirit
         that he may bring true justice to the nations.

If the full quotation from Isaiah 42:1 is understood to influence Luke's thought then his meaning is clear: the promise that God would endow his servant with his spirit is now accomplished in Jesus. Thus Jesus is called and confirmed to inaugurate the time of fulfilment, the awaited time of salvation.

---

5. J. Jeremias, *New Testament Theology* Vol. 1 (London: SCM, 1972) p. 52.

Alongside that prophetic fulfilment, the relationship between Jesus as Son to God his Father is central to this scene, and it is one which Luke addresses clearly in the ministry. When Jesus is 'filled with joy by the Holy Spirit' (10:21) he makes a prayer of thanksgiving to his Father and declares: 'Everything has been entrusted to me by my Father; and no one knows who the Son is except the Father, and who the Father is except the Son and those to whom the Son chooses to reveal him.' (10:22)

The authority for Jesus' word and mission, which is so often questioned throughout the ministry, comes from Jesus' special relationship with God as Abba and forms the basis for his saving outreach to those in need. However, as Bornkamm writes, 'We have to free ourselves from the assumption that Jesus was the first to call God Father in the history of religion. Nor is he the first to have made the idea of all men being children of God the centre of his message.'[6] But as he observes later: 'The nearness of God is the secret of Jesus' language about God as Father. This is also shown in the expression by which Jesus chooses to address God in prayer'.[7] It is precisely Jesus' experience of the nearness of God as Abba which gives authority to the word he speaks and the work he performs. And that nearness is declared by Luke in a dramatic way while Jesus is praying before the ministry. The initiative is seen to be with God who addresses Jesus and owns him as 'my Son, the Beloved'; so Jesus addresses God as 'my Father' – a dynamic that is reflected in the infancy narrative when Jesus is 'called Son of God' by God's messenger (1:35) and is later seen to understand God as 'my father' when he answers Mary and Joseph in the Temple (2:49).

It is that relationship between Son and Father that is put on trial in the wilderness: 'If you are the Son of God' (4:3,9). But again Luke underlines twice in 4:1 the power of the Spirit which fills and moves Jesus. The sequence of the temptations in Luke, wilderness – mountain – Temple, could well serve as a summary for the places where something happens prior to great changes in the Gospel: the wilderness prior to Jesus' ministry in Galilee; the mountain of transfiguration prior to Jesus' journey to Jerusalem; the Temple prior to Jesus' death and exaltation.

6. G. Bornkamm, *Jesus of Nazareth* (London: Hodder and Stoughton, 1973) p. 124.
7. ibid. p. 128.

Whether that sequence is programmatic or not, the important point is that Luke shows Jesus voicing the word of God against the other voice, accepting his Father's way into the future, and emerging from his ordeal to return to Galilee not authorized with the power of Satan, but 'with the power of the Spirit in him' (4:14). Jesus is authentic to his mission.

In the scene in the synagogue at Nazareth (4:16-30; cf. Mk 6:1-6) Luke gives the first concrete instance of Jesus' prophetic activity while at the same time rehearsing the movement of the whole ministry and the various reactions to it.[8] When he is given the scroll Jesus selects the passage from Second Isaiah which sets forth the prophet's anointing by the spirit and his mission to the post-exilic Jerusalem community:

> The spirit of the Lord has been given to me,
> for he has anointed me.
> He has sent me to bring the good news to the poor,
> to proclaim liberty to captives
> and to the blind new sight,
> to set the downtrodden free,
> to proclaim the Lord's year of favour. (4:18; cf Is 61:1-2:58:6)

When he comments on the passage Jesus announces his own claim that he is the anointed one (cf Acts 10:38) and that these words of promise in scripture now find their fulfilment in him: 'This text is being fulfilled today even as you listen' (4:21). Jesus is seen to make himself the object of his own proclamation: the content of his sermon points to himself as the chosen one empowered to accomplish this salvation by heavenly authority. This notice of fulfilment receives the appropriate response of approval from the people.

However, as Luke develops his account the focus moves from the people's reaction to Jesus' gracious words to their assessment of Jesus' identity – 'This is Joseph's son, surely?' (4:23) – which Luke's readers now know to be a wholly inadequate summary of who Jesus is. The people of Nazareth see Jesus without being able to perceive who he is (cf 8:10), which stands in sharp contrast to Simeon who recognised in Jesus

8. Cf. J. Sanders, 'From Isaiah 61 to Luke 4' in *Christianity, Judaism and Other Greco-Roman Cults*, ed. J. Neusner (Leiden: Brill, 1975) pp. 75-106.

the fulfilment of salvation. It was in Simeon's prophetic oracle that Luke first sounded the note of future opposition warning that Jesus was 'destined to be a sign that is rejected ... so that the secret thoughts of many would be laid bare' (2:34,35). That is seen to be true in the synagogue at Nazareth as Luke shows how Jesus interprets the people's question and exposes their hostility to him by anticipating their unbelieving demand for a sign. Jesus' insight leads him to the maxim that highlights the plight of the prophet and, therefore, with his own rejection as a prophet (4:24). The anointed prophet who proclaims the acceptable (*dekton*) year of the Lord is not accepted (*dektos*) in his homeland,

In order to demonstrate the truth of Jesus' maxim Luke appropriates traditional scriptural texts concerning the rejected prophet and then shows how Jesus' word and the word of scripture are all too true in the people's rejection of Jesus: in their hostile behaviour both words become event. Jesus interprets what is going on now in the synagogue in Nazareth by appealing to the experience of Elijah and Elisha (1 Kgs 17:9; 2 Kgs 5:1-19), an appeal to the past which also serves Luke's purpose in another way: as Fitzmyer notes, 'These vv. 25-27 provide a justification from the OT for the Christian mission to the Gentiles.'[9] The townspeople are furious at Jesus' implication that his ministry would have better results elsewhere and that they resemble those who persecuted the ancient prophets; but both points prove to be true. Jesus' own townspeople try to kill him but he makes good his escape and proceeds on his way that will eventually bring him to Jerusalem, the place associated with the death of the prophets (13:33) and his own exaltation.

Although Jesus does not adopt the title of prophet for himself he seems to understand his own mission in prophetic categories in claiming to possess the spirit of God (11:20), in speaking of the prophet's rejection of his own people (4:24), and in tying his own destiny at Jerusalem to the rejection and martyrdom experienced by the prophets of old (13:33). It does seem clear from all the Gospels that prior to Easter Jesus was recognised by the people and understood by his own disciples as a prophet. The people of Nain herald him as a prophet when they witness

9. J. Fitzmyer, *The Gospel According to Luke I-IX*, p. 537.

his authority over death (7:16); Simon the Pharisee wonders if he really is a prophet, given his apparent lack of clairvoyance (7:39); some of the people regard him as one of the ancient prophets or 'Elijah *redivivus* (9:18,19); the Sanhedrin guards taunt him to 'play the prophet' (22:64); the disciples of Emmaus refer to him as one 'who proved he was a great prophet by the things he said and did' (24:19) and go on to speak of their expectation that 'he would be the one to set Israel free' (v. 21).

In their as yet 'pre-Easter' identification of Jesus they would seem to be speaking out of an understanding of Jesus as the eschatological prophet promised by Moses and linking that with the function of the Messiah; or else they are speaking out of their disappointed hopes that Jesus would be the Messiah reverting to seeing him as a prophet. And further to these points, Hill in his study of New Testament prophecy adduces reasons for understanding Jesus as a prophet from certain characteristics of his ministry: his prophetic speech patterns, his visions and ecstatic-prophetic experiences, his prophetic insight and foresight his symbolic acts, and his martrydom.[10]

However, to see Jesus as a prophet does not mean to place him as one among many of the messengers of God: if John the Baptist is 'much more than a prophet' (7:26) *a fortiori* Jesus himself is – something which Luke is at pains to point out in the infancy narrative. Added to that is the consideration that the prophetic ministries of John and Jesus come after a long break in the tradition of prophecy, a factor which puts both prophets into a wholly different category from the classical prophets.

Long before the time of Jesus living prophecy had faded from the life of Judaism; but if the spirit of prophecy was dead, the spirit of expectation was alive nourished by the belief that the prophetic spirit would return at the end of days (cf. Joel 2:28ff; 1 Macc 4:44ff; Ps 74:9). Given that expectation the revival of prophecy in John the Baptist and Jesus gives their witness eschatological significance in signalling the end time. At the heart of that general expectation was a specific hope that one day the prophet would arise in Israel who would be endowed with unique authority and who would fulfil all prophecy: his revelation of the

10. D. Hill, *New Testament Prophecy* (London: Marshall, Morgan and Scott, 1979) pp. 50-
       69.

mysteries of God and his call to repentance would be final as they would point to the approaching kingdom of God. He would be the eschatological prophet through whom God would speak for the last time. That expectation was common in New Testament times and given voice by the people when they ask John: 'Are you the Prophet?' (Jn 1:21). As Cullman has noted, the expectation of the prophet was shared by groups on the periphery of Judaism, 'Samaritans, for instance, and especially the sect which has become better known through the recently discovered Qumran texts.'[11] The ground of that expectation is in God's revelation in Moses:

> Yahweh your God will raise up for you a prophet like myself, from among yourselves, from your own brothers; to him you must listen ... and Yahweh said to me, 'All they have spoken is well said. I will raise up a prophet like yourself for them from their own brothers; I will put my words into his mouth and he shall tell them all I command them.' (Deut 18:15.18)

In the Deuteronomic tradition, which makes such a mark on Luke's writing,[12] a messenger (*angelos*) is promised by God, 'to guard you as you go and to bring you to the place that I have prepared. Give him reverence and listen to all that he says. Offer him no defiance; he would not pardon such a fault, for my name is in him. If you listen carefully to his voice and do all that I say, I shall be enemy to your enemies, foe to your foes.' (Ex 23::20-22) Although the following connections are not advanced as conscious theological parallels, it is interesting to note them. God's name, the Lord, is in the messenger: it is interesting to observe how Luke first calls Jesus *Kyrios* in the ministry when he raises the widow's son and is acknowledged as 'a great prophet' (7:16). Whoever attends to the voice of the messenger ultimately acknowledges God himself; whoever rejects the messenger commits the unforgivable sin (cf. 12:8-10). The people's response to the messenger is definitive: the response to God's final word in Jesus is decisive for all time as Luke demonstrates through the image

---

11. O. Cullmann, *The Christology of the New Testament* (London: SCM, 1973) p. 19.
12. For an exposition of the Deuteronomist tradition cf. M. Weinfeld, *Deuteronomy and the Deuteronomist School* (London: Oxford University Press, 1972).

of those who find themselves outside the locked door (13:25-30).

Schillebeeckx argues that the first followers of Jesus understood him in the readily available Jewish model of the eschatological prophet/messenger and that this was an essential stage in a growing understanding which enabled them to articulate their assessment of Jesus through the messianism of the latter-day prophet, an identification which acted as a matrix for the creeds of the post-Easter period.[13] Schillebeeckx regrets that so many exegetical surveys of Jesus' titles regard 'prophet' as somehow defective, and he tries to compensate for this practice by giving the notion of the eschatological prophet the place he believes it deserved in the tradition:

> That the link between the earthly Jesus and the kerygmatic Christ is the recognition, common to all credal strands, of the earthly Jesus as the eschatological prophet (who does, it is true, surpass all expectations) and that this identification (at least as question and surmise) was most likely made prior to Easter, has enormous consequences. It points to a considerable continuity between the impression that Jesus made during his earthly days and the apparently 'advanced Christology' of the Church's *kerygmata* or affirmations of belief after his death. For from the history of tradition it is still possible to show that all these *kergymata* are in the Judaism of the time already supplied along with the title 'eschatological prophet.'[14]

If Schillebeeckx is accused of making too much of the title,[15] he does exegesis a service in underlining its unique importance in the Jewish tradition and in the early church, particularly as a bridge of understanding between the historical Jesus and the Christ who is proclaimed. And this view would find support in Luke who explicitly identifies Jesus as the eschatological prophet in Peter's sermon at the Portico of Solomon

---

13. Cf. E. Schillebeeckx, *Jesus: an Experiment in Christology* (London: Collins, 1979) pp. 472-499; *Christ: The Experience of Jesus as Lord* (New York: Seabury, 1980) pp. 309-321.

14. E. Schillebeeckx, *Jesus: an Experiment in Christology*, pp. 479-480.

15. Cf. Schillebeeckx's defence of his position, *Interim Report* (London: SCM, 1980) pp. 64-74.

in Acts 3 (quoting Deut 18:19-19) and also in Stephen's address (Acts 7:37).

A reflection of that direct identification could be seen in Luke's Gospel when John the Baptist sends his disciples to ask Jesus: 'Are you the one who is to come, or must we wait for someone else?' (7:19) Fitzmeyer cautiously says that this could be interpreted to refer to the eschatological prophet.[16] More persuasive is Moessner's study [17] in which he argues that in 9:1-50 Luke provides a preview of 9:51-19:44 through which can be traced 'the journey of the prophet Jesus whose calling and fate both recapitulate and consummate the career of Moses in Deuteronomy. We have here nothing less than the prophet like Moses (Deut 18:15-19) in a New Exodus unfolding with a dramatic tension all its own.' [18] In tracing the life of Moses in Deuteronomy Moessner underlines his career as the suffering prophet and mediator who due to the stubborness of Israel in hearing God's voice has to suffer and die to allay God's anger and allow the exodus its completion. Through Moses' death outside the land the people can cross to their promised inheritance.

Moessner underlines four points in the career of Moses: his calling on Mount Horeb to mediate God's word revealed by the voice in the cloud to the gathered assembly; the persistent unwillingness of the people to hear that voice; his calling is disclosed to be a suffering journey to death; his calling will achieve deliverance only for the new people cf the land, the 'children of the mountain'. Moessner sees a profound correspondence in the career of the prophet like Moses outlined in Luke 9:1-50 – Jesus' transfiguration in which a voice from the cloud speaks of Jesus to the disciples representing the 'Twelve'; the disciples are asleep, but the voice of God commands them to obey God's elect in Jesus; Moses and Elijah converse with Jesus about his 'exodus', which involves a journey to Jerusalem and death; only the childlike can heed the voice of the mountain and receive Jesus (9:46-48). This summary does not do justice to Moessner's tightly argued exposition; but perhaps it can serve to point to the transfiguration-exodus pattern of Jesus' life in the frame of the

16. J. Fitzmyer, *The Gospel According to Luke I-IX* p. 666.
17. D. Moessner, 'Luke 9:1-50: Luke's Preview of the Journey of the Prophet like Moses of Deuteronomy' in *Journal of Biblical Literature* 102 (1983) pp. 575-605.
18. *ibid*. p. 582.

prophet like Moses which can be seen from the Gospel itself to consummate the Horeb-exodus pattern of Moses' life.

It must be acknowledged that none of the evangelists directly applies the title of prophet to Jesus in the Gospels – not because they do not believe that Jesus is the eschatological prophet like Moses but because, it is popularly argued, the early church considered 'prophet' to be inadequate as a Christological title for Jesus. However, rather than summing up the title prophet as inadequate to bear the weight of later Christology thereby effectively disabling it, a small shift of emphasis shows the title as one which actually enables people to see further.

This can be seen clearly in John's carefully constructed story of the healing of the blind man in chapter 9 which is more an account of one man's increasing insight into the true identity of Jesus than it is a story of healing. When interrogated by the neighbours the man who has recently emerged from darkness refers to Jesus as 'the man' (v. 11); in the first interrogation by the Pharisees he confesses that Jesus is 'a prophet' (v. 17), while in their second interrogation he defends Jesus by telling the Pharisees that he is 'from God' (v. 33). When in the climax of the story he comes face to face with Jesus for the first time his journey of insight is complete: he comes to see Jesus as 'the Son of man' (v. 35) and addresses him as 'Lord' (v. 38). Rather than interpret the designation of Jesus as prophet to be inadequate, it would seem to make better sense to appreciate its place in the development of insight.

A similar progression of insight is evident in the story of Emmaus which is framed by the theme of recognition and understanding. At the beginning of the story the two disciples do not recognise the risen Christ who journeys with them but they refer to Jesus as a prophet. (24:19). It is only after they hear his word and witness him in the breaking of the bread that they come to see him as Lord. It is not necessary to argue that from the new insight 'prophet' is a wholly inadequate description of who Jesus is now; it can be argued that Luke is illustrating their recognition of Jesus as prophet as a stage in their journey of insight that will soon lead them to recognise Jesus as Lord. Seen in this way, the designation of Jesus as prophet is a bearer of significance rather than a summary of inadequacy.

The disciples are chided by the risen Christ not for their belief in him as a great prophet but because their belief is not educated by the 'full message of the prophets!' (24:25) The full significance of Jesus' prophetic ministry and death is already contained in Moses and all the prophets: the prophetic word can summon up the complete Christ. To show this the risen Lord discloses the full meaning of the word of scripture 'starting with Moses and going, through all the prophets he explained to them the passages of scripture that were about himself.' (24:27) This is shown again in the last instruction of the apostles (24:44). Both teachings illustrate a point made earlier: 'If they will not listen either to Moses or to the prophets, they will not be convinced even if someone should rise from the dead.' (16:31) And both teachings show that there are sufficient Jewish *testimonia* for Christ's passion, death, and resurrection.

The word of eschatological prophecy announced by Moses that God would 'raise up' a prophet like himself (Deut 18:15,18) comes to its full term in the Easter event, and the full significance of that word can be revealed only by the risen Lord because the full totality of what the mighty prophet would achieve could be accomplished only in him. Thus the risen Lord does not marshal new evidence or reveal new titles to explain the meaning of his death and entrance into glory: the full prophetic message is quite capable of supporting the explanation of who he has become because of what he has achieved. Indeed that is its ultimate purpose. In him alone the prophetic word of God rests in fulfilment.

THE AUTHORITATIVE WORD OF JESUS

It is interesting to note that before Jesus proclaims the kingdom of God 'because that is what I was sent to do' (4:43), he is first identified in Luke's scheme as the person who fulfils the Isaian prophecy (4:18). Also, before the risen Christ is depicted speaking to his disciples about the kingdom (Acts 1.3), Luke first shows him identifying himself as the fulfilment of scripture (24:27,32,45). Luke's priority is instructive: in announcing the fulfilment of scripture in Jesus' person and mission at the beginning of the ministry and after the resurrection, Luke sets the stage for the kingdom by declaring the radical unity between God's word and Jesus' mission. In what Jesus says and does, in what he inaugurates and in what is accomplished through him, God is seen to be at work. With the proclamation of the good news comes the event of the kingdom of God: it happens through Jesus' word.

Although none of the synoptics refers to Jesus as God's Word, it is clear from the accounts that Jesus' word enjoys a unique authority in the sacred tradition. Unlike the prophets, Jesus does not use the messenger formula, 'thus says the Lord', nor does he refer to a divine mandate in his preaching with 'the word of God came to me'. Luke refers to the preaching of Jesus as 'the word of God', *ho logos tou theou*(5:1; 8:11,21; 11:28) and also uses the phrase in Acts as a summary of the apostles' preaching (e.g. 4:31; 6:2; 11:1). In using the same phrase to designate the preaching of Jesus and the preaching of the apostles Luke roots the apostolic proclamation in Jesus' own preaching, and, as Fitzmyer notes:

> The phrase suggests the ultimate root of this preaching/teaching is God himself for the phrase means 'God's word' or 'the word coming from God' (a subjective genitive or genitive of author) rather than 'the word telling about God' (objective genitive).[19]

The word that Jesus speaks has a unique authority because it is God's own word.

When people hear the teaching of Jesus they are deeply impressed precisely because of the authority which gives distinction to his words – literally 'his word was with authority' (4:32). Luke omits Mark's comparison 'unlike the scribes' (1:22); but Luke has already shown in his story of the young Jesus in the Temple that the wisdom of his words is not rooted in his intelligence or learning but in his relationship with his Father. Further, the infancy narrative has served to distinguish Jesus from all other human beings: in the power of the Holy Spirit he is called Son of God (1:35). So it is that after his baptism the adult Jesus is recognised as 'my Son, the Beloved' (3:22) and moves 'with the power of the Spirit in him' (4:14) to begin his ministry. It is the power (*dynamis*) of the Spirit that is the source of the authority (*exousia*) of Jesus. That power

---

19. P. Actemeier, 'The Lukan Perspective on the Miracles of Jesus: a Preliminary Sketch' in *Perspectives on Luke-Acts* (Edinburgh: T & T Clark, 1978) pp. 153-167.

endows his teaching with authority and is evident in his call to disciple-ship and his claim on those who hear his words; it establishes his dominion over evil spirits and his mastery over nature; it effects the forgiveness of sins and the healing of sickness. And the power of the Spirit accomplishes all this principally through the word of Jesus.

Luke illustrates the compelling authority of Jesus' word by showing in the tradition of the Old Testament how the power of Jesus' word continues the work of the creative word of God. Luke brings the ancient Hebraism of word-event into his Gospel: the word of God which effects what it affirms is now apparent in the word of Jesus which accomplishes what it says.

This is seen most clearly in the miracle stories prior to Jesus' teaching journey to Jerusalem. In these stories people are seen to recognise in the deeds of Jesus the authority of his imperative word:

> He rebuked the fever and it left her (4:39)
> 'Of course I want to'. 'Be cured!' (5:13)
> 'I order you:get up and pick up your stretcher.' (5:24)
> 'Give the word and my servant will be cured.' (7:7)
> 'Young man, I tell you to get up' (7:14)
> He called to her, 'Child get up.' (8:55)
> Jesus rebuked the unclean spirit and cured the boy (9:42)

Just as in the beginning God created by saying ('God said, "Let there be ... " and so it was'), so Jesus re-creates by saying. The word which he speaks is a power for transfiguration which transforms people into a new creation. Throughout the ministry of Jesus there are many people who meet him but who remain untouched by his deeds and words; but there are many whose encounter with Jesus gives their lives a new signifi-cance. The language used to describe the critical condition of people who come to Jesus or whom Jesus seeks out speaks of disfiguration, of chaos, and of brokenness. Conversely the language appropriate for what happens to people in their encounter with Jesus is that of transfiguration, and of new life:

> the blind   see
> the afflicted   are healed.

the dead	come to life
the lost	are sought out and saved
the poor	hear Good News
the outcasts	experience acceptance
the sinners	are touched by forgiveness
the possessed	regain mastery of their lives

People who are open to the creative word of Jesus leave his presence changed: something happens to them. In that change they see themselves differently, they see Jesus differently and they see their future differently. Jesus' word creates a new beginning; his word brings about the opportunity for people to begin again.

In the miracle stories Luke shows not only how Jesus' word has effective power but often illustrates how the event of the miracle is itself a word of God which in its turn makes for a variety of responses: astonishment, story-telling, faith, praise of God, hostility etc. A good example can be found in Luke's first miracle story (4:3l-37; cf. Mk 1;21-28). Unlike Mark who subordinates the miracle to Jesus' teaching, Luke balances Jesus' teaching and miracle-working, a balance already evident in the programmatic outline of Jesus' first sermon in the Nazareth synagogue. In the synagogue in Capernaum, Luke demonstrates the power of Jesus' word, 'Come out of him!' And the devil ... went out of him' (4:35). Underlining how the word is accomplished in the midst of the assembly Luke depicts their astonished reaction which leads to a question – literally, 'what is this word?' (v. 36). In this example *logos* can be translated as 'thing, word, event', exactly like the Hebrew, *dabar*. This word-event has its own effect in the ensuing witness through the surrounding countryside.

Luke's redaction of Mark in this particular manner extends beyond this episode. As Achtmeier has pointed out in his brief survey on the Lucan perspective on Jesus' miracles, Luke alters Mark's miracle stories in several instances to reflect a studied balance between Jesus' proclamation and his miracle-working.[20] Perhaps it is true to say that Luke, more

20. For a summary article see G. Frost, 'The Word of God in the Synoptic Gospels' in *Scottish Journal of Theology* 16 (1963), pp. 186-194.

than Mark and Matthew, communicates his belief that the miracles are themselves a powerful proclamation of God at work in Jesus and, therefore, have the power to validate Jesus – a view that is supported by the typical Lucan response to miracles in the praise of God.

Two of the most dramatic instances which show how the miracles of Jesus have the power to lead a person to faith are contained in the story of the Gentile centurion's faith (7:1-10) and the story of John the Baptist's questioning (7:18-23). Both accounts are set in the immediate context of miracle-working. The centurion has already heard about the miracle-working of Jesus, and that hearsay makes for a response in faith. In Matthew's account (8:5-13) and in John's (4:46-53) the centurion/royal official goes to Jesus personally to request his help. In Luke 's story the drama is heightened considerably when the centurion remains at his house and communicates with Jesus first through a delegation of elders and then through a group of friends. The focus is on the latter who express the faith of the centurion by telling Jesus not to trouble coming but 'give the word and let my servant be cured' (7:7). In Luke's story two words meet: the expectant word of the Gentile and the powerful word of Jesus. Both words are effective. It is now Jesus' turn to be astonished at 'these words' and he goes on to make a critical observation that he has not found such faith even in Israel. In this pronouncement it is clear that this is not a story of healing but a story of faith – specifically the unparalleled faith of a man who has never met Jesus but who sees his word as inherently effective, thereby unwittingly recognising in the person of Jesus the today of the Lord's year of favour (cf. 4:19).

Luke immediately follows this story by further revealing the extent of Jesus' authoritative word in raising the widow's son at Nain – a foreshadowing of his message to John that 'the dead are raised to life'. In sharp contrast to the word of faith which the Gentile sent Jesus as a result of hearing about his miracle working, Luke now tells the story of the imprisoned John the Baptist who, when his disciples 'give him all this news' (7:18), sends two messengers to Jesus with a word of perplexity. The question which John poses through his delegation is whether the miracles of Jesus validate him as the one who is to come. Luke writes that as the disciples arrive *en ekeine te hora* (v. 21), literally 'in that hour he cured'. The disciples of John are seen to personally witness the miracles of Jesus and are enjoined to relay their personal experience to the Baptist: 'Go back and tell John what you have seen and heard' – in Matthew's version what they hear and see. Jesus' deeds and his words make up his proclamation to John, just as they did to the people of Nazareth (4: 16-30), and will do to the disciples of Emmaus when they answer the question 'What things?' by saying that Jesus was 'mighty in deed and word' (24:19 RSV). And that unity of Jesus' deeds and words is underlined in Luke's portrayal of Jesus as a miracle-worker prior to the call of his own disciples.

WORD AND DISCIPLESHIP

In Mark's bare account of the call of the first disciples (1:16-20) Jesus has just begun his preaching in Galilee when, without any preparation, he suddenly summons four disciples to leave their nets and follow him. There has been no suggestion yet of Jesus' wondrous power. Luke, on the other hand, postpones the calling of the first disciples until after Jesus is seen and acknowledged as a miracle-worker (5:1-11; cf. Jn 21:1-11). Luke's sequence makes the ready response of the first disciples easier to understand – in particular the call of Simon, which follows the cure of his mother-in-law and the miraculous haul of fish. In both events Simon witnesses the unique authority of Jesus' word. The frustrating experience of working hard and catching nothing is set against the fruitful prospect contained in Jesus' word to put out into deeper water and pay out the nets for a catch. The word of Jesus invades that world of Simon which gives him his identity as a fisherman. Simon decides to make Jesus' word, not his recent experience, the deciding factor: 'if you say so' (5:5) – literally 'at your word'. The catch takes place as Jesus said it would, and that miraculous event becomes the turning-point for Simon and his companions. The word now addressed to Simon Peter holds out another prospect – the success of his future mission as a follower of Jesus. Simon is personally called and, with others who had witnessed the great act of Jesus, now leaves the magnificent catch behind to follow Jesus.

There are three examples in Luke's Gospel where Jesus explicitly refers to his own words. Although their authenticity is contested [21] since it is questioned whether Jesus himself referred directly to his own speech in this way, they illustrate the unique claim Jesus' words make on his hearers, a claim whereby people's ultimate relationship with God is dependent on the hearing and doing of Jesus' word.

The first occurs in the presentation of Jesus' sermon on the plain, addressed to the disciples. Luke concludes the discourse with a portrait of the true disciple compared to the wise man who builds his house on rock (6:46-49). The true disciple is defined by his relationship with the person and words of Jesus: the one 'who comes to me and listens to my words and acts on them' (v. 47). Coming, listening, and enacting are three actions with their focus on the word; they are the verbs associated with discipleship not least because they enable Jesus' challenging word to become event.

Secondly, in the context of Jesus' first prophecy of the passion Luke relates the consequences of following Jesus (9:23-27) and the importance of loyalty to his person and words: 'For if anyone is ashamed of me and of my words, of him the Son of Man will be ashamed when he comes in his own glory and in the glory of the Father and the holy angels.' (v. 26) Some manuscripts omit 'words', although it is argued that the omission is unlikely to be original.[22] This close association between the person/ words of Jesus and the glory of the Father is almost Johannine, since people's relationship with Jesus' person/word is seen ultimately to determine their relationship with God. The revelation of God's power is seen in the deeds and words of Jesus which in turn reveal who he is. God's revelation is associated in the closest possible way with the person of Jesus. Thus Luke, in company with Mark and Matthew, witnesses to the same truth that John announces with such powerful clarity in his Gospel: Jesus is the Word of God.

The third instance is towards the end of a complex group of prophetic sayings which make up the last discourse of Jesus: Luke includes the

21. Cf. B. M. Metzger, *A Textual Commentary on the Greek New Testament* (London: United Bible Societies, 1971) pp. 91. Cf. also C. K. Barrett, 'I Am Not Ashamed of the Gospel' in *New Testament Essays* (London, 1972) pp. 132-134.
22. T. W. Manson, *The Sayings of Jesus*, p. 334.

maxim that underlines the enduring validity of Jesus' words: 'Heaven and earth will pass away, but my words will never pass away.' (21:33; cf. 16:17) As Manson has observed: 'it is probable that we should take this saying as having to do with the validity of the teaching of Jesus as a whole rather than with the smaller matter of the correctness of the predictions in the apocalyptic discourse'.[23] Kummel argues strongly for the genuineness of the saying [24] which writes large the authority of the words of Jesus that will never have an end date, but will forever stand true.

The claim underlying Jesus' words is reflected further in two examples in Luke's Gospel where 'the word of God' means Jesus' own preaching (8:21; 11:28). Like Mark and Matthew, Luke has a statement by Jesus about membership of Jesus' family being decided by fidelity to the word of God.[25] In Mark's account Jesus' relatives go to take charge of him convinced that he is out of his mind (3:20-21). When his mother and brothers arrive they stand outside the circle of those who listen to Jesus and pass a message to him; but Jesus responds that those sitting in the circle who do the will of God 'are my mother and my brothers' (3:34). In the Gospel of Mark both the attitude of Jesus' relatives to him and his attitude to them are clearly negative (cf. Mk 6:4).

Although Matthew's account reduces the dramatic tension between Jesus and his family there is still a note of strife (12:46-50). Luke, on the other hand, omits any note of hostility between Jesus and his family: hearing that his family cannot reach him 'because of the crowd' Jesus says, 'My mother and my brethren are those who hear the word of God and do it' (8:21 RSV). Unlike Mark who replaces Jesus' real family with his disciples, Luke shows Jesus praising his physical family because they meet the criterion for membership of his eschatological family – hearing the word of God and doing it. This is fully consistent with Luke's depiction of Mary in the infancy narrative, 'let what you have said be done to me' (1:38), and also with his picture of Jesus' family among the

23. W. G. Kümmel, *Promise and Fulfilment* (London: SCM, 1957) p. 91.
24. Cf. R. E. Brown *et al.* (eds.), *Mary in the New Testament* (London: Geoffrey Chapman, 1978) pp. 167-172.
25. C. F. Moule in *Neotestamentica et Semitica*, ed. E. Ellis and M. Wilcox (Edinburgh: T & T Clark, 1969) p. 100.

community who wait for the Spirit, 'including Mary the mother of Jesus, and … his brothers' (Acts 1:14).

Similarly, in a passage unique to Luke, a woman from the crowd voices a beatitude on the mother of Jesus for bearing such a son and Jesus replies: 'Still happier those who hear the word of God and keep it.' (11:28) Jesus asserts that true beatitude is found not in giving birth to such a child, but in giving response to such a word as the word of God. Again, Luke is hardly implying censure on Jesus' mother: on the contrary, he has portrayed her as the first in his Gospel who meets the criterion of Christian discipleship in letting the word of God become event in her life (1:38). And in Luke's Gospel Mary is the only one depicted wholly in terms of perfect Christian discipleship.

The inseparable link between the word of God and discipleship is elaborated by Luke in the parable of the sower (8:4-8) and its interpretation (vv. 11-15). In Mark (4:1-34) this section is mainly concerned with the teaching of Jesus in parables; Luke shifts the emphasis by omitting the other parables and concentrating attention on hearing the word of God. The parable is addressed to the crowd making their way to Jesus – the first action of discipleship – and in that context Luke focuses on the seed the farmer sows, 'his seed' (v. 5). Underlying the parable is a telling confidence: in spite of all the obstacles present in the various types of soil and in the process of growth, the good news is that the seed succeeds in growing and producing a rich harvest. The word of God preached by Jesus, despite apparent failure and repeated opposition, will enjoy great fruitfulness in the eschatological age – symbolised in the hundredfold of the harvest's yield. The message of Jesus will be heard and enacted; the word of God risked in so many unlikely places will not be an empty word but will succeed indeed.

Opinion is divided among scholars as to whether the allegorical interpretation of the parable is the authentic teaching of Jesus or must be ascribed to the primitive Church. There is general agreement about Luke's shaping of the interpretation which develops the sense of the parable beyond the eschatological to an ethical explanation: why preaching receives such a mixed response; but there is dispute about whether Jesus used allegory in this way. Since the meaning of Jesus' parables was not self-evident it is perfectly feasible to argue that Jesus would use allegory to explain his meaning, a practice familiar to his contemporary rabbis and consistent with Old Testament tradition; so, representing that tradition, Brown, Ellis, and Marshall argue to an original allegorical explanation by Jesus behind Luke's interpretation of the parable of the sower.[26] Jeremias and Fitzmeyer, representative of the opposing view, understand the allegorical interpretation as a construct of the early Church – not least on the linguistic grounds that *logos* 'absolutely is a technical term for the gospel coined and constantly used by the primitive Church; this absolute use ... by Jesus only occurs in the interpretation of the parable of the Sower ... and nowhere else.'[27] In either case the interpretation serves as an analytical tool for examining how the preaching of Jesus and that of the apostolic Church is received.

In the interpretation a variety of responses to the word of God is explored through four types of hearers: those whose response to the saving word does not last because the word is snatched away by the evil opposed to its power; those whose initial enthusiasm for the word cannot withstand trial; those whose first listening never reaches maturity because they are overcome by a litany of distractions; finally, those who listen to the word with a generous heart, make it their own, and yield a harvest through their persistence. The fourth group form the model for true Christian discipleship: in giving the word a secure place in their heart and remaining steadfast to its demands, their cooperation ensures its eventfulness in the Christian life. Again it is discipleship which enables the preached word of God to become a fruitful thing.

The story which illustrates two of those opposing attitudes to the word of God – one of anxious distraction and one of attentive listening – is told by Luke in the responses of Martha and Mary to the word of Jesus (10:38-42). In this special Lucan pericope the portrait of Martha as being worried (*merimnas*) to such an extent that it distracts her from

---

26. Cf. R. Brown, 'Parable and Allegory Reconsidered' in *Novum Testamentum* 5 (1962), p. 40; E. Ellis, *The Gospel of Luke*, p.126; I. H. Marshall, *The Gospel of Luke*, pp. 323-324.
27. J. Jeremias, *The Parables of Jesus*, p.77; Cf. J. Fitzmyer, *The Gospel of Luke I-IX*, pp. 710-712.

attending to the word of God can be seen as a lively commentary on that group which is 'choked by the worries (*merimna*) ... of life' (8:14) when they hear the word of God. Plummer notes of 10:41: 'The verb is a strong one, "thou art anxious," and implies division and distraction of mind, which believers ought to avoid'. [28] In contrast to Martha, her sister Mary adopts the posture of discipleship in sitting at the Lord's feet (cf. Acts 22:3) and listening to his words. She typifies those who 'have heard the word and take it to themselves' (8:15). And that one thing necessary to discipleship shall not be taken from her. Nothing has priority over allegiance to the word of God in Jesus.

Another essential bond between the word and discipleship is taking the word that is heard to others so that they may experience new life. This can be seen in Luke's two accounts of commissioning: the first one depicts Jesus sending out the Twelve and giving them a list of impera-tives to follow (9:1-6; cf. Mk 6:7-13; Mt 10:1-14); the second narrative, peculiar to Luke, records a further mission by seventy-two other disci-ples with instructions for their work (10:1-12). In the first account Jesus summons the Twelve and confers 'power and authority' on them. Luke has already used *dynamis* and *exousia* to describe Jesus' special role and mission; now Luke shows how Jesus gives his chosen followers a share in the dominion which he enjoys as God's chosen one. In empowering them to act and commissioning them to preach the kingdom and heal, Jesus makes them not just messengers but fellow workers. This partici-pation in his mission is a clear foreshadowing of the great commission after the resurrection in 24:46-47. And since the apostles will play such an irreplaceable role in Acts as witnesses and ministers of the word, it is clearly important for Luke to underline their original calling and commission by Jesus himself (cf. Acts 1:21-22).

In Jesus' commissioning of the seventy-two other disciples Luke shows that the task of sharing in the mission of Jesus is not confined to the Twelve – thus Luke roots the spread of the primitive Church in the commissioning word of Jesus. As in the three other commissioning accounts there is a balance between miracle-working and proclaiming,

28. A. Plummer, *The Gospel according to St Luke* (International Critical Commentary; Edinburgh: T & T Clark, 1981) p. 291.

between what the disciples do and what they say. When the apostles returned from their mission they gave Jesus an account of 'all they had done' (9:10) – no mention of Mark's 'and what they had taught'. When the seventy-two disciples return they rejoice that the work achieved through the name of Jesus was effective (10:17). Again Luke seems to give the priority of mention to deeds. And although the pattern of the commission and missionary advice is often ascribed to the early Church, the originality of its intention is not seriously disputed. As Hahn has written in his analysis of Jesus' commissioning words:

> Above all, however, we must regard as authentic the commission to act like Jesus himself in proclaiming that God's kingdom had drawn near and in doing mighty works.[29]

Ultimately, of course, the task of Jesus' disciples to fully participate in his mission will be possible only after the resurrection. That is because they will be unable to make him the subject of their proclamation until after that event which discloses him to be the Christ. Jesus' deeds will never be fully understood until their true significance is disclosed in his death and resurrection. Jesus' words will never be wholly grasped by the disciples until they can understand the word about his suffering and death and resurrection (9:22; 24:26,44). If that word remains an enigma all the other words remain concealed, for it is that word which is given as Jesus' answer to his own question, 'Who do you say I am?' The event of Jesus' death and resurrection will be the supreme expression of God's word in Jesus; understanding that will be the first task of discipleship in the new age. Only when the disciples understand that word will they be able to fully answer the question that moves behind the deeds and words of Jesus to his identity. It is the question which is asked from Jesus' first public appearance in Nazareth to his first resurrection appearance on the road to Emmaus: 'Who is he?'

29. F. Hahn, *Mission in the New Testament* (London: SCM, 1975) p. 36.

PART TWO | # The Experience of Revelation

I N THE STORY of sacred history a priority of place has always been given to the initiative of God in the free offer of revela-tion: it is God who begins, who comes in his visit and speaks in his word. Revelation is historical; faith 'came' into history (Gal 3:23). Only when we recognise the historical actuality of revelation can we talk about the psychological aspects of reaction to this event.

God's visit can be recognised and his word heard only within the perspectives of human experience. Outside the boundaries of human experience there is no revelation. Human experience is necessarily the proper arena for divine revelation as it is for any kind of revelation. If divine revelation is the gradual unfolding of the plan of God, that gradual movement must happen in the midst of the familiar if it is to be recognised and understood for what it is. As human beings we can receive what is disclosed only through the medium of our experience: that is the measure of our humanity.

The development of the biblical narrative can be seen as the unfolding story of those who experienced divine revelation and the account of their experiences interpreted for others as a disclosure of God and an offer of salvation.

Every experience needs interpretation, and although interpretation may be an integral part of the experience itself, many experiences have to await another time when they can be made sense of and understood. The meaning of an experience is not always clear at the time of the experience: it is often later, only after new insight and new experience, that the significance of the experience can be evaluated. In the gradual process of revelation the experience and the interpretation of the experience are mutually dependant. The visit and the word of God are identified in the act of interpretation, and this interpretation itself forms an essential part of revelation which is offered to others as 'a power for salvation' (Rom 1:16). Bornkamm has observed:

The primary and intrinsic secret to which the New Testament message directs us is that God's word has become one with man's word, that it has come to us and become understandable in a human word.[1]

The revelation of God is thus proclaimed through the human word which becomes the graced opportunity of a new beginning for others.

1. G. Bornkamm, *Early Christian Experience* (London: SCM, 1969) pp. 4.5

5 | Experience and Interpretation

THE FACT that revelation is not manufactured from human experience means that we cannot discover Jesus as Lord from a scrutiny of our present experience. As modern Christians we depend in a unique way on the experience of Jesus' disciples who knew him and testified to his greatness through their life, their preaching and their ministry. Our faith is a faith which comes from hearing (Rom 10:17), but a hearing which emerges from the apostolic experience of Jesus as Lord, an experience that was given a name and a historical shape in the tradition of the infant Church. The faith of the apostles was grounded in a litany of experiences at particular times and places, experiences which have become through their expression in the New Testament normative for our faith today. This experience of the apostles makes for a definite religious community and a specific religious tradition, but before experiences become hallowed in tradition they are first new experiences which challenge the inherited expectations and conventional wisdom of the apostles – something which they find difficult to credit (Lk 24:41).

At the beginning and end of his Gospel Luke underlines the irreplaceable importance of those who knew Jesus during his lifetime and who experienced new life in Jesus whom God raised: 'those who from the outset were eye-witnesses and ministers of the word' (1:2), and who were given to understand the central significance of the Easter event: 'You are witnesses to this.' (24:48) Luke's appeal to the quality of witness – that what is proclaimed to others as good news is grounded in what has been experienced and interpreted as truth by accredited witnesses – is an example of the status experience enjoys as the ground of Christian proclamation.

Christianity is rooted in Jesus who is encountered and proclaimed as the Christ. Because of their direct contact with Jesus the first witnesses are uniquely qualified to testify to the saving significance of what has happened to them and others through him, and to offer the central event of his death and resurrection as a liberating message for their hearers. In their proclamation there is no need to prove that Jesus has suffered and died; their testimony centres on the truth that he was raised by God, which is the full interpretation of his passion and death.

Of course, no one is an 'eye-witness' to the resurrection itself: it is not an historical event in the sense that it can be verified by any means available to historical research. However, the reality of the risen Christ is seen as the precondition for the lively faith of the witnesses: that they met again the crucified one whom they knew to have died who disclosed himself as the risen Christ, and that the experience of that self-disclosure in the power of the Spirit utterly changed them. At the beginning of Acts Luke tells us: 'He had shown himself alive to them after his Passion by many demonstrations: for forty days he had continued to appear to them' (Acts 1:3; cf 1 Cor 15:5-8). Later in Acts Peter declares in the house of Cornelius: 'God raised him to life and allowed him to be seen, not by the whole people but only by certain witnesses God had chosen before-hand. Now we are those witnesses – we have eaten and drunk with him after his resurrection from the dead' (Acts 10:40-41). The witnesses' election by God and their experience of the risen Christ credit their status with a unique authority. Although not eye-witnesses to the event of the resurrection, the Easter disciples are chosen as witnesses to the meaning of the resurrection through their encounter with Christ. (But we will leave to the final chapter an examination of Luke's concept of witness.)

However, just as some people could not accept the apostolic testimony from experience when it was proclaimed preferring to believe the apostles to be drunk (Acts 2:13), so some people are suspicious of ascribing importance to experience in revelation because they believe it reduces revelation to a private ecstasy of the spirit. There is a traditional fear that if one begins with experience one ends with experience, and that it is impossible to break out of this enclosure of self to allow for the disclosure of God. The inbuilt assumption in this view is that experience, in contrast to 'objectivity', is unsubstantial and unreliable because it is restricted to subjectivity. That assumption is itself based on a theory of experience which limits experience to a recording of the feelings, ideas, or sense impressions to be found entirely within the mind of the individual, a private recording which is then compared to its discredit with the public world of reality. This dualism precludes a consideration of the independent reality of what is experienced, a reality which is not identical with the subject's private consciousness.

Given that theory, it is no surprise that experience is so often uncritically dismissed as pure subjectivity and, therefore, discounted as an unreliable means of discovering the truth of what happens in the real world. It is precisely that theory of experience which J. E. Smith has scrutinised and rejected in his philosophical study on experience and God, and proposed instead a recovery of experience from a view which has enjoyed a privileged status for too long. He writes:

> The basic roots of religion in experience can be understood only if experience is seen as an encounter with an objective world in the dual sense that the encounter is something objective and that what is encountered at the same time transcends the subjectivity of the individual and of any finite collection of individuals. The reason behind the choice of this term for the description of experience is that it best expresses the fact that in experience we find something already there, we come up against something, we confront persons, objects, events, and we do so with the sense that we undergo or receive whatever it is that we meet without any sense of being responsible for having produced it.[1]

Experience is an encounter with the world beyond the self, not the content of the private mental world of the individual. In experience something or someone other than the self is experienced. When a theory of experience which states that 'what is experienced is identical with the subject who experiences' informs a religious outlook, there follows the inevitable equation between the presence of God and the experience of the individual. This reduces God to a psychological construction with no

1. J. E. Smith, *Experience and God* (London: Oxford University Press, 1968) p. 13

independent existence, an immanent experience which in effect denies the possibility of revelation. To protect revelation from the charge of immanence some people argue to a totally alien intervention ab extra rather like the moment of inspiration portrayed in Rembrandt's painting, St Matthew and the Angel, which depicts the angel whispering the script to the evangelist thus by-passing the process of divine revelation perceived in event and experience, and interpreted in the form of Gospel. This extrinsic concept of revelation betrays a distrust of experience, a distrust based on a theory of experience which, however unelaborated, encloses experience in an incommunicable world of the self reminiscent of Marvell's description, 'The grave's a fine and private place'.

A concern to protect revelation from being reduced to human inventiveness is understandable, but if this concern shows itself in disowning the process of human understanding it denies the historical medium of revelation, the very process which enables the word of God to become flesh. It is self-defeating to argue that the way of perceiving and understanding revelation is totally different from human understanding. Human experience does not create revelation but it is the necessary medium for God's free expression: to discount the medium of revelation is to discount the message. Having its source in God revelation is transcendent of any theory of wisdom derived from human experience, but that does not require understanding in faith to be abnormal. Smith writes:

> Whatever is totally different from all we can experience and apprehend must be something that we can neither experience nor apprehend and, far from calling it God, we should rather call it nothing at all.[2]

Revelation does originate 'from above' but it is received only through the mediating process of human understanding which seeks to name, interpret, and communicate what has been disclosed. Since revelation is always addressed to the human it cannot achieve its purpose outside the process of normal human understanding.

2. *ibid.* p. 69

Writing at a time when Gnosticism and Docetism minimised the historical reality of the Christian message in the fact of Jesus' life, Luke's preface openly reflects on the method he has adopted to accomplish his task: drawing on the many accounts already available, Luke gives priority to the eye-witnesses on whose testimony the other accounts as well as his own are dependant. These eye-witnesses are those who experienced Jesus at first-hand, witnesses to the acts and teachings during his life, and who are also ministers of the word (*logos*), witnesses to the truth and significance of his death and resurrection. As one who regards being an eyewitness an indispensable qualification for the apostolic office (Act 1:21), Luke is clearly aware that what has been handed down to him as tradition (*paradosis*) is precisely a tradition from experience. Thus his whole Gospel is based on the authoritative testimony of those who experienced God's initiative in Jesus.

Luke is not concerned to protect revelation from human experience. As the Emmaus account illustrates in detail the special event of revelation is specifically recognised as a special occasion of experience. Within the confines of the story to discount the experience of the two disciples is thereby to discount the revelation of Christ in his visit and word, and in the breaking of the bread. Given the way Luke has shaped the story it is clear that the disciples do not create what is encountered: at the beginning of the story Christ is not with them, and at the end of the story he disappears from their sight. His approaching them (from 'elsewhere') and his leaving them (for 'elsewhere') serves to underline the truth that Christ becomes part of their experience but is not identical with it. His independent reality transcends the experience of the two disciples. The disciples are seen to respond to the supreme revelation of God in the presence and word of Christ: they come up against someone who is not an extension of themselves; they are confronted by a word they did not author; they are seen to undergo an experience they did not manufacture; they are changed by something they did not cause.

Every disclosure of God, a divine offer embracing event and person, is a special occasion of relationship. What makes the encounter with the Lord at Emmaus a special experience for the disciples is the fact that God has made his presence felt in history in a specific movement which involves them, and he does this by visiting them and speaking his word through the risen Christ. Further, it is clear from the development of the account that the focus shifts from what Jesus says to who he now is: so the climax of the story is the recognition and naming of who they are relating to in this experience. In their relationship to Christ the disciples are not taken out of themselves; rather, it is their involved selves which are changed through the experience of the encounter.

Since the complete experience of revelation includes not only what the Lord offers and who he is but what the disciples bring to that experience and who they are, Luke takes time in his account to describe the condition of the two disciples as they come to encounter the Lord. Revelation is not just about the action of God but about the interaction between who he is and who others are, between what he offers in the event of revelation and what others bring to that experience. I have already mentioned how often Luke describes those who meet Jesus during his ministry in terms of disfiguration and loss, a device which serves to highlight their new experience of transfiguration and new life effected through his ministry. This same dynamic is evident in the Emmaus account.

No one approaches new encounters in a state of total naivety, innocent of a specific past and a received wisdom which act as formative agents in shaping how to react to what happens in experience. Anyone who has had experience brings to new experience a derived way of understanding the world, a complex structure of 'seeing' people and events, and an individual critical ability to make sense of them. People cannot bracket off their human condition, or cancel their previous outlook when they approach new encounters. Past experiences have a way of shaping our capacity to understand and interpret what is going on now in experience. Thus, we all bring an assortment of baggage to any experience: our declared expectations, halting understanding, unformed theology, hesitant insights, clouded resolves, disappointed hopes, frank regrets, and a miscellany of other parts and pieces. These are important factors in what happens in new experience.

Luke is clearly aware that this dynamic is an integral part of the complex experience of revelation since he portrays it in his Emmaus account. Who the disciples are, told in terms of what they bring to this new experience, plays a significant part in the development of the narrative. Who the disciples are before the recognition scene – in the sense of how they see their present and future in the light of how they interpret 'the things that have been happening in the last few days' (24:18) – is portrayed as something which concerns Jesus enough to ask, 'What things?' The question allows us to know the disciples. In articulating their answer Luke shows us how the disciples are not offering a dispassionate summary of recent events; rather they are declaring who they are and how they are through the way they tell the story. Clearly it is their story.

Thus the encounter on the road is told as a meeting between the disciples and Christ through the meeting of different stories: if the two accounts had been similar there would have been nothing at stake when they met. The difference between who the disciples are before the recognition scene and who they are after that event is shown by their conversion and change through coming to understand the full story and coming to see the real story-teller.

Although the Emmaus story is framed as an account of only one eventful experience – but clearly functions as a summary of the growing faith of the early Church – through the journey motif, Luke shows the human process of coming to understand the significance of what has already taken place and what is actually taking place in the experience as it happens. In the journey, Luke shows how it takes time to come to understand what has already been given to the disciples (the word of God); time to recognise the meaning of recent events (the death of Jesus); time to recognise who it is who is with them (the risen Lord). Obviously this is not to suggest that if the disciples had enough time they would eventually grasp everything on their own, but simply to recognise from the text how Luke attends to the human process of understanding in faith what is offered in the experience of revelation. The story of revelation in the Emmaus account is not a story of instant insight, but a story of coming to enlightenment to see the risen Lord in the scripture and in the breaking of the bread.

Emmaus tells the story of one experience (particularity being a standard feature of good story-telling) but we know that no single experience has within it the assurance of its own authenticity. Looking at experience as a participation in the real world does not automatically free experience from the possibility of mistake or error. Finite experience teaches us that error is part of it, and that our interpretation of experience may need to be reviewed radically in the light of new insight. Neither a single event nor an individual person yields up everything there is to know in a single encounter: further encounter is essential, even if that is limited to memory and re-interpretation, because experience requires time for full disclosure. In requiring time experience is necessarily involved in change and development. If experience is a repeated encounter with reality – since we refer to having experience as as a process of learning through time – it makes it possible for future experience or insight to put in question, criticise, or see new significance in past experience. It is the nature of experience that it is always open to new possibility, and it is continually confirmed or constrained by new experience and critical reflection.

Not only is there a critical factor operative in continuing experience but since experience makes for expression it has a social dimension which brings individual experience into relation with other encounters. Edward Schillebeeckx has written:

> A new 'divergent' experience is a challenge, it subjects the prevailing models of experience to criticism. Experience is therefore never 'innocent'. For it is communicable. Anyone who has had an experience ipso facto becomes himself a witness: he has a message. He describes what has happened to him. This narration opens up a new possibility of life for others, it sets something in motion. Thus the authority of experience becomes operative in the telling. The authority of experience has a narrative structure.[3]

Thus, although Luke gives pride of place in his resurrection narrative to the Emmaus story, he does not limit this new experience to the two disciples or to one occasion. People share their experience of Jesus as Lord through story-telling, and the authority of this new experience is

3. E. Schillebeeckx, *Christ*, pp. 37-38

underlined by the fact that it is shared by many, and will continue to show itself in a life lived in the presence of the same Lord (Acts). The future experience of the apostles is seen to confirm their past experience; their shared experiences are seen to corroborate their individual experiences: both are summed up in the communal testimony, 'Jesus is Lord'. Faith needs community, not least because the continuing process of understanding the significance of experience needs the critical discernment and support of the community.

RE-INTERPRETATION: BRINGING THE PAST UP TO DATE

The on-going process of understanding the significance of past events is at the heart of the movement of revelation. As long as there is time, there is the possibility of understanding further the inexhaustible significance of revelation. There is no end point to understanding revelation. Being caught up in the process of revelation is being introduced to a movement that stays awake to the past, the present, and the future. Cullman distinguishes three acts in the process of revelation:[4]

1. The naked event to which the prophet/apostle must be an eyewitness and which is seen by non-believers unable to discern revelation in it.
2. The revelation of the divine plan being disclosed in this event to the prophet/apostle with which he aligns himself in faith.
3. Associating this revelation with previous revelations and the re-interpretation of these in the light of new disclosures.

Cullman adds:

As a rule, the first and second acts take place simultaneously, although this does not always happen. The third may often be brought about in a longer process of theological reflection. Still, a present event recognised in faith as a saving event is fundamental to the third development.[5]

Perhaps Cullman's three acts can be listed from the perspective of witness:

4. Cf. O. Cullman, *Salvation in History* (London: SCM, 1967) p. 90
5. *ibid*. p. 90

1. The witness of event
2. The witness of meaning
3. The witness of scripture

Although the first act (the new event) has a chronological priority, the second act (understanding its revelatory content) may have a logical priority – as in the Emmaus story where the event of Jesus' death is not seen as purposeful until its meaning has been disclosed, as the meeting with the stranger is not fully appreciated until the disciples' eyes are opened to his identity as Lord. In this sense the event functions as a witness only in retrospection: from the advantage of meaning the disciples remember the event with understanding, a dynamic which is a constant theme in John's Gospel.

The circle of association which begins in the experience of new revelation reaches back into past events and re-interprets them in the light of the new perspective gained. Being put in touch with past events in turn throws further light on the new experience by incorporating it into a tradition of certain kinds of revelatory experiences. This process of association and incorporation keeps the past alive by continually bringing it up to date, and recognising how past events can open up new dimensions in the present. In this dynamic the past is not dismissed but adjourned: it waits for new evidence and further disclosure, it postpones final judgement because of the inexhaustibility of new experiences; it waits to be called for again and re-interpreted. The new experience will in its turn become a past experience and be recognised and judged in a new perspective.

The dynamic of understanding whereby because of what is happening now leads to a new appreciation of something which has already taken place is clearly not limited to revelation; rather, because it is an essential part of human understanding it plays an important part in the experience of revelation. Bringing the past up to date is an activity we all engage in from time to time. In the light of new experience and new insight we continually re-assess past judgements and re-shape our understanding of past events, giving new importance to some events that appeared inconsequential at the time, or judging now as insignificant something which hitherto appeared crucial. Very few of our judgements remain immutable because we are changed by continuing experience. Thus the significance of an experience cannot be limited to the significance accorded it at the time of its happening; indeed the experience or event may have to wait years before its true significance can be determined and its influence on subsequent events reliably assessed. As T.S. Eliot has written: 'We have had the experience but missed the meaning'. But the meaning does not have to stay lost: meanings are recoverable in time.

Not only new insight can lead us to re-interpret the past but the absence of insight in our present experience can prompt us to make a journey into the past in the hope of capitalizing on previous experience and insight, and making them available in the present as a source of wisdom. This movement of passing over into the past time and coming back to the present is one which has been explored in depth by John Dunne who has outlined the double journey in search of understanding:

> Passing over is the way a man discovers the shape of the life story in other ages, the story of deeds, and the story of experience, and coming back from this to his own time is how he discovers by contrast its current shape, the story of appropriation. This is ultimately how he brings time to mind, how he searched through time and memory, for passing over avails him of the time and memory of others, and coming back leaves his own time and memory enriched.[6]

This movement serves to underline that we are not limited to our own time for insight, or to our own story for wisdom: if the past does not disengage us from further appreciation it can be a source of present revelation. Memory keeps the past available as this source, as a discerning interpretation converts it into insight. That is why memory and intelligence are so closely associated: unless we remember we cannot understand.

Keeping the past available – as opposed to keeping the past as past – is of central importance in both Testaments as an aid to understanding

6. J. Dunne, *A Search for God in Time and Memory* (Indiana: University of Notre Dame Press, 1977) p. xi; cf. also *The Way of All the Earth* (New York: Macmillan, 1972)

the whole story of the present. If we must be open to new experiences to grow in wisdom, we must be open to past experiences to grow in understanding: it has always been folly to limit enlightenment to those who happen to be walking around at the moment, or to suggest that discernment is something of a modern discovery. We need the past in order to understand the kind of people we have become, just as we need to update it through re-arranging our reading of it in the light of new experience.

This process of updating the past runs through all historical writing which attempts to do more than simply record what happened. It may be sufficient for the annalist to record what took place, but the historian must try to evaluate the significance of what happened and put it into some kind of evaluative perspective. In this light Marsh makes the distinction between 'what took place' and 'what was going on'[7] arguing that to understand any event we must appreciate what was going on in what took place. One can develop that distinction to show the mutual dependence between:

what takes place	what is going on
the experience	its meaning
the fact	its significance
the view	its evaluation
'seeing and hearing'	'perceiving and understanding'
eyewitness of event	*witness to meaning*

This way of thinking is similar to E. M. Forster's distinction between story and plot, a distinction which is not limited to the literary form of the novel, but one which serves equally well in the present discussion:

We have defined a story as a narrative of events in their time-sequence. A plot is also a narrative of events, the emphasis falling on causality. 'The king died and then the queen died' is a story. 'The king died, and then the queen died of grief' is a plot. The time-sequence is preserved, but the sense of causality overshadows it ...

7. Cf. J. Marsh, *Jesus in His Lifetime* (London: Sidgwick & Jackson, 1981) pp. 27-28

Consider the death of the queen. If it is in a story we say 'and then?'
If it is in a plot we ask 'why?'[8]

Similarly it is a distinguishing mark of the Christian faith not only to know that Jesus died, but to understand 'that Christ died for our sins, in accordance with the scriptures' (1 Cor 15:3). Thus in the Emmaus story it is not enough to know that Jesus suffered, but the why of his suffering: 'Was it not ordained that the Christ should suffer and so enter into his glory?' (24:26). Knowing what happened and understanding why it happened, being an eyewitness to the event and a witness to its meaning, form a necessary preliminary for Luke to the apostolic proclamation of the Gospel.

EXPERIENCE AND INTERPRETATION IN LUKE 24

The continuing process of understanding past words and events through insight gained from new experience is one which Luke uses as a unifying thread through his three resurrection narratives. In each of the episodes told as stories of experience Luke illustrates dramatically how the resurrection cannot be understood in the absence of an interpretation which discloses its redemptive meaning. By themselves, the empty tomb (24:4.11.12) and the resurrection appearances (24:16, 37) lead no one to belief in the resurrection; they need the accompanying word of God to interpret them. Thus the pattern of Luke's resurrection narratives is a combination of unintelligible events which stand in need of an interpreting word. Event and interpretation stand in mutual dependence, and from Luke's account it can be clearly seen how there are three effective interpretative words which disclose the saving significance of the death and resurrection of Jesus:

1. The new word of the risen Lord recalling and opening
2. the word of Jesus during his ministry and
3. the word of the scriptures.

In sharp contrast to the word of the risen Lord, the word of the two angels (interpreting the meaning of the empty tomb and recalling the

8. E. M. Forster, *Aspects of the Novel* (New York: Harcourt, Brace & World, 1955) p. 86

words of Jesus during the ministry), the word of the women (recalling their recent experience), and even the word of the disciples themselves (sharing the story that the Lord is risen), are insufficient to arouse in others an Easter faith in the resurrection. Neither the angelic word nor the human word can lead anyone to believe that Jesus is Lord. So it is that Luke shows in his resurrection tapestry not only how Christ is the link between the ancient scripture and the new proclamation and how the resurrection is a fulfilment of his own prophetic word, but also how it is through the certifying word of the risen Lord that the prophetic witness is effectively disclosed. Without the word of the risen Lord the death of Jesus is vacant of meaning, a dumb reality; but through his word it becomes a message for salvation.

EXPERIENCE AS PUZZLE: THE EMPTY TOMB

All four Gospels agree that the visit of the women to the tomb on Easter morning acts as a first disclosure in a chain of puzzling events.[9] In Luke's account the women go to the tomb expecting to find the corpse of Jesus, and we know that these are the same 'women who had come from Galilee with Jesus' (23:55), who followed Joseph of Arimathaea as he took the body of Jesus from the place of crucifixion to the tomb, and who 'took note of the tomb and the position of the body.' (23:55) The importance of the women as eye-witnesses at the burial of Jesus is further underlined by Luke's explicit mention of them as eye-witnesses at the death of Jesus: 'and they saw all this happen' (23:49). Further back in the Gospel these women are first identified as those who experienced in themselves the effects of Jesus' healing power and who, with the Twelve, were 'with him' (8:1) on his Gospel journey. Thus their credentials as eye-witnesses are carefully established in the developing stages of the story. When the women go to the tomb on Easter morning prepared to complete the embalming of Jesus' body their expectations are con-

9. In John's Gospel Mary of Magdala makes her way alone – which P. Benoit argues is a version of the empty tomb story that is earlier than Mark's: 'Marie-Madeleine et les disciples au tombeau selon Jean 20:1-18' in W. Eltester (ed.), *Judentum, Urchristentum, Kirche, Beiträge zur Zeitschrift für die neutestamentliche Wissenschaft* 26, (Berlin: A Töpelmann, 1964) pp. 141-152

founded when they find that the stone has been rolled away and discover there is no body to anoint. Paradoxically, their discovery is of an absence. In Mark (15:5-6) and Matthew (28:2-6) it is the young man/angel who points out to the women the empty place where the body of Jesus was laid. In Luke's account the women's reaction to what they can see for themselves is one which points to their inability to make sense of what they can see: they stand 'not knowing what to think' (24:4).

By itself the empty tomb leads these eye-witnesses only to perplexity: they can see but not perceive; they are confronted by an unintelligible fact which calls for an interpreting word. The perplexity of the women sets the scene for the appearance of two men in brilliant clothing. The women's reaction of fear is a typical element of angelophanies (1:12,29; 2:9); they also 'bowed their faces to the ground' (24:5 RSV).

It is worthwhile recalling at this point the apocalyptic setting of Daniel's vision:

> When I, Daniel, had seen the vision, I sought to understand it; and behold, there stood before me one having the appearance of a man. And I heard a man's voice....and it called, 'Gabriel, make this man understand the vision.' So he came near where I stood; and when he came, I was frightened and fell upon my face. But he said to me, 'Understand, O son of man, that the vision is for the time of the end. (Dan 8:15-17)

The purpose of the appearance of the angel(s) has a double function in the stories: to disclose the meaning of puzzling events, and by their presence to point to the eschatological significance of what has happened. This double function is also evident in the accounts of the transfiguration and ascension.

The transfiguration is preceded by statements about the final visit of the Son of Man (9:26). In the transfiguration itself the visitation of two heavenly figures has the function of revealing the purpose of Jesus' *exodos* to be accomplished in Jerusalem (9:31). The three disciples 'saw his glory' (9:32), a clear confirmation of the final part of the passion announcements that Jesus' mission will not end in death. In this context 'glory' is a description of the status of the risen Christ (24:26). The presence of two men in white at the ascension leads the disciples to an understanding of what has happened before their eyes pointing out to how Jesus will come in the same way at the parousia (Acts 1:9-11). In recalling the prophecies Jesus made during his ministry, the angels at the tomb refer to their subject as the Son of Man. Dillon observes: 'It is clear that the use of the Son of Man in these formulas coincides with the duration of the passion's concealment.'[10] When the risen Lord refers directly to the passion prophecies the reference is no longer to the Son of Man but to 'the Christ' (24:26,46). Following the revelation of the risen Christ the angels can refer to the final visit of the Son of Man by directly speaking of the final coming of Christ who has ascended.

It can be seen from the table below how the angels' summary to the women at the tomb relates to Jesus' three passion prophecies:

Luke 24:7 (RSV)	Passion Prophecies (RSV)
that the Son of Man must be delivered	9:22 saying, 'The Son of Man must … 9:44 be delivered
into the hands of sinful men and be crucified	into the hands of men 18:33 and kill him,
and on the third day rise.	and on the third day he will rise.

Unlike Mark and Matthew, Luke does use the title Son of Man in his resurrection narrative, and he does this only before the risen Lord has revealed himself. This device underlines the hiddenness of the meaning of the passion and death which will be revealed only by the risen Lord himself.

Luke structures the story of the angels' appearance in such a way that there are three witnesses to the resurrection emerging from their confrontation of the women. The angels question the women about why they seek the living in the place reserved for the dead (the witness of the empty tomb); they disclose what has happened by telling the frightened women that Jesus is risen (the witness of their proclamation); they recall the words Jesus spoke in Galilee about his death and resurrection (the witness of Jesus' prophetic word). The purpose of remembering past

10. R. Dillon, *From Eye-witnesses to Ministers of the Word* (Rome: Biblical Institute Press, 1978) pp. 39.40

words is to understand what is happening in the present. Can the women see how the words of Jesus (9:22) interpret the present event, 'He is not here; he has risen' (24:5), and, conversely, how this new event thus interpreted makes sense of the words of Jesus by fulfilling them, 'raised up on the third day' (9:22) Rather than pointing towards the appearances of Christ in Galilee (Mk 16:7; Mt 28:7) the angels point backwards to the words of Jesus in Galilee which pointed to this moment. This shift is clearly in keeping with Luke's overall plan, not just to ensure the integrity and centrality of Jerusalem, but since these 'women of Galilee' come from a Galilee where Jesus' passion prophecies were not understood, they still have to make a journey of understanding to a Jerusalem associated with the accomplishment of Jesus' mission. Can the women of Galilee become the women of Jerusalem?

The women do remember the words of Jesus (24:8), but the words they remember are a prophecy of the passion, the meaning of which was hidden, and it is an unwarranted departure from the text to argue that their recollection memory adds up to a 'genuine faith' [11] or is 'implied' [12] by their response. Dillon rightly observes that 'If those 'words' were not comprehended by the disciples when they were uttered, the 'remembrance' of them now cannot be taken to imply faith or understanding unless the shift is explicitly noted.' [13] There is no suggestion by Luke that the eyes or minds of the women are opened to a new understanding as experienced by the disciples of Emmaus (24:31) or the gathered assembly (24:4).

The beginnings of Easter faith can be seen in Luke's resurrection account only when the risen Lord himself is seen as the source of the disclosure. The experience of perplexity and misunderstanding will continue, for it is Luke's interest to show the risen Lord as the origin of Easter faith.

The women return from the tomb to the Eleven and all the others (24:9). This return at the conclusion of each of Luke's three resurrection

11. Cf. P. Perkins, *Resurrection: New Testament Witness and Contemporary Reflection* (London: Geoffrey Chapman, 1984) p. 155

12. Cf. E. L. Bode, *The First Easter Morning: The Gospel Accounts of the Women's Visit to the Tomb of Jesus* (Rome: Biblical Institute Press, 1970) p. 67

13. R. Dillon, *From Eye-witnesses to Ministers of the Word*. p. 51

narratives (24:9,33,52) is one which focuses on the centrality of the
Jerusalem community and gives a unity to the concluding episodes of the
Gospel. That same Jerusalem circle will act as a link between the Gospel
and Acts. Although the women in Luke's account do not receive any
commission to 'go and tell his disciples and Peter' (Mk 16:7) they
nevertheless tell their experience of 'all this' (24:9) to the assembled
gathering. Luke has been at pains to establish the credibility of these eye-
witnesses who now give a full acount of their own experience – one
which would include, therefore, the prophetic words of Jesus which his
followers heard for themselves. The 'apostles' are again mentioned in
verse 10 to underline who it is doing the rejecting. And in rejecting the
story of 'all this' the apostles are thereby rejecting the triple witness
contained in it. However, their disbelief at this point in the story does
have a positive function: it preserves the independence of the apostolic
witness. When the apostles do come to proclaim the resurrection of
Christ it will not be on the basis of the women's testimony of what
happened at the tomb but from their own experience of encountering
him whom God raised (Acts 10:41).

As Luke specifies the apostles among the assembled group, he sharpens the focus further to concentrate on one individual within the Eleven:
Peter (24:12). This verse is missing from some important manuscripts
and scholars argue for and against its inclusion.[14] Within the context of
Luke's resurrection pattern of showing how Jesus' followers cannot
make sense of their experience by themselves, it is wholly appropriate
that Luke concludes this first account by showing how the principal
apostle – even after personally checking the empty tomb for himself –
cannot come to an Easter faith without the personal disclosure of the
risen Lord (24:34). As one of the Eleven Peter's first reaction is to dismiss
the story of the women, but now he runs to the tomb to see for himself
(Cf Jn 20:3-10). All he sees are 'the binding cloths but nothing else' and
he returns home. Thus the last reaction of this first resurrection account

---

14. Representing the case for inclusion, cf. A. R. C. Leaney, *The Gospel according to St
Luke* (Oxford: Blackwell, 1977) pp. 28-31; for the case against cf. R. Mahoney, *Two
Disciples at the Tomb. The Background and Message of John 20:1-10* (Bern/Frankfurt-
am-Main: Herbert/Peter Lang, 1974) pp. 41-69.

is wonder. Wonder is wonder is wonder. It does not have within it the specific declaration of faith.

In this first resurrection narrative the risen Lord does not appear. His absence is important because, among other things, it gives Luke time to explore what happens when the Lord is risen but not yet present to his followers, and what happens when the event of the resurrection is not yet accompanied by the authoritative interpretation of Christ. Thus the stage is carefully prepared by naming the triple witness and showing the different reactions of the women: bewilderment at what is not there, fear at who is there, and recollection memory of the prophetic words of Jesus. Without stating how the women evaluate the angels' testimony (their reaction of fear is to the angels' presence), Luke portrays them simply as messengers, and shifts the focus to the reaction of the apostles which is one of frank disbelief. The final reaction is Peter's amazement at what has happened.

In summarising the account in the following way one can see clearly how Luke explores the conflict between paschal witness and human reaction:

Paschal Witness	*Human Reaction*
1. The empty tomb	bewilderment
2. angels' appearance (and proclamation)	fear
3. Jesus' prophetic words	recollection, memory
Story's Conclusion	
'all this' as message	disbelief
empty tomb checked by Peter	amazement

All the reactions are still a long way from acceptance, and at the moment nobody can make sense of what has happened. Clearly something more is needed for resurrection faith.

6 | Emmaus: Experiencing the Risen Lord

THE EMMAUS ACCOUNT follows directly on the story of the empty tomb, and its twenty-three verses form the central section of Luke's resurrection narrative. It has no parallels in the other Gospels apart from the Marcan postscript (16:12), although as a private christophany which has no commissioning it has elements in common with John 20:11-17.[1] The format of the story in which a divine being is encountered as a wandering stranger, reveals his real identity and disappears after the delayed recognition, is one which has parallels in ancient literature[2] and can be identified in three Old Testament stories: the appearance to Hagar (Gen 16:7ff); the visit of God to Abraham (Gen 18:1ff); the appearance of the angel of the Lord to the parents of Samson (Jg 13:2ff).

More closely parallel to the Emmaus story, perhaps, are stories from the hellenistic tradition of someone who appears after undergoing death, and A. Ehrhardt discusses two of these as analogous to Luke's story.[3] The first is the Greek legend of Romulus in which a man of blameless reputation is on his way from his farm when he recognises Romulus in his full armour leaving the city. Romulus approaches the farmer and reveals his message of hope that his protective spirit will lead those who have died into the presence of the gods. The second story concerns the two disciples of the martyred Appolonius of Tyana who are walking along the shore discussing the events leading to the trial of their master, who was executed for treason on the order of the Emperor Domitian. When the two disheartened disciples reach their destination

1. Cf J. E. Alsup, *The Post-Resurrection Appearance Stories of the Gospel Tradition* (Stuttgart: Calver-Verlag, 1975) pp.190ff.
2. Cf. H. Gunkel, *Zum religiongeschichtlichen Verständnis des Neuen Testaments* (Göttingen: Vandenhoek & Ruprecht, 1903) pp. 71ff.
3. A. Ehrhardt, 'The Disciples of Emmaus' in *New Testament Studies* 10 (1963-64) pp. 194-201

at the nymph's grotto, Appolonius appears to them, invites them to touch him to prove that he is no shadow, and convinces them that he is alive.

However, no matter how interesting these comparisons might prove to be, our main concern must be to understand the story of Emmaus within the theological framework of Luke's Gospel and the development of his own resurrection narrative.

The majority of modern scholars accede that Luke probably had available to him a tradition of a private christophany, an appearance to two disciples who were not official witnesses. This tradition he has reformulated and elaborated in his characteristic way - especially in the development of the conversation (24:19-27) which follows Luke's well-used device of 'argument from prophecy' and which can be seen as a summary of the early Church's preaching in Acts. In the infancy narrative we saw how Luke borrowed from the Old Testament tradition and from events in the public ministry to develop his theological argumentum. Likewise we shall see in the Emmaus story the same backwards and forwards movement as Luke demonstrates the historical continuity of the tradition.

In the company of many I am persuaded of P. Schubert's working hypothesis that the narrative section of the meal scene constitutes the story's traditional nucleus, while the dialogue section is the story's enlargement and Luke's own composition.[4] The studies of J. Wanke [5] and R. Dillon [6] which analyse in detail the language, style and motifs of the Emmaus story, leave one in no doubt about the clear hand of Luke throughout every part of this story. This in itself makes it difficult to draw a clear line between tradition and composition, as does the fact that since the story has no Gospel parallels it is not easy to detect Luke's particular contribution.

We must leave it to the exegesis of the story to yield an understanding

4. P. Schubert, 'The Structure and Significance of Luke 24' in W. Eltester (ed.) *Neutestamentliche Studien für Rudolph Bultmann* (Berlin: A. Töpelmann, 1954) pp. 174ff.

5. Cf. J. Wanke, *Die Emmauserzählung. Eine redaktionsgeschichtliche Untersuchung zu Lk 24, 13-35* (Leipzig: St. Benno-Verlag, 1973)

6. R. Dillon, *From Eye-witnesses to Ministers of the Word*, pp. 69-156

of the Emmaus account as, perhaps, the most formidable statement of Luke's theology and a further development of what we saw in the story of the empty tomb: the dramatic tension between the witnesses to the paschal events and the human reaction to them, between being part of those events and knowing what they mean.

THE JOURNEY FROM JERUSALEM   VERSES 13-14

> That very day two of them were going to a village named Emmaus, about seven miles from Jerusalem, [14]and talking with each other about all these things that had happened. (RSV)

It is clear from the first verse of the Emmaus story how Luke maintains continuity with the preceding account through the triple connection of time ('That very same day'); persons ('two of them'); place (Emmaus, seven miles from Jerusalem). The time is still 'the first day of the week' (24:1) identified as 'the third day' in the Galilean prophecy (v. 7). The group 'of them' to which the two travellers belong is not the Eleven but the wider group of disciples who also heard the women's story (vv. 9.23). By the end of the Emmaus story these two disciples will have rejoined 'the Eleven assembled together with their companions' (v. 33). The destination of the two disciples is located in relation to Jerusalem, which is maintained as the focal point not only of the fulfilment of Jesus' mission, but of its theological understanding.

The exact location of Emmaus, which used to engage the attention of commentators out of all proportion to its significance in the story, is of peripheral interest since, as Lohfink points out, the geographical note serves to ensure the appearance of Jesus within the vicinity of Jerusalem.[7] The two places which have the most appeal to scholars are Amwas, located about twenty miles from Jerusalem and favoured by ancient tradition,[8] and El-Qubeibeh, a village seven miles north-west of Jerusalem, although tradition has hallowed this place only from the time of the crusades.[9] It is well known that Luke's knowledge and interest in the

---

7. G. Lohfink, *Die Himmelfahrt Jesu* (München: Kösel-Verlag,1971) pp. 207f., 264f.

8. Cf. G. Dalman, *Sacred Sites and Ways* (London: SPCK, 1935) pp. 226-232

9. Cf. A. Plummer, *The Gospel according to Saint Luke*, pp. 551-552

geography of Palestine are minimal, whereas his redactional interest in Jerusalem is central to his entire Gospel as it is to this chapter. This is all the more evident when we appreciate that the real destination of the two disciples is the rediscovery of the significance of their starting-point: Jerusalem.

It is worth noting at this point that the only other instance where Luke gives an indication of distance is when he brings his appearance accounts to a close in the story of the ascension, the final act of Jesus' exaltation: 'So from the Mount of Olives, as it is called, they went back to Jerusalem, a short distance away, no more than a sabbath walk' (Acts 1:12). Again activity is related in reference to Jerusalem which is maintained as the central location. And not only is Jerusalem the vicinity for the acts of Jesus' exaltation, but the starting point for the witness of the Church where the apostles make their 'beginning from Jerusalem' (24:47).

Jerusalem is neither a neutral place in saving history nor a peripheral spot in Palestine's geography. Luke's distinctive concern to show Jerusalem as the place where God's saving visit is accomplished and God's visitation of judgement is focused has already been pointed out in the first chapter. The visit of God in Jesus first heralded by Zechariah as a visit of salvation (1:68-75) and recognised by the people in Jesus' prophetic activity (7:16) is one which will be accomplished in Jerusalem (9:31). Jesus resolutely sets his face towards Jerusalem (9:51), and when advised to diverge from his decreed course for safety's sake replies: 'for today and tomorrow and the next day I must go on, since it would not be right for a prophet to die outside Jerusalem.' (13:33) As Conzelmann has noted: 'The prophets do not perish merely in, but by means of Jerusalem.' [10] Thus the double significance of Jerusalem: not only is it the place of God's visit, but as a body it is accountable for its failure in religious insight because it did not recognise the time of its visitation (19:42-44).

If seeing Jerusalem as denoting the theological significance of the visit of God in the life and death of Jesus is the reference point of the story, the setting of the journey to/from Jerusalem is the story's framework. The disciples are 'on their way', but the direction of their way is away from

10. H. Conzelmann, *The Theology of Saint Luke*, p. 133

Jerusalem. This is in sharp contrast to what Luke has already presented as the necessary direction of Jesus' way: 'I must go on my way … it cannot be … away from Jerusalem.' (13:33 RSV) When the time and the place eventually drew near, Luke introduced the third passion prophecy with Jesus saying, 'Now we are going up to Jerusalem' (18:31), and underlined the apostles' reaction to the prophecy, 'But they understood none of these things; this saying was hid from them, and they did not grasp what was said.' (18:34)

Closely tied together are the way of the Lord, Jerusalem, and the inability of Jesus' disciples to understand his appointed course. Further, when Luke described the way of the cross itself, Jesus lead the way, with Simon from Cyrene carrying the cross behind Jesus, followed in turn by large crowds of people (22:26-27). And if the condition of following Christ is for the disciple 'to take up his cross every day and follow me' (9:23), that necessarily means coming face to face with Jerusalem.

Given the pull of Jerusalem in Luke's theology it can be said that the two disciples are going in the wrong direction. But if they have put distance between themselves and Jerusalem they cannot distance themselves from what has happened there. The journey they are making is not only an outward journey: since they cannot leave behind the recent events but talk about 'all that had happened' they make an inward journey to see if they can make sense of the events for themselves. So the journey to Emmaus is

>from without to within
>from confusion to understanding
>from death to life
>from hopelessness to hope
>from blindness to recognition
>from absence to presence
>from Jerusalem to Jerusalem
>from separation to community.

The destination of the inward journey is insight, and it will become clear when the disciples recount their version of events that they cannot reach understanding by themselves. Thus the narrative dynamic of Luke's first resurrection account between event and interpretation, between seeing and understanding, is developed further as we are prepared for hearing the story of the two disciples.

THE MEETING ON THE ROAD   VERSES 15-16

> While they were talking and discussing together, Jesus himself drew near and went with them. [16] But their eyes were kept from recognising him. (RSV)

Luke tells us that while the disciples talk about the recent events Jesus himself draws near and walks by their side. Before a word is exchanged between the two parties we are told that the appearance of the risen Lord, this fourth witness in Luke's resurrection account, is by itself insufficient to bring the disciples to a belief in the resurrection. Jesus is present, but he is not yet present to the disciples as Lord. His presence does not cause alarm or fear as it will later (24:37); for the time being he is a fellow-traveller, a stranger who draws near and accompanies them on their journey.

It is worth noting that the phrase 'drew near' is one which Luke uses three times in the last stage of Jesus' journey to Jerusalem (19:29.37.41) which culminates in his pronouncement of the visitation of God.

> And when he drew near and saw the city he wept over it, saying, 'Would that even today you knew the things that make for peace' But now they are hid from your eyes.' (19:41-42 RSV)

In the above passage Jesus is drawing near his destination but the significance of what is about to be accomplished will be lost on Jerusalem. Luke points to the divine agency at work in the phrase, 'they are hid from your eyes.' Jesus' action of 'drawing near' seems to correspond to his true identity and his mission remaining hidden.

Similarly, the literary-theological tension is held in the Emmaus story between Jesus' drawing near the disciples and their inability to recognise him. The contrast between 'their eyes were kept from recognising him' (24:16) and 'their eyes were opened and they recognised him' (24:31) dominates the whole story. The use of the passive tense indicates that the disciples are subjected to the force of supernatural power, and this highlights Luke's point that when they finally do see, it will not be because they have 'got it' at last, but because it has been gratuitously revealed to them. There are no substitutes for 'Jesus himself' in Luke's resurrection account.

Luke has already stated, prior to the teaching journey to Jerusalem (9:45) and towards the end of the journey (18:34), that the meaning of Christ's passion was hidden from his followers. Although the time of the Emmaus journey is the third day after the passion, the journey is still within the time of the hiddenness of Jesus' passion and death. This hiddenness of meaning, rather than some form of disguise adopted by Jesus as in the Marcan postscript (16:12), is at the heart of Luke's purpose. The delayed recognition will dramatically highlight the moment of revelation when it does come, as it will focus on the unique source of revelation being in the person of the risen Jesus.

The image of Jesus drawing near and accompanying the disciples on their journey is also a biblical image of God's initiative in the story of revelation: he must make the beginning in his visit or word if people are not to be abandoned to the experience of his remoteness and left to the limitations of their own insight.

The beginning of revelation is marked by the presence of God as he enters history and reveals his hidden purpose. For Luke, two of the clearest distinguishing marks of God's visit of salvation in Jesus are the mission of Jesus in reaching out to people on the fringes of society (19:10) and his familiarity with them (7:34). Luke will portray 'Jesus himself' who has risen as he portrayed Jesus during the ministry: the wayfarer who comes to share his life-giving word with two unknown disciples on the fringes of the apostolic group, and who ultimately gives himself away in the breaking of the bread.

Before examining the sequence of dialogue that leads into the conversation on the passion and death of Jesus and the meal, it will be worthwhile to look first at another meeting on the road from Jerusalem: the meeting between the itinerant preacher, Philip, and the Ethiopian eunuch (Acts 8:26-39). Just as Luke's portrayal of the risen Jesus is necessarily influenced by his presentation of Jesus in the ministry, it can be argued that these two stories of encounter, which have striking resemblances, are influenced by the experience of the early Church in meeting Christ in word and sacrament. Certainly both stories follow the basic pattern of the christological interpretation of Scripture centring on the passion and death of the Messiah which leads into the sacramental action.

Modern biblical scholarship has acknowledged that among the various interests which influenced the writing of the evangelists must be included the early Christian liturgy.[11] Luke gives us a summary of the earliest Christian community at Jerusalem:

> These remained faithful to the teaching of the apostles, to the brotherhood, to the breaking of bread and to the prayers. (Acts 2:42)

Jeremias argues to the probability 'that Acts 2:42 describes the course of an early Christian service. The sequence was (1) the instruction by the Apostles; (2) the offering, cf. Acts 6.1; (3) the celebration of the meal; (4) the prayers.'[12]

Although, as Haenchen points out, the apostolic teaching was not limited to the ritual meal but carried out in the temple,[13] another instance in Acts suggests that the *didache ton apostolon* was closely linked with the breaking of the bread. In Acts 20:7-12 Luke gives a further description of a gathering for 'the breaking of bread': it takes place on the first day of the week; there is a lengthy teaching by the apostle Paul which goes into the night; Paul breaks bread and eats; he continues preaching until daybreak. Although this liturgical assembly seems to be independent of the community's meal which formed the context of the early setting of the Eucharist (cf. 1 Cor 11:20-21), at the heart of the celebration is the apostolic teaching and the breaking of bread.

Paul speaks of participation in the Eucharist in terms of proclamation: 'Until the Lord comes, therefore, every time you eat this bread and drink this cup, you are proclaiming his death' (1 Cor 11:26). D. Stanley

---

11. Cf. D. Stanley, 'Liturgical Influences on the Formation of the Four Gospels' in *Catholic Biblical Quarterly* 21 (1959), pp. 24-38; R. Orlett, 'An Influence of the Early Liturgy upon the Emmaus Account' in *Catholic Biblical Quarterly* 21 (1959), pp. 212-219
12. J. Jeremias, *The Eucharistic Words of Jesus* (Oxford: Blackwell, 1955) p. 83.
13. Cf. A. Haenchen, *The Acts of the Apostles* (Oxford: Blackwell, 1971) p. 191

argues that the Eucharist can be seen as proclamation from one of the forms the 'liturgy of the Word' assumed from the earliest days. This was passion recital, which would in its turn account for the unusual phenomenon of the structural similarity of the passion narratives in the Gospels:

> The most probable explanation of this phenomenon, which can be verified by a rapid reading of the four Passions, is that in relating the story of Jesus' suffering and death, these sacred writers had of necessity to guide themselves by some previous written account or accounts, which were already popular in the Christian communities. Why did the story of these events, beginning with the Last Supper and culminating in Jesus' death and burial, assume a definite, written form so early in the apostolic age? The best answer, I believe, is to be found in the creation of a Christian liturgy. This time-honoured association of the recital of the Passion with the sacramental re-presentation of 'the death of the Lord' explains why Paul can refer to the eucharistic liturgy as a 'proclamation.' [14]

And it is clear from Acts and the writings of Paul that the apostolic preaching and teaching both have at their centre the passion and death of Jesus. For Christians who had never met Jesus when he was alive on earth, the experience of the two disciples in the Emmaus account will tell the story of their belief: that in the passion recital accompanied by authoritative teaching and in the breaking of the bread they will encounter Christ. A similar story is told in the meeting between Philip and the Ethiopian (cf. Table 1 on facing page).

In both stories a meeting with a stranger on the road from Jerusalem begins a sequence of events: the stranger's questioning reveals the inability of his travelling companion(s) to understand the passion story recited; the conversation focuses on a christological interpretation of Scripture with particular attention to the meaning of the Messiah's passion; the authoritative interpretation is followed by an invitation from the hearer(s) which leads to sacramental action; the stranger then disappears. In both stories there is a meeting with Christ in the opening

14. D. Stanley, *art. cit.*, pp. 27, 28

Table 1

Luke 24:13-35	Acts 8:26-39
	Philip is commissioned to make a journey from Jerusalem to Gaza (v. 26).
Two disciples are on their way from Jerusalem (v. 13).	The Ethiopian eunuch is returning by chariot from Jerusalem (vv. 27-28).
They talk about recent events in Jerusalem: the death of Jesus (v. 13).	He reads Isaiah 53:7-8, the death of the Suffering Servant (vv. 28.32-33).
	Philip is prompted by the Spirit to meet the chariot (v. 29).
The stranger, Jesus, joins the disciples and asks them what they are discussing (vv. 17-18).	The stranger, Philip, runs up and when he hears the Ethiopian reading from Isaiah asks him if he understands it (v. 30).
The disciples tell Jesus about the recent events which they cannot understand (vv. 19-24).	The Ethiopian admits he cannot understand the Scripture without a guide and invites Philip into the chariot (v. 31).
Jesus explains the full message of the prophets that Christ's suffering was for glory. Starting from Moses, his teaching about himself goes through all the prophets (vv. 25-27).	Starting with the text of the prophet Isaiah, Philip explains the Good News that refers not to the prophet Isaiah but to Jesus (vv. 34-35).
When the disciples draw near to their destination they invite Jesus to stay with them (vv. 28-29).	When they come to some water, the Ethiopian invites Philip to baptize him (v. 36).
Jesus accepts the invitation; he breaks some bread and gives it to them; their eyes are opened (vv. 30-31a).	Philip accepts the invitation; they both go down into the water; Philip baptizes the Ethiopian (v. 38).
Jesus vanishes from their sight (v. 31b).	Philip disappears and the Ethiopian sees him no more (v. 39).
The disciples recall their burning hearts and return to Jerusalem (vv. 32-33).	The Ethiopian eunuch continues his journey rejoicing; Philip passes on to to preach the Gospel (vv. 39-40).

of Scripture and in the sacramental action, and these same opportunities for meeting the Lord are available in liturgical gatherings where the Scripture is opened, where the bread is broken, and where the Spirit is present.

Finally, it is worth noting a further nuance to the meeting and acceptance of the stranger in the suggestion that in both stories Luke is outlining continuity with the travelling disciples of Jesus' ministry – 'Anyone who listens to you listens to me' (10:12) – but, more especially, representing the mission of the unknown, travelling apostle in the early Church: 'Those who receive him with hospitality and listen with faith to his word in the explanation of the Scripture come to know Christ himself, especially in the Eucharist.' [15]

THE OPENING DIALOGUE   VERSES 17-19a

And he said to them, 'What is this conversation which you are holding with each other as you walk?' And they stood still, looking sad. [18] Then one of them, named Cleopas, answered him, 'Are you the only visitor to Jerusalem who does not know the things that have happened there in these days?' [19]And he said to them, 'What things?'   (RSV)

As the stranger makes the first move in approaching the two disciples so he takes the initiative in the first word. In his opening question the connection between recent events and the journey is rehearsed again (vv. 13f), and the way is opened for the disciples' account of what has happened. The stranger's question, which literally reads, 'What are these words?' (cf 24:44; Acts 5:5,24), gives immediate direction to the whole conversation which will be marked by the juxtaposition of the disciples' words which are unable to give life, and by the stranger's words which will lead them to new life.

Before we hear the disciples' words Luke draws our attention to their condition. The stranger's question brings them to a standstill, and before we hear their story we are asked to look at their faces: they are disciples

15. J. Grassi, 'Emmaus Revisited (Luke 24,13-35 and Acts 8,26-40)' in *Catholic Biblical Quarterly* 26 (1964), p. 467

'with gloomy looks' (cf. Mt 6:16). The disciples have faces to match their story: their looks give them away and reflect the condition of their heart, 'slow of heart to believe all that the prophets have spoken!' (v. 25). How the disciples look puts them clearly within the frame of the passion's concealment of meaning: they are followers of Jesus, whose significant story in life is lacking the good news that leads to joy (24:52).

One of the two disciples is identified as Cleopas. The name of one traveller, like the name of the Emmaus locale, would seem to point to the original tradition that was available to Luke. Is Cleopas the same person as Clopas, whose wife Mary is mentioned in John 19:25? Plummer argues against this on the grounds that the name in John's Gospel is Aramaic while the name in Luke's account is Greek,[16] but there is no reason why Luke should not use an equivalent to the Semitic form. Eusebius identifies Clopas as the father of Simeon, who succeeded James as the leader of the Jerusalem community.[17] Certainly, it seems unlikely from the text that the unnamed disciple is Simon (v. 34).

No matter where speculation about the identities of the two disciples may lead scholars, it is much more important for Luke to focus on the identity of the stranger. And it is that identity which Cleopas tries to guess when he conjectures that the stranger must be the only visitor to Jerusalem who does not know what all the festival pilgrims have been talking about these last few days.

In meeting the disciples Jesus is first seen as a stranger; now he is seen as a 'visitor' to Jerusalem who is inexplicably ignorant of what has been happening there. The term 'visitor' suggests a person whose relationship to Jerusalem is that of someone who inhabits the place as a stranger – which, paradoxically, will remain a true description of Jesus until the significance of his presence there is revealed in the Easter perspective. Jerusalem did not recognise the true identity of the one who entered the city not quietly as a casual visitor but publicly as a king destined to bring peace (19:31-34). Jerusalem failed to recognise in the coming of Jesus the gracious visit of God offering a last opportunity for repentance; so, there will be a different kind of visitation (19:44).

16. A. Plummer, *The Gospel according to St. Luke*, p. 553
17. Eusebius, *Historia Ecclesiastica*, 3.11

Luke's emphasis on the public nature of recent events in Jerusalem – 'after all, these things were not done in a corner' (Acts 26:26) – stands in marked contrast to another public fact in their meaning being lost on the people and the disciples. Again Luke repeats the argument of his resurrection narrative: the significance of these events as God's saving visit will be understood only when their meaning is revealed by the risen Christ. And that revelation is not rushed: we first have to hear how those events are interpreted in the absence of belief in the risen Christ. The stranger provides the occasion with his question, 'What things?'

THE DISCIPLES' STORY: 'CONCERNING JESUS OF NAZARETH'
VERSES 19b-21a

And they said to him, 'Concerning Jesus of Nazareth, who was a prophet mighty in deed and word before God and all the people, [20]and how our chief priests and rulers delivered him up to be condemned to death, and crucified him. [21]But we had hoped that he was the one to redeem Israel.   (RSV)

In the first part of their story the disciples give a summary of Jesus' life, his death, and their own hope. It can be seen from the following list of connections (Table 2, below) how their story echoes Luke's Gospel

Table 2		
	Gospel of Luke	Acts of the Apostles
Jesus of Nazareth	4:34	2:22; 4:10
a prophet	4:24; 7:16; 13:33	3:22; 7:37
powerful	4:1.14.36; 5:17; 6:19	1:8 4:7.33; 10:38
in deed and word	4:36; 7:22; 10:24	1:1; 2:22; 7:22; 10:37ff
before God	1:6	10:38
and all the people	cf. 4:14	cf. 10:38
chief priests and rulers	23:13	13:37
delivered him up	9:44; 24:7	3:13
to be condemned to death	(cf. Mk 10:33)	
and crucified him	23:21.33; 24:7	2:23.36; 4:10
our own hope		28:20
the one to redeem Israel	1:68; 2:38; 21:28	7:35; 28:20

portrait of Jesus and also summarises part of the preaching of the early Church in Acts.

From the backwards and forwards movement of the disciples' summary it is clear how Luke's hand is responsible for the story. The notable exception is the phrase 'to be condemned to death' (*eis krima thanatou*) which is probably taken from the only Marcan prophecy where Jesus' condemnation is specifically mentioned.

There are three parts to the disciples' recollection:

1. the portrait of Jesus as a prophet mighty in deed and word;
2. the rejection and death of Jesus;
3. their own hope in redemption.

We have already reflected on Luke's treatment of the prophetic ministry of Jesus (pp. 80-89) and Jesus' authoritative word (pp. 89-94). It will be sufficient here to understand them in the context of the disciples' problem which is at the heart of Luke's resurrection narrative. The question is how to hold together the fact that Jesus proved himself in word and deed to be a prophet and the fact of his rejection and death. It is precisely their inability to hold these two facts together that accounts for the collapse of their hope.

At the opening of the ministry Luke marked Jesus' prophetic mission by the endowment of the Spirit (3:22; 4:1) and by the opposition of the devil (4:2ff). Jesus emerged from that conflict 'with the power of the Spirit in him' (4:14); thus accredited, he began his powerful ministry of deed and word. Immediately following, however, is the programmatic scene in the Nazareth synagogue in which is writ large the prophetic role of Jesus and the people's opposition and rejection. The fact that Jesus is a prophet mighty in deed and word does not discount opposition and rejection. It is here that Jesus is seen to make the observation that will summarise the continuing conflict in his mission: 'no prophet is ever accepted in his own country.' (4:24) Even at this early stage prophecy and rejection are seen to go hand in hand, a necessary alliance which is seen in the travel narrative to have its historical focus in Jerusalem (13:33.34).

The statement of the two disciples of Emmaus brings together their experience of Jesus as a mighty prophet (v. 19) and the messianic hope of Israel (v. 20). Is the mighty prophet also the Messiah? The hope in the eschatological prophet like Moses (Deut 18:15ff) is one which Luke sees fulfilled in Jesus (Acts 3:22,26; 7:37). So, too, Luke understands Jesus to be the fulfilment of the messianic hope of Israel (2:11.26; 24:26.46). The disciples' expectation is that the prophet like Moses was to redeem Israel in the same way as the prophet Moses who was 'sent to be both leader and redeemer' (Acts 7:35). The prophet like Moses is described in messianic terms as the eschatological deliverer. So, too, the task of the Messiah is understood in terms of the function of the eschatological prophet, a fusion of two originally separate traditions.[18] That fusion is echoed in the Gospel when the people of Nain proclaim Jesus as 'a great prophet' while acknowledging that 'God has visited his people' (7:16), a visit which Luke has already framed in eschatological terms (1:68).

That conjunction of Jesus' prophetic activity with messianic hope is further confirmed in the following story when, in answer to the Baptist's disciples about whether Jesus is 'the one who is to come', the evidence is furnished to show how Jesus who has just been proclaimed as the great prophet is also the one who fulfils messianic expectations through his mighty deeds and words which can be seen and heard (7:22). The eschatological prophet is the Messiah. And Luke brings that section on the two prophets to a close by noting how the people reject both prophets (7:31ff).

In 9:1-50, which acts as a preview to the travel narrative, the exodus of the mighty prophet and his rejection are regarded as necessary steps in the accomplishment of Jesus' mission. Prior to the miracle of the loaves in which Jesus is seen to be mighty in deed and word before all the people, the question of Jesus' prophetic identity is posed (9:7-9); after the miracle comes the disciples' report that Jesus is one of the ancient prophets and Peter's christological confession (9:18-21). Immediately following is the first prophecy of the passion which stresses the note of rejection and death (9:22). In the transfiguration scene the exodus pattern of Jesus' life recapitulates the exodus pattern of the career of Moses: both men are called to face a journey of severe suffering so that through their rejection God's plan will be accomplished (9:28-36).

18. Cf. R. H. Fuller, *The Foundations of New Testament Christology* (London: Collins, 1969) pp. 46-49; 50-53

After another miracle showing Jesus mighty in deed and word (9:37-43) the second prophecy of the passion underlines rejection and death alongside the fact that 'they did not understand him when he said this; it was hidden from them so that they should not see the meaning of it' (9:45). Thus Luke's pattern is firmly established: the Mosaic prophet/messiah, mighty in deed and word, is destined for rejection and death – a destiny which is beyond the comprehension of the disciples. And it is that incomprehension that is reflected in the statement of the two disciples on the road to Emmaus.

Luke's pattern establishing the identity of the mighty prophet/messiah, his greatness evident in his deeds and words, and his public rejection, is one which is paralleled in Stephen's speech in Acts which speaks of Moses:

— God's visit of salvation was set in motion through Moses' mission to Egypt. (7:34)
— Moses was sent as leader and redeemer. (7:35)
— He performed wonders and signs leading the people in the exodus. (7:36)
— He was mighty in deed and word. (7:22)
— But he was rejected and thrust aside by his own people. (7:39ff)

In both cases Moses and Jesus are the two mighty prophet/redeemers through whom God's visit of salvation takes place; throughout their *exodos* their greatness is evident in their powerful deeds and words; they both suffer rejection and death which enables Israel to know redemption. It will be no surprise, therefore, that, in his exposition of Scripture, the risen Jesus will begin with Moses and go through all the prophets (24:26). As Dillon observes: 'Moses, as prototype of the rejected prophet, is the key to the passion mystery which is about to be broken.' [19] Christ's exposition emphasising the necessity of suffering will be addressed directly to the disciples' problem of understanding: holding together the vision of Jesus as a mighty prophet, his rejection, and the messianic hope for Israel's redemption.

19. R. Dillon, *From Eye-witnesses to Ministers of the Word* p.132

Luke's account of the disciples' story can also be interpreted as an excellent portrait of discipleship living in the absence of a resurrection faith. In giving a summary of Jesus' story from his first emergence as a prophet until his death at the hands of the authorities the two disciples are in effect answering the question: 'Who do you say I am?' Their experience of Jesus as a mighty prophet funded their hope in the redemption of Israel, but neither their experience nor their hope can cope with the death of Jesus which is a stumbling block on their road to understanding. They cannot advance on that road simply by recalling the recent events that have happened.

The two disciples do not interpret the death of Jesus as having any saving significance; rather the death of Jesus is offered to account for the collapse of their hope. The death of Jesus discloses no possibilities: it stands unrelated both to the experience of Israel and the fate of the prophets, as it does to Jesus' own prophetic words about his passion and death. Neither the word of Scripture nor the word of Jesus is used by the disciples as a tool to interpret the recent events. Their memory is such that they cannot remember to hope. What has happened is an obscure text to them and yet they believe it is the definitive edition. And it comes to a dead end.

In telling the story of Jesus the disciples are also telling their own story: they give away how they see themselves. As disciples the two travellers found their identity in Jesus: because of what Jesus did and said, because of who he was, they saw themselves in the light of 'discipleship'. Their direction in life was in following him; their hopes were invested in his redemption of Israel. Necessarily, their discipleship was tied to Jesus: they did not create it and they cannot re-create it now.

Their story is not only about the death of Jesus, therefore, but about the death of their relationship with him. Their groping for meaning can be seen as a cry for relationship. That relationship is no more; so their discipleship is no more. They see themselves as ex-disciples of a dead prophet, and that takes them away from Jerusalem. Their experience did not match their expectation, and their hope cannot be reclaimed because it is buried with Jesus of Nazareth. They no longer have a presence to live by, one in which they can invest their hopes. They have nothing by which the death of Jesus can be interpreted to mean anything more than it appears – the sorry end to so much promise.

Given that fundamental inability to interpret the death of Jesus, it is no surprise that the second part of their story gives no ground for hope.

THE DISCIPLES' STORY: CONCERNING THE EMPTY TOMB
VERSES 21b-24

> 'Yes, and besides all this, it is now the third day since this happened. [22]Moreover, some women of our company amazed us. They were at the tomb early in the morning [2]and did not find his body; and they came back saying that they had even seen a vision of angels, who said that he was alive. [24]Some of those who were with us went to the tomb, and found it just as the women had said; but him they did not see. (RSV)

In the absence of present hope in Jesus – that hope which points to the resurrection to account for itself (Acts 23:6; 26:6-8) – the disciples cannot make sense of the more recent events at the tomb. Their story is brought up to date by incorporating a summary of what Luke has already written in 24:1-12: the experience of the women at the tomb in not finding the body of Jesus; the two angels who assert that Jesus is alive; the women's report to the disciples; the reaction of amazement when it is found that the tomb is indeed empty; the fact that no one sees Jesus.

In comparing the two stories there is only one apparent discrepancy – between v. 24 stating that several disciples went to the tomb and v. 12 stating that Peter went alone. However, v. 24 can be understood as an example of the tradition that there was more than one disciple who went to the tomb (cf Jn 20:3-10), while v. 12 can be understood as Luke's alteration of the tradition to bring out the importance of Peter – a form of double reference which is evident in Luke's story of the calls of Peter and of the disciples (5:1-11).

There can be little doubt from the language and style of vv. 21b-24 that they are Luke's work, and through the repeated connection of time, place and people, Luke reinforces the link between the Emmaus episode and the tomb incident. Moreover, Luke's *argumentum* is developed: in bringing together the summary of Jesus' ministry and death (vv. 19b-21a) and the summary of the Easter events so far (vv. 21b-24) Luke shows how all the events together still do not add up to words of evidence accounting for an Easter faith. The gap between all the recent events and an Easter faith is impressive.

Paradoxically, hidden in the disciples' story is the Easter proclamation that Jesus is alive. As Sr Jeanne D'Arc has noted:

> The crucial word has been spoken, the word that our faith will repeat till the end of time, but it springs from a fourth-hand testimony! Luke (1) tells us that Cleopas (2) has related that the women (3) had affirmed that the angels (4) had told them that he is alive. The essential truth hardly emerges after being attenuated by and filtered through so many intermediaries.[20]

It is as if Luke is impressing the reader with the rehearsal of the paschal witnesses thus highlighting the disciples' failure to understand. They are near, yet so far; they have the Easter information but not the Easter faith. And their story finishes with a description of what is their problem: given all this, plus the new dimension of the presence of Jesus, him they do not see. What is dramatically highlighted in all this is the necessity for the interpretative word of the risen Jesus. And it is that word which is now heard.

THE CHRIST STORY   VERSES 25-27

> And he said to them, 'O foolish men, and slow of heart to believe all that the prophets have spoken! [26]Was it not necessary that the Christ should suffer these things and enter into his glory?' [27]And beginning with Moses and all the prophets, he interpreted to them in all the Scriptures the things concerning himself. (RSV)

Apparent in the disciples' story 'concerning Jesus of Nazareth' was their inability to move from their experience of Jesus as a mighty prophet to

20. Sr Jeanne D'Arc, 'Catechesis on the Road to Emmaus' in *Lumen Vitae* 32 (1977) pp. 150,151 – a corrective to the original passage in *Les Pèlerins d'Emmaüs* (Paris: Editions du Cerf, 1977) p. 60

the messianic hope of Israel via the suffering and death of Jesus. Their christological understanding proved itself essentially defective because they could not go that route, a route of understanding which reflects the course of Jesus' own journey to Jerusalem. The Jerusalem course of Jesus' journey was not optional but necessary; likewise the disciples' road to understanding cannot bypass the mystery of the passion. If they are to see their hopes fulfilled they must first see the essential place of suffering in the redemptive plan of God. And in opening up the Scriptures the stranger will focus on the purpose of the Messiah's suffering in the revealed plan of God.

After hearing their story, the stranger calls the disciples 'senseless' and 'slow of heart to accept all that the prophets have spoken'. The disciples are portrayed as being selective in remembering the promises referring to a victorious Messiah while ignoring the prophecies related to his sufferings. Cleopas and his companion are familiar with the prophets and they have heard the women's report about the empty tomb; but they remain unconvinced. Acceptance of the full message of the prophets should have enabled the disciples to accept the women's report.

Their disbelieving attitude finds a peculiarly Lucan parallel in the parable of the rich man and Lazarus in which Abraham says: 'If they will not listen either to Moses or to the prophets, they will not be convinced even if someone should rise from the dead.' (14:31) This is manifestly true of the two disciples. The stranger cannot, therefore, reveal himself as the risen Christ at this point; he must first open the eyes of the disciples to the witness already available to them in 'all that the prophets have spoken.'

The appeal to Scripture sets what has happened within the prophetic reach of Israel. Clearly the need was felt in the early Church for testimonia supporting Christ's death and resurrection. Peter's sermons at the Portico of Solomon and in the house of Cornelius show how what happened to Jesus had been foretold in Israel by 'all the prophets' (Acts 3:18.21.24; 10:43). The expression 'all that the prophets have spoken' is also found in Acts 24:14; 26:22.27; 28:23. The testimonia which can be discerned from all the prophets serve to underline further the incomprehension of the two disciples. Just as Jesus, in spite of being a prophet mighty in deed and word 'before all the people' was not fully understood by the disciples, so the witness of 'all the prophets' is insufficient to lead the disciples to understanding. Again, the dramatic juxtaposition between the widespread publicity of testimonia and the disciples' failure in understanding.

However, just as the disciples' ignorance is matched by the ignorance of the Jewish people in putting Jesus to death (3:17), so, in both cases, God will use that ignorance for the fulfilment of God's own purposes (3:18).

As Peter's sermon goes on to teach: just as the principal prophet, Moses, declared that 'God will raise up a prophet like myself' (3:23),so indeed 'God raised up his servant' (3:26). It is entirely appropriate, therefore, that it is the eschatological prophet/messiah himself who will open up the testimonia of Scripture because it is only in his risen person that Scripture finds its true accomplishment.

In v. 26 the destiny of Christ is summarised as briefly as possible: the Messiah's suffering was necessary in his appointed course to glory. The very thing that destroyed the disciples' hope is what makes for Scripture's fulfilment. The Messiah's destiny is declared to be the same as the prophet's destiny. Luke has already stated how Jesus cannot avoid the traditional destiny of the prophet – rejection and death at Jerusalem (13:33.34).

Luke's familiar sequence of powerful word and deed followed by rejection is, in turn, the inevitable vocational pattern of the early missionaries. As the preaching of Paul and Barnabas is supported by 'signs and wonders' (Acts 14:3), so it is, in turn, followed by rejection (14:5).

The sequence is repeated in the next episode (Acts 14:8ff): during his preaching Paul performs a wondrous deed which is acclaimed by the people; however, Paul is soon stoned and left for dead outside the town by his would-be executioners. It is immediately declared that what has happened is part of a destined course: Paul and Barnabas 'put fresh heart into the disciples encouraging them to persevere in the faith. "We all have to experience many hardships," they said, "before we enter the kingdom of God".' (14:22) That prophetic course is summarised later in a truly Lucan format as Paul gives his farewell address to the elders of Ephesus: 'I am on my way to Jerusalem ... imprisonment and persecution await me ... when I finish my race I have carried out the mission the Lord Jesus gave me.' (20:22-24) Between the ancient prophets and the early missionaries stands Christ on his destined course.

The disciples are accused of being ignorant of prophecies relating to the necessity of the Messiah's suffering. Luke is alone in unambiguously declaring the necessity of the Messiah's suffering (also 24:46; Acts 3:18; 17:3; 26:23), something which is warranted by Scripture. The place of suffering in the basic pattern of the Messiah's experience is a troublesome issue since it seems unlikely that pre-Christian Judaism really expected the Messiah to suffer.[21] Luke does not adduce any scriptural texts to support his claim, perhaps because there are none:

> Nowhere is it even intimated that the Messiah should suffer, neither in the Bible as written nor in the Bible as read in first-century Judaism.[22]

In spite of the absence of any specific scriptural proof Luke's persistence could be interpreted as a counter measure to an objection in the early Church, one which is at the heart of the two disciples' story: how can the crucified prophet from Nazareth be identified as God's anointed ruler?

That question is answered by Luke in his appeal to the larger theological concern which dominates his writing: that God's salvific plan is fulfilled in the person of Jesus. In the specificity of his person and his way, several apparently divergent titles and expectations come together. Thus it is clear that the Christ should (*edei*) suffer since Jesus himself is the Christ. As Tiede states:

> The most crucial proof that the Messiah must suffer may even be that Jesus, in whom all the Scriptures are fulfilled, suffered. Since the promises of a servant-prophet and servant-Messiah both come to fulfilment in the one Jesus, clearly the Messiah also had to suffer for '*everything* written about me in the law of Moses and the

---

21. Cf. H.H. Rowley, 'The Suffering Servant and the Davidic Messiah' in *Oudtestamentische Studien* 8 (1950), pp. 100-136
22. L. Gaston, *No Stone Unturned: Studies in the Significance of the Fall of Jerusalem in the Synoptic Gospels*, Supplements to *Novum Testamentum* 23 (Leiden: E. J. Brill, 1970) p. 292

prophets and the psalms must be fulfilled' (Luke 24:44, emphasis added). The answer may precede the question. But in the face of a chaotic and contested history, even this effort to speak of the divine will and plan must be acknowledged as testimony to the faithfulness of God.[23]

And since the object of going through 'Moses and all the prophets' is to point to passages that are about 'himself', it is the mysterious 'self' which in its turn is opening the Scriptures retrospectively. Christ himself is the warrant for Scripture.

The 'must' (*dei*) of God's governing providence refers both to the suffering of Christ and to his glory. The revelation of that divinely appointed way is the gift of the risen Lord: the picture of the Messiah is now understood in Christian terms because it is determined by the crucifixion and resurrection of Jesus of Nazareth. The time of the passion's concealment is now over. That theme of divine necessity in the Messiah's journey is repeated in Acts when Paul is in the synagogue in Thessalonica where he 'developed the arguments from Scripture for them, explaining and proving how it was ordained that the Christ should suffer and rise from the dead.' (17:2-3) Paul's argument is recited again before King Agrippa (26:23).

The two parallel formulations in Acts do not speak of the Messiah's glory but of his rising from the dead. Resurrection, however, is the Messiah's entrance into glory. That view is first stated by Luke in the transfiguration scene when Moses and Elijah appear 'in glory' and speak of Jesus' exodus which is to be accomplished in Jerusalem (9:30ff). The three apostles have a vision of the glory of Jesus alongside the glory of the two vindicated prophetic figures. And the necessary steps to that glory for Jesus, as declared in the three passion prophecies, is his suffering, rejection and death. In the resurrection the eschatological prophet is vindicated and the Messiah enters into glory (*doxa*).

In the interpretation of recent events the stranger takes a stand for purpose over absurdity, for life over death, for glory over desolation. His story does not deny the centrality of death, but interprets it as significant

23. D. Tiede, *Prophecy and History in Luke-Acts*, pp. 102f

in the saving plan of God. It is a story which makes sense of pain and rejection and brokenness by seeing these as stages in a journey to life with God. Unlike the story of the disciples, the stranger's story does not rest in death; the story moves on – as the journey of Jesus moved on, as the journey of faith must move on – to new life on the far side of the Messiah's death. If there is to be Gospel then it must begin with the essential ingredient which is missing from the disciples' story, the proclamation of the resurrection. The contrast between the disciples' story and the stranger's story is the difference between non-Gospel and Gospel. The beginning of Gospel is marked by the affirmation in faith of Jesus' identity: that he is Christ the Lord (2:11).

So the risen Lord interprets recent events not only as the central witness of those events but as the one to whom witness is borne by the ancient writings. For the first time Scripture is read in a Christian way. In Christ all the previous words are authenticated. In the light of the new event of the resurrection there is a new interpretation of all Scripture: everything that happened before has tended to this event, just as everything that will happen in the early Church will be an unfolding of this event. The risen Christ's interpretation of the Easter events in the light of Scripture will form the basis for the apostolic proclamation of Gospel.

In opening the Scriptures in such a way that as past words they throw light on recent events Jesus is not simply engaging the disciples in an instructive seminar: he is at the same time illuminating their own experience. They do not stand apart from the subject of the discussion: who they are and how they call time to mind depend on their ability to make sense of the recent events. In the story of the risen Christ they are forced to think again, to see again, and to understand anew. The fact that their hearts burn within them as they listen to the stranger is a testimony to how that new story addresses their real selves in a direct and uplifting way. It is a story which takes them out of their former selves. Thus it is a story which restructures and renews discipleship itself.

In presenting the Christ story, Luke has been careful to show that the crucifixion and resurrection are not events just added on to previous words and events. Rather, this necessary exodus exercises unprecedented power over past words and events by re-interpreting them in the light of accomplishment and thereby yielding up their deepest significance. Luke shows that the true 'evidence' for the resurrection is the prophetic witness of the word of God as interpreted by the risen Jesus. Without that, the death and resurrection are 'non-events' in that they are words which have been uttered but not understood.

This disclosure to the disciples about Jesus is not yet, however, a disclosure for the disciples by Jesus. He is still the stranger. Thus the fifth witness in Luke's resurrection narrative, the witness of disclosing the meaning of Scripture, is still not sufficient to lead to Easter faith. Again the conflict is rehearsed between paschal witness and human reaction: something more is needed before Easter fact and Easter faith can meet together in Easter proclamation.

HOSPITALITY TO THE STRANGER   VERSES 28-29

So they drew near to the village to which they were going. He appeared to be going further, [29]but they constrained him, saying, 'Stay with us, for it is toward evening and the day is now far spent.' So he went in to stay with them.   (RSV)

Since the interpretation of Scripture focused on the Christ we would naturally expect the identity of the stranger now to be revealed to the two disciples. However, since the climactic Easter event is the appearance of the risen Lord at a meal, the recognition will take place in the breaking of the bread. This is not to suggest that Luke has simply postponed the recognition for his own purposes; rather, as noted earlier, the recognition scene as part of a meal with the risen Lord would seem to come from the Emmaus tradition called on by Luke. And the link between a stranger being with the disciples on their journey and the Lord being with them at table is the disciples' offer of hospitality.

In v. 15 Jesus as the stranger unexpectedly 'drew near' the disciples and joined them on their journey. The journey motif is repeated in v. 28 as the disciples and their mysterious travelling companion draw near the village of Emmaus. When the disciples come to recognise that they are sharing their table with Jesus, that recognition will signal the beginning of another journey; but first they must offer hospitality to a stranger.

Interestingly, the phrase 'with them' is repeated three times in vv. 29-30. Just as the Easter faith will be nourished not only by the words of Christ but by his presence, so the focus will now turn to his staying 'with them.' But the stranger makes to continue his journey without them. In beginning to move on, the stranger does not impose his presence on his companions but gives them the opportunity to make the offer of hospitality.

If hospitality in Luke's Gospel is primarily a response to the one who speaks the word of God (10:1ff), then it is appropriate that these two disciples should themselves respond to this word by offering hospitality to the one who brings it.

From the following list it can be appreciated how Luke uses the motif of hospitality as a way of talking about the response to the visit of God in Jesus and as a way of showing how Jesus himself receives others, particularly those on the fringes of society:

— Jesus experiences inhospitality from his own people at Nazareth. (4:24.29)
— By contrast there is pressing hospitality from the people of Capernaum. (4:43)
— The great reception given by Levi for Jesus and tax-collectors. (5:29ff)
— The fasting of John the Baptist and the feasting of the Son of Man. (7:33)
— Jesus prefers the extravagant hospitality he receives from the woman who is a public sinner to the inhospitality of the righteous Simon. (7:44-48)
— A group of women, all of whom have been healed by Jesus, accompany him and the Twelve and provide for them as they journey through the towns and the villages. (8:1ff)
— Inhospitality in the country of the Gerasenes when the people ask Jesus to leave them (8:37) while 'On his return Jesus was welcomed by the crowd' (8:40).
— Jesus instructs the Twelve to rely on the welcome of those to whom they minister and to leave those towns where the people are inhospitable. (9:1ff)

- The crowds come to Jesus and 'he made them welcome' (9:11).
- As the day is wearing away the disciples ask Jesus to send the people away but Jesus gives them food after he has blessed it, broken it, and handed it to his disciples. (9:12ff)
- At the beginning of his journey to Jerusalem Jesus rebukes his disciples for wanting to meet the inhospitality of a Samaritan town with fire from heaven. Instead, they move on.(9:52ff)
- 'The Son of Man has nowhere to lay his head' (9:58).
- Jesus instructs the seventy-two disciples about the radical life-style of their wandering mission. Because of their work they have a right to board and lodging and their hearers have an obligation to share their hospitality with the wayfaring preachers. In so doing they are welcoming Christ. (10:1ff)
- The hospitable action of the wayfaring Samaritan is given as an example of being a neighbour. (10:29ff)
- Jesus is received at the house of Martha and there are clear instructions that the hospitality offered the itinerant preacher is not to be so attentive that the word of God is not welcomed. (10:38ff)
- The hospitality that insists on searching for bread in the middle of the night until it can be found. (11:5) 'Knock and the door will be opened to you.' (11:9)
- At table with a Pharisee Jesus gives a collection of criticism of both Pharisees and lawyers. (11:37ff)
- The master who rewards his attentive servants by putting on an apron and waiting on them at table. (12:37)
- While at table with a leading Pharisee Jesus tells the guests how to choose places at table and the kind of people to invite to their dinners. (14:1ff)
- Responding to the complaint about how he welcomes sinners and eats with them Jesus tells three parables each of which has its climax in sharing an individual joy by showing hospitality to others. (15:1ff)
- To guarantee that 'there will be some to welcome me in their homes' (16:4) the crafty steward readjusts his arithmetic.
- The rich man is condemned because Lazarus lives and dies in the absence of hospitality that could have saved him. (16:19ff)

- The disciples try to keep children away from Jesus but he says, 'Anyone who does not welcome the kingdom of God like a little child will never enter it.' (18:17)
- Zacchaeus welcomes Jesus joyfully but the people complain, 'He has gone to stay at a sinner's house' (19:7).
- On his final visit to Jerusalem the people welcome Jesus by throwing their garments on the road. (19:35)
- Teaching in the Temple Jesus tells the parable of how the tenants of the vineyard receive the master's servants and how they kill the heir. (20:9ff)
- Jesus who has longed to eat the passover with his apostles takes his place at table. 'Then he took some bread, and when he had given thanks, broke it and gave it to them' (22:19).

Understandably, hospitality is usually associated with meals. Throughout Luke's Gospel Jesus never seems far from table: he frequently accepts invitations to dinner and uses the occasion as an opportunity for fellowship, teaching, and forgiveness. Not only is he a guest at the table of others, but Luke presents him as the indiscriminate host who welcomes those outside the boundaries of religious and social approval. When Jesus is at table something happens – so it is that people often wonder about his real identity, for table fellowship offers Jesus the opportunity for epiphany.

As the one who comes 'to seek and save what was lost' (19:10) Jesus has a clear purpose in sharing table fellowship: how people receive Jesus therefore is an indication of how they see him. Hospitality is not just a social virtue for a people who were once nomadic; for Luke it becomes a witness of faith and a christological affirmation. This is directly related to the itinerant preachers of the early Church who regarded it as essential for their ministry to travel on the principle that whoever welcomed them because of their work was in fact receiving the person of Christ (10:16; Mt 10:40; 25:31-46). Hospitality became an act of faith. As Dillon points out in the company of many others,[24] that missionary situation in the early Church has been bequeathed to Luke in his sources and influences

24. Cf. R. Dillon, *From Eye-witnesses to Ministers of the Word* pp. 238-249

the importance he ascribes to hospitality.

As they approach their destination the two disciples see the stranger as an itinerant preacher who has opened up the Scriptures to them. Clearly, their offer of hospitality is not consciously addressed to Jesus but to a stranger – an action which finds its equivalent in Matthew's scene of the last judgement where those who offered hospitality to the stranger are told that in so doing they welcomed the Lord himself (25:40).

For the two disciples of Emmaus, however, their companion is more than a stranger: he has revealed himself as a journeying preacher through his opening of the Scriptures. So the disciples urged (*parebiasanto*) him to stay (*meinon*) with them. The same terms are used in one of the 'we' passages in Acts where Luke describes how Lydia receives the missionaries during their visit to Philippi:

> And when she was baptized, with her household, she besought us, saying, 'If you have judged me to be faithful to the Lord, come to my house and stay.' And she prevailed upon us. (Acts 16:15 RSV)

The similarities between the two stories are striking, and it would seem that Luke is making a connection between Jesus' staying and the staying of the missionaries at the house of a believer. It is worth noting further that after their eyes are opened the disciples reflect how their hearts burned while listening to Jesus. As for Lydia, 'The Lord opened her heart to give heed to what was said by Paul.' (Acts 16:14) In both instances the Lord is seen as the source of the opening, and the effect of the preachers' words is registered in the hearts of the listeners.

Jesus responds to the entreaty of the two disciples by going in to stay with them (cf. 19:5). Because of who he is and because of who they are it will be a significant visit. It will be similar to the Lord's visit depicted in Revelation: 'Behold, I stand at the door and knock; if any one hears my voice and opens the door, I will come in to him and eat with him, and he with me.' (3:20)

RECOGNITION IN THE BREAKING OF THE BREAD   VERSES 30-32

> When he was at table with them, he took the bread and blessed, and broke it, and gave it to them. [31] And their eyes were opened and they

recognised him; and he vanished out of their sight. [32] They said to each other, 'Did not our hearts burn within us while he talked to us on the road, while he opened to us the Scriptures?'   (RSV)

As Luke devotes more attention than the other evangelists to Jesus' presence at meals during the ministry, it is hardly surprising that he clearly associates the presence of the risen Jesus with meals (24:30,41-43; Acts 1:4; 10:41). The meal serves the purposes of Jesus: its social setting provides a natural occasion for Jesus' self-revelation and the disclosure of why he has come; as a time for fellowship it is also an offer of salvation; it is an event where the word of God is shared as a word which brings life.

The two outstanding occasions in the ministry when Jesus and his disciples share a meal are the feeding of the five thousand (9:10-17) and the Last Supper (22:14-38). It can be seen from Table 3 (below) how the

Table 3		
The Feeding of the Five Thousand (Luke 9)	Last Supper (Luke 22)	Emmaus (Luke 24)
v. 14 'Make them sit down ... '	v. 14 He sat at table,	v. 30 When he was at table
	and the disciples with him.	with them
v. 16 and taking the five loaves and two fish he looked up to heaven,	v. 19 And he took bread,	he took the bread
blessed	and when he had given thanks	and blessed
and broke them,	he broke it	and broke it
and gave them to the disciples.	and gave it to them.	and gave it to them.

The connection between the feeding of the five thousand and the meal at Emmaus is further supported by the same time setting. Luke's expression occurs only in these two places:

9:12 'Now the day began to wear away.'

24:29 'The day is now far spent.'

action of the stranger at the Emmaus meal is clearly reminiscent of what Jesus does at the other two meals: he takes, he blesses, he breaks, he gives. (The only divergence to note is that in the Last Supper account Jesus says the Kiddush, the Jewish blessing which marks the beginning of sacred time; in the feeding account, the object of Jesus' blessing is the bread and the fish together, while in the Emmaus account it is the bread alone.) For Luke, these verbs which have Jesus as their subject and bread as their object – taking, blessing, breaking, giving – serve as cues for the recognition scene itself.

The three stories are connected in further ways. The feeding of the multitude is set immediately prior to the first prophecy of the passion in which the question of Jesus' identity is raised by Jesus himself. In revealing his own answer to his own question Jesus speaks of his suffering, rejection and death as necessary experiences before being raised on the third day (9:22) and goes on to instruct his disciples that any followers of his must take up their own cross if they are to be acknowledged by the Son of Man when he comes in 'glory' (9:26).

A similar sequence – the event of a meal followed by a word of self-disclosure involving the disciples – is clear in Luke's account of the Last Supper. Jesus speaks of the decreed destiny of the Son of Man (22:22,37) and how his followers will share in that destiny themselves until they 'eat and drink at my table in my kingdom' (22:30). Again fellowship in the meal is immediately followed by Jesus' revelation about himself and his own destiny, and how his disciples will share in that themselves.

This sequence is reversed in the Emmaus account. In the first part of the story Luke shows how the disciples are not disinterested in what has happened to Jesus: their interpretation of events, however, emerges from a radical misunderstanding of who Jesus is. When the stranger instructs the disciples that it was necessary for the Messiah to suffer and so enter his glory, this self-revelation is directly related to the disciples since it is seen as a response to their story of dashed hopes. In the journey narrative Luke shows that the christological revelation involves the disciples directly because who they are depends on their understanding of who Jesus is. After the instruction on the mission and destiny of the Messiah there is the meal. In this brief scene there is no mention of eating;

this allows the focus to fall entirely on what the stranger does. His particular actions make up the divinely appointed moment for his identity to be revealed.

The pattern of the Emmaus account looks backwards into the ministry when the Messiah's identity and mission were hidden from his followers – in spite of the meals and passion instructions. This pattern also looks forward to the time when the risen Jesus will be present to his followers at a meal which is followed by instruction:

Luke 24:36-49
a) The risen Jesus appears to his apostles.
b) Jesus asks them for something to eat. They offer him a piece of broiled fish, which he eats.
c) As a way of revealing himself he opens their minds to understand the Scriptures.

Acts 1:1-8
a) For forty days Jesus appears to his apostles.
b) During this time he eats with them.
c) He instructs them to wait for the coming of the Spirit when they will become his witnesses.

Acts 10:41-43
a) Peter recalls how God allowed the risen Jesus to be seen by chosen witnesses;
b) how these witnesses ate and drank with the risen Jesus;
c) how Jesus instructed them to testify to his true identity, one to which all the prophets bear witness.

Apart from the reference in the Marcan postscript to Jesus showing himself to the Eleven while they were at table (16:14), there is further support for a tradition of the risen Jesus appearing at a meal of bread (and/or fish) in John 21:1-14. What is read as a consecutive story would seem to be a combination of two original narratives: firstly, the miraculous catch of fish which provides the occasion for Jesus to reveal himself to the disciples – with the further symbolism of the apostolic mission to catch men (cf. Lk 5:10); secondly, the story of a meal at which Jesus is recognised by his disciples – with the sacramental symbolism evocative of the Eucharist.

There is a striking similarity between the meal of bread and fish at which Jesus is recognised as the risen one (Jn 21) and the meal of bread and fish after the multiplication when Jesus is recognised as the mighty prophet (Jn 6). The language describing the action of Jesus as he 'took the bread and gave it to them, and so with the fish' (Jn 21:13 RSV) echoes Jesus' other action as he 'took the loaves, and when he had given thanks, he distributed them to those who were seated; so also the fish' (Jn 6:11 RSV). Further, as Brown points out: 'The fact that the scenes in vi and xxi are the only ones in the Fourth Gospel to occur by the Sea of Tiberias naturally helps the reader to make a connection between the two meals.'[25]

The majority of scholars would agree that the two meal-scenes in John are framed in such a way that they are deliberately evocative of the Eucharist, just as Luke's description of how the two disciples came to recognise Jesus in the breaking of the bread would also remind his readers of the Eucharist. However, more to the present point is that Luke's account of the risen Jesus revealing himself at a meal shared with his disciples is independently attested by John 21, both of which describe what happens in terms reminiscent of the feeding of the multitude. What emerges from both accounts, which rest on independent traditions,[26] is a pattern of the risen Jesus being recognised at a meal. John 21, therefore, can be seen as giving independent support to the story which came to Luke, one which he has shaped according to his own purposes. Dillon argues:

> The hypothesis is quite plausible that Luke's Emmaus tradition was the account of the risen Christ encountered as a wayfaring stranger entertained as a house-guest (in the house of Cleopas?) and, while reclining at table with his host, re-enacting the miraculous feeding of bread and fish, whereupon his astonished hosts-turned-guests recognized his identity.[27]

Dillon's hypothesis about the historical tradition of Emmaus is in

25. R. E. Brown, *The Gospel according to John XIII-XXI* (Anchor Bible; New York: Doubleday, 1970) p. 1099
26. Cf. J. Wanke, *Die Emmauserzählung. Eine redaktionsgeschichtliche Untersuchung zu Lk 24, 13-35.* pp. 103ff.
27. R. Dillon, *From Eye-witnesses to Ministers of the Word* pp. 152,153

keeping with the close relationship between Luke's finished account and the feeding of the five thousand: the two disciples would not have been present at the Last Supper and, therefore, the divine action which induces recognition is seen to be related to an experience shared with Jesus. More importantly, the tradition which Luke received placed special emphasis on Jesus' pastoral strategy of visiting a house where the meal gave him an opportunity of 'visiting' people with God's saving power – an outreach which is seen to be repeated by the disciples in the ministry and by the missionaries in the early Church. The meal at Emmaus stands at the point where the whole movement of Jesus' life, death and resurrection is first revealed in its full significance, and as a pointer to how the Christian community will meet the risen Lord in the christological interpretation of Scripture and in the breaking of the bread (cf. pp. 127-130, 148 ff.). And just as the Christian community's encounter with the risen Lord will be focused in the one sacramental action of word and meal, so the two disciples will recognise the risen Jesus in the one encounter of Scripture and meal.

The time of concealment is ended as the eyes of the two disciples are opened to recognise their table companion as the risen Lord. In 24:16, Luke also used the passive voice, implying divine power at work preventing the two disciples from recognising the identity of the stranger. That witholding of recognition was consistent with Luke's careful schedule of concealment which he maintained throughout the ministry of Jesus. Luke declared that concealment before the major journey to Jerusalem began (9:45) and again at its conclusion (18:34): the meaning of Christ's passion was hidden from his disciples. That teaching journey was made within the framework of two terms of concealment: the journey began in mystery and ended in mystery.

Now that that major journey has been repeated in the company of the risen Christ who has fulfilled his destiny, Luke shows us that this journey is different: it begins in mystery and ends in revelation; it moves from hiddenness to openness. The disclosure of Jesus' mission and identity is the destination of this journey, an objective which is reached not through the contrivance of the two disciples but through the fact that their eyes are opened. This is the second 'opening' in the story: first, the

Scriptures were opened because of what Jesus said; now, their eyes are opened because of what Jesus does. Divine determination is seen to be at work in the word and deed of Jesus.

Once he has been recognised the risen Jesus vanishes (*aphantos*). This is the only place the word appears in the New Testament, and Plummer has commented:

> Something more than a sudden departure, or a departure which they did not notice until He was gone, is intended. We are to understand disappearance without physical locomotion.[28]

The disappearance of the risen Jesus points to the accomplishment of his mission: the two disciples now recognise who he is and that their hopes in him have now been fulfilled. The disappearance also emphasises who Jesus is – as Marshall indicates, 'It is as a supernatural visitor that the risen Christ is portrayed.'[29] Jesus approached the two disciples as a companion on the journey, and he now leaves them as the risen Lord. The effect of his presence during that time is registered in the pronounced change which the two disciples have experienced. Now they are able to see the truth of the earlier testimony they rejected: 'He is not here; he is risen.' (24:5)

It is only when Jesus reveals himself in the breaking of the bread that an event at the same time becomes a word of life for the two disciples. In this, the sixth witness of Luke's structured resurrection narrative, Jesus is finally recognised as the risen Lord in the midst of human experience. Because of what is happening in their present experience the disciples are able to discern what was really going on in recent events. In the light of their new experience they are enabled to see their past experience as the source of significance rather than the memory of disappointment, as a word of life rather than a word about death. Only retrospectively do the disciples realise that who was with them on the road was indeed the Lord, and what they heard was indeed the word of the Lord. Their recognition of the Lord has not only opened up their present experience by giving a name to it, but uncovered the true name of what had already

28. A. Plummer, *The Gospel according to Saint Luke*, p.557.
29. H. Marshall, *The Gospel of Luke*, p. 898.

taken place in the recent events they discussed on the road.

The previous five witnesses which formed an integral part of their story (the empty tomb, the angelic proclamation, the prophetic words of Jesus, the presence of Jesus as a travelling companion, and the christological disclosure of Scripture) can be recognised as witnesses only now because the disciples have experienced for themselves who and what these witnesses were attesting to: the risen Lord.

The disciples' recognition of Jesus is used immediately to account for what happened within them as they listened to the Scriptures being opened – how their hearts burned. They are now able to identify what they have experienced. In speaking of the word of God registering in the heart, Luke is calling on a traditional biblical image which refers to the penetrating power of the word of God which has its effect in a change of heart (cf. p. 101). Before Jesus joined his disciples on the road their own reflection on recent happenings could not make their 'hearts burn'. After Jesus has been with them, their reflection is radically different. They have a new way of telling the time. They have a new awareness of Jesus as the risen Lord; they have a new memory which liberates them from absurdity and failure because it can now call upon the value of Jesus' suffering and death; they have a new hope because their own future is now perceived differently.

In short, they are different. Throughout the ministry Luke has shown us who Jesus is through showing us what happens to those who are transfigured by his saving power. Now, in the time of the resurrection, 'That very day', that experience is seen to happen in a new way. At the beginning of the journey the two disciples saw themselves as ex-followers of a dead prophet; now they are disciples of the risen Lord. Their hopes had been dashed; now their hope is alive. They left Jerusalem as the place where everything they hoped for had foundered; now they can return to the place where the Messiah's destiny has been fulfilled. Through their experience of renewal, Luke tells us the good news that Jesus is Lord.

And they rose that same hour and returned to Jerusalem; and they found the Eleven gathered together and those who were with them, [34]who said, 'The Lord has risen indeed, and has appeared to Simon!' [35]Then they told what had happened on the road, and how he was known to them in the breaking of the bread.   (RSV)

Just as the first verse of the Emmaus account maintained continuity with the preceding story by the triple connection of time, place and persons, so Luke now repeats his editorial framework in vv. 33-35 to serve as a conclusion to the present story and to set the scene for the Jerusalem appearance. 'That very day' (v. 13) becomes 'that same hour' as Luke underlines the disciples' urgency to communicate their experience and share their joy. Their destination is Jerusalem, the same place they left behind them earlier in the day. Their return there will reunite them with the apostolic circle of the Eleven and the wider group of disciples (cf. v. 9).

Clearly, it is not enough for the two disciples to reflect on their experience; they must carry it to others, specifically to the community they suppose is still enclosed in the same disappointment they themselves experienced. They do not hoard the revelation of Christ because it is not something that has been given to them for their exclusive benefit. Seeing the Lord is a dismissal for ministry. So they do not try to build a booth to mark the spot, thereby associating the presence of the Lord with one particular place; that presence has now become part of their experience and it is their interior change which marks the spot.

By their decision to return, the pace of the story is changed: before the recognition scene things happened at a leisurely pace; now the pace quickens dramatically as recognition makes for the immediate return of the two disciples. The telling of what they have experienced is in marked contrast to the silence that prevailed during the period of concealment. When the three apostles witnessed the glory of Jesus in his transfiguration 'they kept silence and told no one in those days anything of what they had seen.' (9:36 RSV) 'Those days' are now over because this hour of 'this very day' is the time when the mystery is revealed by the risen Christ himself and the disciples are compelled to tell what they have seen and heard. Their new hope releases a new energy in them; it takes them back to community.

The act of returning by the two disciples is also an example of Luke's editorial technique whereby he often concludes an episode with the return of the principal characters. Luke is clearly fond of the verb 'to return' (*hypostrephein*) for it serves his narrative purpose well. None of the other evangelists uses the word; Luke uses it twenty-one times in his Gospel and eleven times in Acts. From Table 4 (following page) we can see a representative example of Luke's motif of return.[30] The instances I have listed go beyond the return of the main characters to include some form of report or response. The implication of this development would seem to be that Luke is concerned to note that what has happened in the event goes further – in declaration or prayer – than the immediate characters involved. When the return motif is framed in this way it serves a further purpose in underlying the witness value of the participating characters.

It can also be seen clearly how the return motif is refined in the resurrection narratives to a 'return to Jerusalem'. Again Jerusalem is maintained as the geographical and theological centre: all the participants in the Easter drama are deliberately drawn there as if to account for themselves and be accounted as authentic. The risen Lord himself will appear in Jerusalem where he will speak of the future missionary outreach 'beginning from Jerusalem. You are witnesses of these things.' (vv. 47b-48) Jerusalem and the original nucleus of witnesses are inextricably tied together, just as Jesus and Jerusalem were inseparable in the ministry (13:33). So when the women returned from the tomb it was to the Eleven and the rest that they returned. When the two disciples return – like the women they have been away from the full assembly – it is to a Jerusalem where the Eleven are gathered with the rest. After the ascension – when they had been led out as far as Bethany – the full gathering of disciples returns to Jerusalem. All three narratives conclude with the return to Jerusalem and with the full gathering of the assembled disciples. And it is worth noting in passing that the return to Jerusalem

---

30. References to returning not included in table: Lk 1:23,56; 2:15,20,39,43,45,51; 4:1; 7:10; 19:12; 23:56; Acts 4:23; 5:23; 12:25; 13:13; 14:21; 17:15; 20:3; 21:6; 23:32.

Table 4

The Event	The Return	Report/Response
After the baptism and the temptations	'Jesus returned in the power of the Spirit to Galilee	and a report concerning him went out through all the ... countryside.' (4:14)
After the healing	the paralytic 'went home' (5:25)	and the people praise God.
When the demoniac is cured	Jesus says, 'Return to your home,	and declare how much God has done for you.' (8:39)
Jesus sends out the twelve	'On their return	the apostles told him what they had done.' (9:10)
After their mission	'The seventy returned with joy' (10:17)	to tell Jesus of their success.
When he saw he was healed	the leper 'turned back' (17:15)	to praise God and thank Jesus.
When they saw the crucifixion	the crowds 'returned home	beating their breasts.' (23:48)
After the angels' proclamation	'returning from the tomb	they told all this to the eleven and all the rest.' (24:9)
After recognising the risen Jesus	the two disciples 'returned to Jerusalem' (24:33)	to tell the eleven and the rest.
After the ascension	the disciples 'returned to Jerusalem with joy	and were continually in the temple blessing God.' (25:52.53)
After the ascension	'they returned to Jerusalem' (Acts 1:12)	where they pray with the women.
After Peter and John testified	'they returned to Jerusalem	preaching the Gospel to many villages of the Samaritans.' (Acts 8:25)
After his conversion	Paul 'returned to Jerusalem' (Acts 22:17)	where the Lord commissions him to preach to the Gentiles.

continues to exercise Luke's redactional style when he tells the story of the early Church in Acts.

Like the women, the two Emmaus travellers are reunited with the assembly of followers which has the Eleven as its core group. This assembly forms the gravitational centre of the Easter events.

From the momentum of the narrative we would expect that the two new arrivals would first relate their Easter experience to the corps of disciples; but, without waiting to hear what the newcomers have to say, the assembly takes the initiative and proclaims the first Easter confession: 'The Lord has risen indeed, and has appeared to Simon!' Not only do the two disciples find the Eleven gathered with the others, they also find that the focus of this gathering is the experience of one member of the apostolic group: Simon. From the wider group of disciples Luke sharpens his focus on the Eleven; from the Eleven the focus is sharpened further to the person of Peter. The two disciples of Emmaus were seen earlier in the narrative to be part of this wider group (v. 22) but from their story it became clear that there was no reason to keep the group together.

The event that now brings this gathering together is seen to be the Lord's appearance to Peter. Thus what might appear in v. 34 to be an unnatural break in the sequence of events actually serves Luke's theological purpose: it gives primacy to the apostolic group by making them the first speakers of the Easter confession; it gives primacy of place to Peter showing that the Easter faith of the community is founded on the Lord's appearance to him.

When the Eleven and all the rest heard the story of the women at the tomb, they did not believe what they judged to be an idle tale (v. 11). However, Peter was singled out as the one who checked the tomb for himself, after which he returned home wondering what happened (v. 12). Verse 34 recalls both reactions and celebrates the new Easter response which is related not to the empty tomb but to an appearance of the Lord to Peter. As Peter was the last to visit the empty tomb, so he is the first to believe in the risen Lord.

The primacy which is acknowledged in v. 34 is framed in confessional language and is similar to the kerygmatic formula in 1 Corinthians 15:3-5 in which Paul appeals to what he himself has received as Gospel quoting the tradition, 'that he was raised ... and that he appeared to Cephas'. Both Paul and Luke declare that the appearance to Peter is the foundation of the community's Easter faith. The shared unbelief of the disciples in 24:11 is now changed through Peter's experience to a communal belief in the risen Lord. Neither the visit to the tomb nor the experience of the Emmaus disciples is the foundation for the Easter faith: that unique privilege is accorded to Peter.

Unlike the confessional text in Corinthians which refers to Cephas, Luke refers to Peter as 'Simon'. At first this seems inconsistent with Luke's own practice: after the call of Simon (5:1-11) the leading apostle is referred to as Peter. But there is a notable exception to this in the Gospel. In the Last Supper account Jesus says: 'Simon, Simon, behold, Satan demanded to have you, that he might sift you like wheat, but I have prayed for you that your faith may not fail; and when you have turned again, strengthen your brethren.' (22:31-32 RSV)

In using 'Simon', the apostle's given name, at the time of his call when he turns away from his past life and also before the passion when he is called on to turn away from denying Jesus, perhaps Luke is saying that Simon has now fulfilled both calls. He has honoured his call at the beginning of the ministry and at the end of the ministry. Certainly the confessional statement of v. 34 points to the fact that Simon has indeed turned and has strengthened the assembled brethren. Their Easter proclamation is wholly dependent on the personal testimony of Peter.

It is only after they have heard the Easter confession of the apostolic assembly that the newly returned disciples relate the story of their own experience. The priority that Luke has given to the apostolic testimony ensures that the account of the two disciples is incorporated into that story, not vice-versa—even though Luke gives us the disciples' story first, and like the other New Testament writers has no detailed story of an appearance to Peter. However brief, the story of Peter confirms the truth of the two disciples' new experience, as the story of their experience will confirm the truth of what has happened to Peter. Their rehearsal of what has happened (cf. Acts 10:8; 15:12.14; 21:19; Jn 1:18) is a concise summary of the two parts of the story and is a good example of Luke's device of concluding an account with a report from the returned characters (cf.

Table 4, p. 190).

First, the disciples tell of the meeting on the road and then tell how the Lord was made known to them in the breaking of the bread. Again the passive voice is used to underline the fact that this recognition was a divinely managed action rather than a ritual sequence by Jesus which acted as a trigger for the disciples' recognition-memory. The disciples recognised Jesus because God visited them. As the concealment at the story's beginning was by divine appointment (v. 16), so the recognition at the story's climax is by divine action (v. 31), a truth that the story's conclusion rehearses again (v. 35). Throughout the development of the story God is seen to be at work, and the Lord's action in the breaking of the bread is the moment chosen by God fully to reveal the mystery of the divine purpose in Jesus.

Finally, the two-stage encounter of the disciples' story also functions as an eloquent summary of the two openings in the Eucharist: the followers of Jesus will continue to be instructed in the destiny of Christ in such a way that their own destiny is also opened up; they will continue to meet the Lord in the fellowship of the sacred meal which will enable them to meet the demands of discipleship (cf. Acts 2:42). In the 'liturgy of the word' and in the 'liturgy of the Eucharist' God will continue to speak his word and visit his people. In word and in sacrament, the opportunity of encountering the risen Christ will be available for all the followers of Jesus.

CONCLUSION

As we summarised Luke's first resurrection narrative in terms of how he explores the conflict between paschal witness and human reaction (p. 120), we can conclude our study of the Emmaus narrative by summarising the story in exactly the same way to show how Luke has developed his theme:

Paschal Witness	*Human Reaction*
4. Jesus' presence on the road	non-recognition
5. Jesus' interpretation of Scripture	burning hearts
6. Jesus breaking the bread	recognition

Paschal Witness	*Human reaction*
Story's Conclusion	
return to tell all this	proclamation of new paschal witness by apostolic assembly
7. 'The Lord has risen indeed, and has appeared to Simon'	disciples tell their story which confirms proclamation

In dramatic contrast to the first resurrection narrative, which concluded with the disbelief of the apostolic circle and the story of Peter's amazement at the empty tomb, the Emmaus narrative closes with the belief of the apostolic circle centring on Peter's encounter with the risen Lord. Into the conclusion of his Emmaus narrative, Luke has inserted a new paschal witness, one which is fundamental to the faith of the growing community of believers. The human reaction of the Eleven and the others to the Easter experience of Peter allied to the response of the two disciples to their own experience makes for a community gathered around Peter and the apostolic circle, sharing a belief in the risen Lord. All seems well. But whether 'all this' is going to be sufficient to maintain an Easter faith is called into immediate question in the third resurrection narrative.

PART THREE

From Experience to Message:

He Is Proclaimed

7 | Becoming Witnesses: Luke 24:36-53

IN HIS THIRD resurrection narrative Luke follows on the Emmaus story without a break. He shows how Jesus' self-disclosure to Peter and the two disciples is now confirmed to the Eleven and their companions as Jesus gives his final instructions and prepares his company for the sending of the Spirit after he has finally departed. The experience of the whole group encountering the Lord corroborates the two previous christophanies and will become a communal testimony after Pentecost (Acts 2:32). However, by first showing the disciples' manifest inability to make sense of what is happening to them, Luke repeats and stresses the unity of event and interpretation in the person of the risen Jesus. In this Luke rehearses again the conflict that has dominated his resurrection narrative so far: the dialectic between paschal witness and human reaction, between Easter event and interpretation.

In beginning his third resurrection *pericope* as if nothing has already happened Luke manages to question the perception which presumes that what has happened so far is sufficient for the beginning of faith. Clearly it is not. As Luke frustrates attempts to arrive too quickly at a witnessing faith, he tells us again that something more is needed for Easter faith. Luke exercises tight control of his narrative as he moves it to the threshold of a witnessing community. But he does not cross that threshold in the Gospel. Instead he gradually prepares for that moment by first showing the risen Jesus present to the assembly of followers and opening their minds to the meaning of the Scriptures. In the light of the interpretative word of Jesus the disciples are able to interpret their past experience of Jesus and their present experience of him as Lord. Their experience of him then and their experience of him now, interpreted aright through the word of the Lord and the power of the Spirit, will become the sure ground for witness.

JESUS APPEARS TO THE ASSEMBLED DISCIPLES   VERSES 36-43

As the risen Lord joined the two disciples on the road to Emmaus while they were discussing recent events, so he now stands in the midst of his chosen ones while they are discussing more recent events. The risen Lord's standing among them is the same idiom used in the Septuagint for the heavenly visitors who come to relay a divine message or interpret the meaning of an event (cf. Gen 18: 2; Dan 8:15; 12:5; Tob 5:4; Zech 2:3), a construction which Luke brings into his own writing (1:11; 24:36; Acts 10:30; 16:9). Of course this is not an angelic visitation but a visit by the Lord himself, but Luke has adopted the Old Testament pattern of angelic apparition: appearance and greeting; reaction of fear; heavenly visitor identifies himself; message is given; objection is made; objection is overruled by a sign (cf. pp. 31-32). As Boismard has pointed out, this literary pattern is used not only to announce divinely appointed births but also to announce divine commissions.[1] And the message of revelation from the risen Lord in this passage has the divine commission as its principal objective.

The opening greeting of peace, framed in the historic present, is found in John 20:19 – leading some scholars to argue that 'the possibility of an interpolation has to be admitted'.[2] However, as A. George has pointed out,[3] the peace motif already proved important in Luke's Gospel: when Jesus sent out the missionaries to the places he was to visit, he told them that their first words to the house they entered must be a greeting of peace and that they must accept what food and drink were offered them (10:1-7). Thus the kingdom of God was announced. The risen Jesus is seen to follow his own instruction as he greets the present company with peace, eats the food offered him, and commissions them to preach to all nations. As Dillon has observed:

> Moreover, in his role of 'proto-missionary', the risen One justifies the echoes of the Old Testament visitations by divine messengers

1. Cf. M.-E. Boismard, 'Le réalisme des récits évangéliques' in *Lumen Vitae* 109, (1971) pp. 31-41

2. J. Jeremias, *The Eucharistic Words of Jesus*, p. 98.

3. A. George, 'Les récits d'apparitions aux Onze à partir de Luc 24,36-53' in P. de Surgy et al., *La résurrection du Christ et l'exégèse moderne* (Paris: Editions du Cerf, 1969) p. 77.

which have been produced in this narrative. Indeed it may not be accidental that, at the beginning of the Gospel's 'journey' section, the theme of Jesus' dispatch of 'messengers' to precede him comes into its own straightway in the idiom of Old Testament angelic embassies ... (Lk 9:52; cp.Lk 7:27/Mal 3,1).[4]

The appearance of the visitor and his greeting of peace do not make for Easter joy as Luke portrays another human reaction to paschal witness. The reaction of the disciples is undisguised fear and confusion as they interpret what they see to be a spirit. That is their answer to the eternal question, 'Who do you say I am?' (9:20) Again, Luke serves notice that the appearance of the risen Lord is not by itself a convincing or compelling demonstration of his reality. By itself the appearance does not open the disciples' eyes and dispel the mystery of Jesus' real identity; it did not do that on the road to Emmaus, neither will it do it here.

In Luke's three resurrection narratives the main participants undergo questioning: the women are questioned by the angels (24:5); the Emmaus disciples are questioned by the stranger (24:17.19); the assembled disciples are questioned by the visitor (24:38). In asking the disciples why they are 'troubled' (cf. 1:12) and why there are doubts rising in their hearts (cf. 2:35), Jesus continues to be the questioner who resists the unyielding outlook of others, the one who stays to insist that others must look and look again in order to understand. To demonstrate that he is not a spirit, he first invites the disciples to look at his hands and feet so that they can see 'it is I myself' (v. 39; cf. Mk 6:50).

He then invites his followers to touch him so that they see who it is they are touching. The plea to see and to touch is followed by an appeal to reason: spirits do not have bones and flesh. A ghost cannot be touched; the risen Christ has a presence that can be felt not only by the heart but by the hand. The appeal to the disciples' sight, their touch, their reason, actually operates as a foil in the narrative's progression towards the climax because it will not be until after the disciples hear the christological interpretation of Scripture that their minds will be opened.

Luke does not say that any of the disciples touch their mysterious

---

4. R. Dillon, *From Eye-witnesses to Ministers of the Word* p. 188

visitor; after Jesus speaks his word of appeal he makes a gesture of display showing his hands and feet to the bewildered gathering. V. 40 is missing from the 'Western' text and some Syriac manuscripts, and some scholars believe it to be an interpolation patterned on John 20:20 where Jesus shows his disciples his hands and his side. However, Luke does not mention the pierced side of Jesus (cf. Jn 19:34) and since he has already mentioned hands and feet in 24:39, v. 40 is clearly in harmony with the tradition he has received. The purpose of this demonstration is to show 'it is I, myself', identifying the mysterious visitor who is alive with the crucified Jesus. The one who appears before them is the same Jesus who was crucified. The risen Christ is the wounded one; even now he carries the marks of the suffering he experienced on the cross (cf Jn 20:25-27).

To this paschal display by the risen Jesus, Luke recounts the human reaction of the disciples. Again the dialectic between revelation and human experience is explored as the disciples' doubt is not dispelled by focusing on the identification marks of the mysterious visitor. In John's account, the invitation to touch and see leads to the recognition of the Lord by the disbelieving Thomas (2:27-28). Luke's assembly of disciples, however, 'still disbelieved' (cf. 24:11) and 'wondered' (cf. 24:12).

Such reactions respectively echo the response by the group of disciples to the women's message and the response by Peter to what he saw in the tomb. Although Luke softens the disciples' disbelief by saying their joy prevented them from believing, disbelief is still operative. Luke remains consistent with his declared position in the resurrection narratives that the moment of recognition does not come from the Easter appearance itself (cf. again 16:31). Something more is needed.

The disciples' continued disbelief leads the action of the narrative into the visitor's request for something to eat. 'They gave him a piece of broiled fish, and he took it and ate it before them.' (24:42-43 RSV) In John 20 there is no parallel to the eating scene, although the possibility is admitted that if the meal was part of the tradition available to John, he could.have excluded it in the interest of his own Easter account.[5] The postscript of John's Gospel, however, includes a request by the risen

5. Cf. J. A. Bailey, *The Traditions Common to the Gospels of Luke and John* (Leiden: E. J. Brill, 1963) pp. 92ff.

Jesus for food (fish) from disciples who fail to recognise him (21:5).[6]

In Luke's account, if the purpose of eating the fish 'before them' is to demonstrate the physical reality of Jesus to the disciples, one which is reminiscent of the occasion when Jesus directed that the newly raised daughter of Jairus should be given something to eat (8:55), then the demonstration fails in its objective. The absence of any response from the disciples cannot be read to imply faith. Luke has not developed his narrative with such evident care to let the moment of recognition pass without calling attention to it. We are again in the time of concealment, and that time is prolonged until Luke's narrative explicitly notes its conclusion.

What then is Luke's purpose in the eating scene? Moving away from what he calls 'that scholarly fixation on the *manducatio* as physical demonstration and apologetic *tour de force*'[7] Dillon argues that in the phrase 'before them' the 'preposition is a septuagintal idiom for "in the presence of," or "with," especially in situations of meals taken by guests "before" their host. This is the usage we observe in Lk 13,26S; and Acts 27,35 also involves table fellowship … We propose, therefore, that the parallel texts and the range of the preposition's idiomatic usage in Lk both urge the sense: "he ate it at their table," or "in their company," "… as their guest," in Lk 24 43.' [8]

If Dillon's argument seems to strive too anxiously in favour of this eating as an Easter meal, he is surely right in arguing that the physical substance of the risen body is not Luke's principal concern. Luke is clearly unsympathetic to the argument that Jesus' demonstration of his corporeal reality leads anyone to belief – as it does in John's Gospel – and, therefore, hardly serves as a telling apology against the docetist position. There is an undoubted physical realism in the account, but if that realism was used in Luke's tradition as an effective paschal witness then Luke has clearly altered its use here. Perhaps it is sufficient to see Jesus' receiving food from his disciples as a distant echo of the meals in the

---

6. *Pace* I. H. Marshall who refers to this as 'the recognition scene' in *The Gospel of Luke*, p. 904

7. R. Dillon, *From Eye-witnesses to Ministers of the Word* p. 202

8. ibid., pp. 101,102

ministry and an anticipation of the early missionaries becoming guests in various households.

We have already considered Luke's portrayal of Jesus as a visitor/ guest during the ministry, as the one who uses the context of the meal as an occasion of fellowship and an opportunity for teaching. More to the point in the present discussion is the association of his table-fellowship with forgiveness (5:2; 7:39; 19:10), an association which will prove to be important in the present pericope. Jesus as a visitor/guest who receives food can also be seen as anticipation of the early missionaries who will continue the work of Jesus in their itinerant mission and be visitors/ guests themselves who have already been charged to eat what is set before them (10:7). The prime example of this is when Peter is called away from staying at the house of Simon to stay as a guest at the house of Cornelius (Acts 10:22). Even though Peter acknowledged that it is unlawful for a Jew 'to visit anyone of another nation' (Acts 10:28), he eats what they offer him. In that household he recalls how the disciples 'ate and drank with him after he rose from the dead.' (Acts 10:41). Peter goes on to state that all the prophets bear witness to Jesus and that whoever believes in him will receive forgiveness of sin (Acts 10:43). That sequence of visiting, eating, and preaching the fulfilment of Scripture and forgiveness to Gentiles, is one which would seem to be grounded in this resurrection narrative. Thus rather than seeing Jesus' eating 'before them' as a proof that failed, if it is seen in the wider context of this pericope it becomes more susceptible to nuances from elsewhere in Luke's writing. From Jesus' eating what is offered him, Luke moves the narrative into Jesus instructing his disciples.

JESUS' FINAL INSTRUCTION   VERSES 44-49

The appeal to the disciples now shifts as the risen Jesus invokes their memory of what he said during the ministry. Luke has recounted how the first instruction of Jesus, which took place in the synagogue in Nazara, was a teaching on Scripture and its fulfilment (4:21). Now in the today of the resurrection (24:1.13.36) the risen Jesus recalls his own words spoken during the ministry and interprets the hidden object of Scripture as himself.

Luke's narrative focus is on the interpretative word of the risen Jesus, a word that develops previous words in the resurrection account. The women at the tomb were reminded that Jesus had predicted the death and resurrection of the Son of Man during the ministry (24:7). The Emmaus disciples were told how Moses and the prophets had predicted that the messiah had to suffer to enter his glory (24:25-27). Now, more explicitly, the whole assembly of disciples is told that 'everything written about me in the law of Moses and the prophets and the psalms must be fulfilled.' (24:44) This passage sums up the two previous passages and adds 'the psalms' which will be used by the witnesses in Acts as the principal source from the Hebrew Bible to testify to the resurrection and exaltation of Jesus (cf. Acts 2:25-29; 2:34f; 4:11.25; 13:33.35). The whole corpus of Scripture finds its fulfilment in the risen Christ, and as the object of that revelation he is the first subject to interpret its full meaning. In his risen person Christ is the definitive revelation of all the Scriptures.

The risen Jesus opens the disciples' minds to understand the meaning of Scripture, a meaning that is based on the prophetic character of all the Scriptures and which is summarised in the necessity of the Messiah's suffering – Luke's christological summary of Jesus' mission (24:26; Acts 3:18; 17:3). The veil of mystery is now drawn back to reveal the fulfilment of all the scriptures and the meaning of the passion prophecy which was hidden and, therefore, incomprehensible to the disciples (9:45; 18:34).

Again, the direct intervention of the risen Christ is essential for Luke if the disciples are not going to be confined to the period of concealment. They cannot make that move for themselves; they cannot cross the border between incomprehension and insight precisely because that border is divinely established. Only the risen Christ can take the disciples from mystery into revelation through opening their minds to the divine purpose in scripture and the divine purpose in the journey of Jesus. There is no substitute for the interpretative word of the risen Jesus. Only through that word do recent events, the word of Jesus during the ministry, and the words about the Messiah in the scriptures, reveal their redemptive meaning (cf. pp. 114-115).

The word of God cannot be separated from the event: the word was given as promise; the event happens as fulfilment. Both need the complementary word of authoritative interpretation. And it is in this, his most comprehensive statement about the progressive pedagogy of Scripture, that Luke includes the future mission of the Church.

Included in the biblical prophecy of what is written is the charge 'that repentance and forgiveness of sins should be preached in his name to all nations, beginning from Jerusalem. You are witnesses of these things.' (24:48-49) For Luke the universal perspective of the mission is based not only on Jesus' command but on scriptural prophecy. Luke has taken the 'must' of preaching to all nations from the apocalyptic setting in Mark 13:10 and placed it in his own framework of prophecy/fulfilment. The visit of salvation, proclaimed in the power of the Spirit by Zechariah, was already attached to the forgiveness of sins (1:77). And as that salvation was recognised by the Spirit-filled Simeon to be prepared for all the nations to see (2:31) so the forgiveness of sins and the Gentile mission are explicitly brought together in the new word of the risen Jesus.

The proper response to the offer of salvation in God's visit is repentance, and the preached appeal to repent was at the forefront of the ministry (5:32; 10:13; 11:32; 13:3) as it will be at the forefront of the mission of the early Church (Acts 3:19; 20:21; 26:20). In both programmes repentance is the desired response, and as Hahn has pointed out, 'in Luke, when it is joined to "the forgiveness of sins" on the one hand and to faith and new life on the other hand, it becomes the term for conversion.'[9] And that conversion, like the response of the disciples to the new word of the risen Jesus, is a response to a decisive word which calls its hearers away from their present way to a new way 'in the name of Jesus'.

The effective power of the name of Jesus has already been demonstrated during the time of the ministry (9:49; 10:17). Early in the missionary programme, when Peter and John are ordered by the council 'to speak no more to anyone in this name' (Acts 4:17 RSV) they reply that they 'cannot but speak of what we have seen and heard' (v. 20). That necessity of speaking in the name of Jesus is rooted in the Easter mandate of the risen Jesus.

9. F. Hahn, *Mission in the New Testament*, p. 131

So is the mission's 'beginning from Jerusalem'. The role that Jerusalem played in the death of the prophets (13:33) and its ignorance of the time of its visitation (18:44) were decisive factors in the death of the eschatological prophet. But his way to Jerusalem and his death there were destined by divine purpose. Similarly, the way from Jerusalem is destined by the plan of God and is part of biblical prophecy. And Jerusalem will be seen to validate biblical prophecy further as its energetic hostility drives the missionary effort away from its centre in the city (Acts 8:1ff; 13:45-46). The missionary journey from Jerusalem will have the same biblical compulsion as Jesus' journey to the city of his death. For Luke neither is accidental; both have their sure purpose in the plan of God for the name of Jesus will be experienced as a power by the Gentiles.

The new word of the risen Jesus, which opens up his word spoken during the ministry and the prophetic word of Scripture, is the central revelation of the Easter event. That word of opening is itself an event that moves the assembly of disciples from fear and perplexity to Easter understanding. The physical demonstrations by the risen Jesus were clearly insufficient as an argument to belief: what the disciples are witnesses to, therefore, is the Easter opening of scripture which makes sense of all the recent events. Appearance and interpretative word necessarily go together, and it is that word which also sets the programme for the new missionary outreach. 'You are witnesses of these things.' (We will develop the theme of Luke's concept of witness in the next chapter.)

Unlike the other evangelists (Mt 28:19-20; Mk 16:15; Jn 20:21) Luke does not present the risen Lord now sending his disciples on mission. They cannot begin this new mission now; something more is needed. Again Luke's care is apparent in developing his theological programme. Before the disciples are sent to witness, Jesus must first send them the power to witness: 'And behold, I send the promise of my Father upon you; but stay in the city, until you are clothed with power from on high.' (24:49 RSV) The promise of the Father (cf.Acts 1:4) and the power from on high are identified in Acts 1:8 as the Holy Spirit. At the moment Jesus sends this promise (futuristic present) – and the tense underlines the note of expectancy and sets the scene for the gathering after Pentecost (Acts

2:1). Only after Jesus has completed his mission in the exaltation can he send the Spirit that he has received from his Father (Acts 2:32). That pouring out of the Spirit has its own place in biblical prophecy (Joel 2:28ff; Is 32:15; Ez 39:29). The missionary will see a dramatic extension of this pouring out of the Spirit (Acts 2:16ff.) as a new people are born in its power.

So it is that the universal mission cannot be undertaken on the present resources of the disciples: they must stay in Jerusalem until something happens to them, for as Jesus began his mission in the power of the Spirit (4:14) so his witnesses will begin their missionary journey in the same power (Acts 1:8). They will be empowered to witness through the gift of the Holy Spirit. That gift is the something more that is needed. In the meantime they must stay in wait for the power that will enable them to move from experience to message and proclaim Christ as the word of salvation for all peoples.

JESUS' FINAL DEPARTURE   VERSES 50-53

Luke concludes his third resurrection episode with Jesus' final departure in the ascension, a departure which also functions as a solemn conclusion to the whole Easter narrative. The departure scene has no parallels in the Easter accounts of the other three gospels (excluding 16:19 in the Marcan postscript). But, unlike Luke, none of the other evangelists has declared such a literary interest in concluding apparition scenes with the apparition's departure (1:38; 2:15; 9:33; 24:51; Acts 1:9 10:7; 12:10). Like his redactional interest in the motif of return (p. 156), the motif of departure brings the sequence of apparition and revelation to a natural conclusion. More importantly, not only is Jesus' Easter appearance brought to a conclusion, but his whole mission to Jerusalem is now to be completed. That journey began 'when the days drew near for him to be received up' (9: 51 RSV). The phrase 'the days' denotes a period of time rather than a single occurrence, and refers to the complete paschal mystery of passion, death, resurrection and ascension.

Now in 'the third day' the time has come for the completion of the paschal programme. The word *analempsis*, 'to be received up' (9:51), recalls the assumption of Elijah, the Spirit-endowed prophet who was taken up to heaven when he completed his work on earth (2 Kgs 2:9-11). The corresponding verb is used by Luke to speak of Jesus' ascension (Acts 1:2.11.22). The Elijah typology gains ground in view of his presence with Moses (also assumed) before the journey begins (9:30) and in its immediate context (9:54). Further, Luke has shown himself clearly influenced by an Elijah tradition in his portrayal of Jesus (7:11-17) and Peter (Acts 9:36-43) and Paul (Acts 20:7-12) as they re-enact the miraculous raising from the dead of Elijah and Elisha (1 Kgs 17:17-24; 2 Kgs 4:8-37). The language used by Luke for Jesus' ascension, particularly in Acts 1, is similar to the Elijah texts [10] and it seems likely that Luke was conscious of the parallelism.

The bodily ascension of Elijah is also celebrated by Ben Sira (Sir 48:9-10) whose writing, particularly chapter 50, is associated with Luke 24:50-53.[11] In his mediation on saving history thus far, Ben Sira recalls the mighty deeds of great men (44-50), celebrating in particular the miraculous works of the anointed prophets beginning with Moses. This litany of the great words/deeds of the prophets is solemnly concluded by the priest Simon: he lifts his hands over the assembled sons of Israel to pronounce the blessing, and the people bow down in worship (Sir 50:20-21). That worship is followed by blessing God, the prayer for 'cheerful hearts' and for the restoration of peace to Israel.

As Ben Sira brings the history of salvation to a solemn conclusion, so Luke concludes his story of salvation with the one who sums up in himself the whole tradition of biblical prophecy and the history of salvation: 'lifting up his hands he blessed them. While he blessed them, he parted from them and was carried up into heaven and they worshipped him' (24:51b-52a). That worship is followed by the. return of the disciples in great joy to Jerusalem where they are continually in the temple blessing God.

Luke has waited for this moment to display Easter faith as he shows the gathering of disciples united in worshipping the one who is visibly

10. Cf. J. G. Davies, *He Ascended into Heaven. A Study in the History of Doctrine* (New York: Association Press, 1958) pp. 52ff.
11. Cf. P. Van Stempvoort, 'The Interpretation of the Ascension in Luke and Acts' in *New Testament Studies* 5 (1958-59) pp. 30-42; R. Dillon, *From Eye-witnesses to Ministers of the Word* pp. 179ff.

taken up into heaven. All the responses so far recounted in the Easter narrative point to this triumphal conclusion. Luke's determined care in postponing the Easter response to the risen Jesus works to a dramatic conclusion of prayerful adoration. By keeping alive the tension in this one day between paschal witness and human reaction, between Easter revelation and incomprehension, Luke has created a longing for reconciliation in the fulness of faith. That reconciliation between revelation and understanding is now evident in the response of the disciples. As Lohfink has noted: 'Only now have the disciples grasped the height and depth of what has occurred. Only now do they find the real answer to the fact of the resurrection.'[12] As in the two previous Easter accounts, the process leading to this response can be seen as follows:

Paschal witness	Human reaction
8. Jesus' appearance and greeting of peace	alarm and fear
9. Jesus invites disciples to see and touch him. Displays wounds.	They disbelieve for joy
10. Jesus eats the fish offered him	(no reaction)
11. Jesus interprets scripture	their minds are opened
Conclusion of Easter Account	
12. Jesus blesses them and is carried up to heaven.	the disciples worship him and return with great joy to Jerusalem

   Thus the Easter account is closed as the Gospel itself is closed with the end of the story of Jesus in the ascension. The visit of God's salvation in Jesus, heralded at the beginning of the Gospel by Zechariah (1:68.78) is now concluded with Jesus' final departure. The visit is over because the visitor's mission is now accomplished, and he will not return until the final visit at the end of time (21:27-28). The ascension will be viewed from a different perspective in Acts where it will be recognised as the beginning of the story of the church. As the ascension in the Gospel closes one epoch of saving history so it will open a new epoch in Acts. As

12. G. Lohfink, *Die Himmelfahrt Jesu*, p. 114

Flender has observed:

> The exaltation of Christ is more than an end of Old Testament redemptive history. It is, as Luke sees it, the transcendental fulfilment of the Old Testament prophecies. With the reign of Christ, salvation ceases to be confined to a particular nation in history, and now extends to the whole cosmos.[13]

In the Gospel Luke has celebrated the fulfilment of God's saving promise in the person of Jesus. In the Acts he will celebrate the extension of that salvation to all peoples beginning from Jerusalem.

So the disciples return to Jerusalem. They will begin their missionary endeavour where the visit of salvation was accomplished. In Jerusalem they are continually in the temple blessing God; they occupy the centre of Israel's religion in the new understanding that promises have been fulfilled (cf. 2:37). The disciples' reaction to all that has happened is summarised in the phrases 'with great joy' and 'blessing God', terms characteristic of the eschatological atmosphere which permeated the infancy narrative (1:14,64; 2:10,28). They now wait for the creative presence which dominated the infancy narrative: the Holy Spirit. It will be in that creative power that they will become a witnessing community.

---

13. H. Flender, *St Luke: Theologian of Redemptive History* (London: SPCK, 1967) pp. 102, 103.

8 | Being Witnesses

IN THE GOSPEL OF LUKE the appearances of the risen Jesus and the ascension brought to a completion the visit of salvation in Jesus. As a scene of farewell the ascension marked the end of the appearances on Easter Sunday night; it also looked forward to the new beginning promised in the words of the risen Jesus (24:49). In the opening verses of Acts, however, Luke tells us that Jesus appears to the apostles for a period of forty days staying and eating with them (v.4a) and speaking to them about the kingdom of God before he is taken from their sight. The new story of appearance and ascension serves a new function: the appearance of Jesus in this second part of Luke's work shows how the future life of the Church has its foundation in the risen Lord, while the ascension shows that what marks the fulfilment of Jesus' personal mission in his exaltation makes the beginning of his disciples' pastoral mission in the sending of the Spirit. If Acts tells the story of the work of the Spirit in the followers of Jesus, the beginning of Acts announces how that programme is rooted in the authoritative word of the risen Jesus.

At the beginning of this second part of his work Luke repeats something he did at the beginning of the first part. Just as he brought the Law and the Prophets into the beginning of the Gospel to demonstrate how the expectations represented by Zechariah and Elizabeth and Simeon and Anna were fulfilled in the person of Jesus, so now Luke brings Jesus into the story of the beginning of the Church to show how Jesus' promises are indeed fulfilled in the beginning of the new age of the Spirit.

In the Gospel and in Acts there is a bridge between the past and the present, between promise and fulfilment, between word and event. Both beginnings convey the idea of fulfilment. Thus the story of the beginning of the Church is not told in the absence of Jesus; rather, his presence is seen to direct the operation from the very beginning and his words are seen to account for its spread to the ends of the earth.

The beginning of Acts, therefore, is not just an example of how Luke adopts the stylistic convention of ancient historiography by opening a new work with a brief review of the previous book and a preview of the present one.[1] Luke makes his own theological use of this literary convention by declaring the person of the risen Jesus to be a summary of all the deeds and words of the Gospel while at the same time previewing the new age through the words of the risen Jesus. Luke maintains the position he developed so carefully in the final chapter of his Gospel: the precondition for being a witness is encountering the risen Lord and being opened to his revealing word.

The content of the risen Jesus' instructions focuses on the kingdom of God [2] and this makes way for the important exchange in Acts 1:6-8. In the Gospel Luke has reserved the first preaching of the kingdom to Jesus – 'because that is what I was sent to do' (4:43; contra Mt 3:2). The Twelve were sent out 'to proclaim the kingdom of God' (9:2); discipleship itself was 'for the sake of the kingdom of God' (18:29). Although Luke believed that the kingdom was already present in the ministry of Jesus (11:20; 16:16; 17:21) – a view that Conzelmann has disputed at length [3] - the evangelist retains the traditional understanding of the kingdom as a future reality (22:18), an action of God in establishing his rule at the end time when the Son of Man will come in glory at the final visit (21:27). It is the future aspect of the kingdom that the risen Jesus is seen to address himself to, a subject which is important to Luke's readers. Is the kingdom coming soon? Is the expectation of an imminent *parousia* a concern which should dominate the lives of the followers of Jesus?

The subjects of the kingdom of God and the coming of the Spirit give

1. Cf. H. J. Cadbury, *The Making of Luke-Acts*, (New York: Macmillan, 1927) pp. 198-199
2. Cf. O. Betz, 'The Kerygma of Luke' in *Interpretation* 22 1968) pp. 131-146; C. H. Dodd, *The Apostolic Preaching and its Development* (London: Hodder and Stoughton, 1936); W. G. Kümmel, *Promise and Fulfilment*; N. Perrin, *Jesus and the Language of the Kingdom: Symbol and Metaphor in New Testament Interpretation*, (Philadelphia: Fortress, 1976).
3. Cf. H. Conzelmann, *The Theology of Saint Luke*, pp. 95-136; for a critique cf. W. G. Kümmel, 'Current Theological Accusations against Luke' in *Andover Newton Quarterly* 16 (1975) pp. 131-145.

rise to the disciples' question: 'Lord, has the time come? Are you going to restore the kingdom of Israel?' (Acts 1:6). Haenchen has noted:

> The earliest Christians regarded the outpouring of the Spirit as a sign that the end of the world was at hand. With this in mind it is easy to understand why they should ask, 'Is the kingdom coming now, at the same time as the Spirit?' The question thus brings up the problem of the eschatological near-expectation, which is however linked with a second problem: 'Is the kingdom restricted to Israel?'[4]

In Luke's source the outpouring of the Spirit is understood as a sign that marks the beginning of the end, 'before the great Day of the Lord dawns' (Acts 2:20 quoting Joel 3:4). In Joel's prophecy the eschatological outpouring of the Spirit will put new life into a broken Israel; it will signal the final salvation of all who call on the name of the Lord; it will announce the time of the final visit when God will sit in judgement over the nations 'for all they have done to Israel, my people and my heritage' (Joel 4:2). Whereas God identifies himself with Israel, he is judge and prosecutor of the nations; and Israel's exclusive restoration will coincide with the Gentile decline. God's favour is focused in one place: 'Jerusalem will be a holy place, no alien will ever pass through it again.' (Joel 4:17) Thus in the prophecy of Joel the outpouring of the Spirit signals the *parousia* and the exclusive restoration of Israel, both of which are reflected in the disciples' questions.

Both of these are reinterpreted by Luke in the reply of the risen Jesus: 'It is not for you to know times or dates that the Father has decided by his own authority, but you will receive power when the Holy Spirit comes on you, and then you will be my witnesses not only in Jerusalem but throughout Judaea and Samaria, and indeed to the ends of the earth.' (Acts 1:7-8)

In the final words of the risen Jesus two things are clear: the outpouring of the Spirit does not signal the *parousia*, and salvation is not limited to Israel but extended to everyone in the universal mandate. Conzelmann makes the comment:

---

4. E. Haenchen, *The Acts of the Apostles*, p. 143

The Spirit Himself is no longer the eschatological gift, but the substitute in the meantime for the possession of ultimate salvation; He makes it possible for believers to exist in the continuing life of the world and in persecution, and He gives the power for missionary endeavour and for endurance.[5]

Certainly, the outpouring of the Spirit will begin a new time when the message of salvation will be taken by witnesses to the ends of the earth – a spatial image of a process that takes a considerable time. And this re-interpretation of Joel's prophecy will be confirmed by events in the event of Pentecost itself and in the development of the missionary programme.

The last words of the risen Jesus challenge the preoccupation of those who continue to look for an impending *parousia* and face the disappointment of those who cannot understand why it has not already come. In Mark's Gospel when Jesus was speaking in the ministry of the coming of the Son of Man at the end of time he warned: 'But as for that day or hour, nobody knows it, neither the angels of heaven, nor the Son; no one but the Father.' (Mk 13:32) Luke omitted that logion at the expected place in 21:25ff. to save it for the present context. Speculation about the time of the *parousia* is not only a useless pastime, it is forbidden.

The focal point of Christian concern must be the task of a missionary programme to spread the message of salvation. This spread accords with the progress of Acts itself: Jerusalem (chapters 1-7); Judaea and Samaria (8-9); the ends of the earth (10-28).So the risen Lord who visits and instructs his disciples for forty days is seen to be source and guide of the future way of the Church.

Immediately Jesus gives his disciples the universal mandate to mission he is lifted up and a cloud takes him from their sight (Acts 1:9). The story of the ascension is connected without a break to Jesus' final words. Jesus is lifted up (aorist passive); it is not something he does of his own initiative or power. A cloud, a sign of God's presence (cf. Ex 13:21; 24:15-18; Lk 9:34f.), takes him out of their sight. Thus the disciples are eye-witnesses of this visible conclusion to the visit of God in Jesus, the account of which can be seen as a careful response to the problem of the

5. H. Conzelmann, *The Theology of Saint Luke*, pp. 95.96

delay of the *parousia*.[6]

In his eschatological discourse Luke used the imagery of Daniel 7:13-14 to speak of the visible end of history when 'they will see the Son of Man coming in a cloud with power and great glory. When these things begin to take place, stand erect, hold your heads high, because your liberation is near at hand.' (Lk 21:27-28) Luke appropriates this *parousia* imagery for the final departure of Jesus; but the disciples' stance of gazing into the heavens is precisely the one that is questioned by the two angels. The sudden appearance of the two men in white serves the same function as it did in the first resurrection narrative (Lk 24:5-7): they question the attitude of those who are looking in the wrong place for the risen Jesus; they interpret the meaning of what has happened and point to its eschatological significance.

Clearly Luke has no intention of diminishing the unique importance of Jesus' final coming in judgement at the *parousia* (cf. Acts 3:20f; 10:42; 17:31); but staring into the heavens is not an appropriate attitude for the Christian community to adopt until that day comes. That immobile stance has just been dismissed in the missionary charge of the risen Jesus as it is dismissed now by the two angels. The angels, however, do speak of the *parousia*. In the tomb the angels referred to Jesus' prophecies of the Son of Man; now that the meaning of the passion has been revealed by the risen Jesus himself bringing to an end the time of the passion's concealment, the angels speak of the final coming of Jesus who has ascended into heaven (cf. pp.116-117). This Jesus will come in the same way – in a cloud – as he went (cf. Dan 7:13; Mt 24:30; 1 Thess 4:17; Rev 1:7; 14:14-17). The angels establish a bond between the ascension of Jesus and his return at the end of time. Thus the ascension marks the visible beginning of the period between the saving visit of God accomplished in the exaltation of Jesus and the visible visit of Jesus at the last day.

The link between the ascension and the *parousia* is reinforced when we learn in v. 12 that Jesus' departure took place from the Mount of

6. A. L. Moore, *The Parousia in the New Testament* (Leiden: E. J. Brill, 1966); D. E. Aune 'The Significance of the Delay of the Parousia for Early Christianity' in G. F. Hawthorne (ed.), *Current Issues in Biblical and Patristic Interpretation* (Grand Rapids: Eerdmans, 1975) pp. 87-109

Olives. In the Jewish eschatological tradition the Mount of Olives is the place where God will come on the last day. Second Zechariah tells of how God's people will be purified before they enter his kingdom, but first the final battle of Jerusalem must take place before the day of the Lord. All the nations will be gathered in Jerusalem for battle and God himself will take to the field: 'On that day, his feet will rest on the Mount of Olives, which faces Jerusalem from the east ... Yahweh your God will come, and all the holy ones with him.' (Zech 14:4.5b) The Mount of Olives is the chosen place for the final visit of God. Luke has already referred to the Mount of Olives in the story of Jesus' entry to Jerusalem (19:29.37) and recounted Jesus' own lament over a Jerusalem that did not know the time of its visitation (19:42). Now we learn that Jesus will return from heaven to the Mount of Olives where he will exercise final judgement on the last day.

Up to this point in Acts the reader could suppose that the apostles were the only witnesses to Jesus' ascension. However, in vv. 13-14, after naming the Eleven, Luke adds two further groups: firstly, the women; secondly, the family of Jesus, his mother Mary and his brothers. These three groups – the Eleven and the women and the family of Jesus – form the one community that prays and waits for the coming of the Spirit. The gathering of these three groups into one community that waits in the upper room in the city of Jerusalem serves an important function for Luke's editorial plan for Acts: from the very beginning of his second book this community serves to demonstrate the unbroken continuity between the story of Jesus and the story of the Church. Together, they will constitute the basic community of the Church.

The Eleven enjoy a unique importance because they were chosen by Jesus to be his apostles (Lk 6:14) and were with him 'right from the time when John was baptising until the day when he was taken up from us' (Acts 1:22). But the apostles' experience does not cover the whole narrative of Luke's Gospel – which is why the other two groups are important for Luke's purpose. The women were the first to hear the message of the resurrection in the empty tomb (Lk 24:1-11) – an important scene not witnessed by the apostles. Mary was the first in the Gospel to hear God's message about Jesus and, together with Joseph, was

responsible for the formation of Jesus' early life. All this she kept in her
heart (Lk 2:52). The apostles were not witnesses to this time in Luke's
Gospel. Thus the apostles and the women and the family of Jesus bring
Luke's Gospel in its entirety into the beginning of Acts.

Mary is present at the beginning of the story in the infancy narrative,
during the ministry, and now at the end of the story. One of the brothers
of Jesus, James, will play an important part in the early Church as the
head of the Church in Jerusalem; he is included in Paul's list of those to
whom Jesus appeared (1 Cor 15:7). However, John states in his Gospel
that not even the brothers of Jesus believed in him (7:5); and in Mark's
Gospel the mother and brothers of Jesus are depicted as a group outside
the circle of Jesus' real family (3:34; cf. Mt 12:49) – an exclusion that Luke
alters dramatically in his account (Lk 8:19-21). For these stories to be
preserved, clearly there must have been some tension in the early Church
about the role of the family of Jesus – perhaps over the question of who
had authority to speak and act in his name, the family or the disciples. All
four Gospels agree that discipleship (being chosen by Jesus), not family
(being related to Jesus), constitutes the real authority for speaking and
acting in the name of Jesus. Since Luke has already presented Mary as the
disciple who hears the word of God and keeps it, he avoids this tension
in the Gospel. And now he presents the family of Jesus united with the
apostles and the women.

BEGINNING WITH THE TWELVE   ACTS 1:15-26

In spite of its togetherness, however, there is something radically incomplete about this gathering, an incompleteness that must be remedied
before the coming of the Spirit at Pentecost. With the vacancy left by the
defection and death of Judas there are now eleven apostles, and if Luke
is going to preserve the symbolic continuity between the old Israel and
the new Israel of the Church, he cannot start with the number eleven. He
must show how the central significance of the Twelve is found intact in
the new community from its beginning. This he does in his account of
the election of Matthias.

Peter, who will be the most prominent figure in the first part of Acts
as Paul will be in the second part, addresses the wider group of the

brothers. The fate of Judas is understood as a necessary fulfilment of God's will revealed through the Holy Spirit in the Scripture - although the manner of his death and why the field of blood was so called are clearly of little historical importance (cf. Mt 27:3-10). The focus is now on the replacement for Judas to the office of membership of the Twelve, and Peter announces the criterion for choosing the new candidate (1:21-22). So that the new candidate can act with the eleven apostles as a witness to the resurrection, he must be chosen from among those who have had the requisite experience: those who, like the Eleven, can fulfil the historical requirement of associating with Jesus from the beginning (the time of John's baptism) to the end (the time of the ascension).

The criterion of apostleship obviously supposes that other disciples can meet this historical requirement; at the very least, two of them. The names of Joseph called Barsabbas and Matthias are put forward – by the apostles or by 'the whole assembly' (cf. 6:4) is not clear. In the prayer before the lots are drawn (1:24.25), Luke signifies that it will be the Lord's choice that will be made (as it was his choice that made the Eleven apostles). As the lot falls on Matthias, he is now numbered with the Eleven. The Twelve are now reconstituted.

With almost half of this opening chapter devoted to the election of the new apostle, it must seem strange that the choice of Matthias has no importance for the subsequent story of Acts: he never appears again in the New Testament. The importance of Matthias is not due to his person but to the fact that he completes the Twelve. Matthias has no individual importance, and this is something he shares with the majority of the Twelve about whom we know so little. Their importance lies in the fact that together they constitute a unique group. The lists of the names of the Twelve vary (Mt 10:2; Mk 3:6; Lk 6:14; Acts 1:13), and there is no doubt that after some time their names could not be remembered precisely. John does not give a list but refers to the Twelve (6:67.70.71) and names Thomas as one of them. But he has nothing further to say about them.

However, no matter how the lists of the names of the Twelve vary, there are always twelve names. The arithmetic is more important than the individuals – just as the names of the patriarchs vary with different circumstances (Gen 49; Deut 33; Jg 5) while the number twelve remains a constant.

All four Gospels agree that Jesus chose twelve close companions. Luke tells us that the reason Jesus chose twelve was an eschatological one related to the kingdom: 'you will eat and drink at my table in my kingdom, and you will sit on thrones to judge the twelve tribes of Israel.' (Lk 22:30) The choice of the Twelve is related to the kingdom and to Israel – thus the question before the ascension, 'Are you going to restore the kingdom to Israel?' (1:6) The choice of twelve would seem to indicate that their work was confined to Israel. Their role as the Twelve (to sit on thrones judging the twelve tribes of Israel) is clearly not synonymous with their role as apostles ('sent' to preach to all nations, beginning from Jerusalem). If the primitive Church believed that the kingdom was indeed coming soon and that the judgement would take place at Jerusalem on the Mount of Olives, there would be little point in the twelve apostles leaving the city. The function of the Twelve would appear to be a stationary one; the function of the apostle would appear to be a missionary one.

Perhaps the tension between the two functions goes some way to explain why 'the Twelve' disappear so soon in the story of the Church. After they supervise the appointment of the seven (Acts 6:1-6) they play no discernible role in the growth of the Church and take no active part in the development of the missionary programme. The tension exists in Luke's writing because he identifies 'the Twelve' with 'the apostles' and ascribes that designation to Jesus in the ministry (Lk 6:14), a delimitation of apostleship which would seem to have its origin in the early Church.[7]

The twelve apostles do not appear in Acts as a group that spearheads the missionary programme to the Gentiles. Peter and John are sent to Samaria to lay hands on the Samaritans who have accepted the word of God (8:14-17) and Peter is the first to preach to the Gentiles (Acts 10); but as a group the apostles are identified with Jerusalem and the ministry to Israel (8:1; 11:1). And in Jerusalem, it is James the brother of the Lord, not one of the twelve apostles, who heads the community of believers (cf. Acts 12:17; 15:19; Gal 1:19; 2:9).

7. Cf. J. Dupont, 'Le nom d'apôtres a-t-il été donné aux Douze par Jésus' in *L'Orient syrien* 1 (1956) pp. 267-290, 425-444.

After the council at Jerusalem 'the apostles' fade out of the scene and Luke makes his last reference to them when Paul carries their instructions to the communities of Asia Minor (16:4). Later, when Paul visits Jerusalem to report what God has done among the pagans in his ministry, his visit is to 'James, and all the elders' (21:18). By this time the twelves apostles are absent even by reference in the story of the Church; the focus is on the missionary activity to the ends of the earth, a move which is credited to the dynamic leadership of Paul who, along with Barnabas, is called 'apostle' (14:4,14).

The 'apostolic' function of the Twelve in the early Church is clearly not Luke's primary interest. The importance of the Twelve, those who were with Jesus from the beginning of his ministry until his ascension, is that they can act as a corporate 'witness to his resurrection' (1:21; cf 10:39). They constitute the historical foundation of the new Israel which will be built on their witness in the power of the Spirit. But the corporate witness of twelve also points to the end time. The Church exists between two functions of the Twelve: their function as apostolic witnesses to the resurrection and their function as judges at the coming of the kingdom. Once the college of the Twelve is reconstituted, its membership remains unchanged.

There is succession to the apostolic mission of exercising authority in the name of Jesus, but there is no succession to the office of the Twelve. When James the son of Zebedee, a member of the Twelve, is beheaded by King Herod Agrippa (Acts 12:2), there is no election to fill the vacancy. The fact that the Twelve are not a perpetual institution in the life of the Church is not simply because the conditions of membership can be met only by first generation followers of Jesus.

More importantly, the Twelve cannot be replaced because of their eschatological role, one which they shall exercise in the kingdom. When the Twelve die they will take the places reserved for them in the kingdom: no one can sit in their places. They have a unique place and an irreplaceable role in the kingdom which they enjoy as members of the Twelve. That is why it is important for Luke to have the college of the Twelve complete when the new age of the Spirit begins, a period of time that will last until the final day.

BEGINNING WITH THE SPIRIT: PENTECOST

In the setting of the pilgrimage feast of Pentecost, the Feast of Weeks, Luke unfolds the story of the beginning of the Church in the outpouring of the Spirit. Luke introduces his account on the note of fulfilment – literally, 'When the day of Pentecost was fulfilled' (2:1), a formula which he used to announce the birth of Jesus (Lk 2:6) and the beginning of Jesus' exodus to Jerusalem (Lk 9:51; cf.9:31). The mysterious visitation of the Spirit at Pentecost will be an event which fulfils the word of the risen Jesus (Lk 24:49; Acts 1:5,8) and the word of ancient prophecy (Joel 3:1-5; Is 2:2). This fulfilment marks a new beginning at Pentecost in the birth of a new Israel; it is the moment when the chosen followers of Jesus will become the accredited witnesses of his resurrection.

The setting of the Feast of Weeks is important for Luke's theological purposes. Numbered in the list of the three principal feasts in Exodus 23:14-27 is the Feast of Harvest, which celebrates the first fruits of the grain harvest. Since a good harvest was a sign of God's blessing (Gen 26:12; Ps 128) and a bad harvest or famine a sign of God's judgement (Jer 5:17; Joel 1), the time of harvest was perceived as a visit of God. The Feast of Harvest, or the Feast of Weeks (Ex 34:22), was a community celebration to give thanks to God for the blessing of new produce. Its timing was reckoned by counting seven weeks from the beginning of the grain harvest (Deut 16: 9) or fifty days (Lev 23:16) from the Passover and the offering of the first sheaf. Eventually the feast became known as Pentecost, from the Greek word for 'fiftieth' (Tob 2:1).

Because it was an agricultural feast it would have been celebrated by the Israelites only after they had settled in Canaan; later, however, it assumed historical significance as a commemoration of the covenant given to Moses at Sinai when God revealed his way in the Law and ratified his choice of Israel as his people. The basis for celebrating Pentecost as a memorial of the covenant was the reckoning according to Exodus 19:1 that the Israelites arrived at Sinai in the third month after their exodus from Egypt, and the Feast of Weeks was seen to coincide with that arrival. In the texts of the Book of Jubilees and Philo Judaeus, as well as the tradition of rabbinic Judaism in the second century, the giving of the Law on Sinai was understood as having taken place on the fiftieth day after the exodus, thus giving the Feast of Weeks a new religious dimension as the Feast of the Renewal of the Covenant.[8]

More interesting for our present purposes is the collection of the Dead Sea Scrolls, in particular the eleven columns of the QS scroll from cave 1 which make up the Rule of the Community.[9] The community, dedicated to the Law of Moses and the teaching of the prophets, believed that they formed the remnant of God's elect, the last of God's chosen ones. God had revealed his will to the Teacher of Righteousness who was the only one able to interpret the mysteries of the Scriptures and so outline the way of holiness. Symbolically divided into twelve tribes, the Qumran sect believed that they constituted the one true Israel chosen by God to inherit the covenant and ultimate salvation. The community represented the New Covenant, and entry into this New Covenant, reserved to Israelites, meant becoming a candidate for admission into the community. The whole community assembled on the Feast of the Renewal of the Covenant, their most important feast, which they celebrated on the Feast of Pentecost. On this feast, new members were accepted into the community:

> On entering the Covenant, the Priests and Levites shall bless the God of salvation and all his faithfulness, and all those entering the Covenant shall say after them, 'Amen, Amen!' (1 QS 1)

It is also worth noting that the Rule of the Community refers to an entrance rite attached to entry into the Covenant, a ceremony of purification that is similar to baptism:

> For it is through the spirit of true counsel concerning the ways of man that all his sins shall be expiated that he may contemplate the light of life. He shall be cleansed from all his sins by the spirit of holiness uniting him to His truth ... And when his flesh is

---

8. Cf. R. le Déaut, 'Pentecôte et tradition juive' in *Spiritus* 7, (1961) pp. 127-144; K. Hruby, 'La fête de la Pentecôte dans la tradition juive' in *Bible et Vie Chrétienne* 63, (1965) pp. 46-64; E. Schweizer, 'Pneuma' in *Theological Dictionary of the New Testament* VI

9. Quotations from the Qumran scrolls will be taken from the translation of G. Vermes, *The Dead Sea Scrolls in English* (Harmondsworth: Penguin, 1977)

> sprinkled with purifying water and sanctified by cleansing water, it shall be made clean by the humble submission of his soul to all the precepts of God. (1 QS 3)

Thus for the Qumran community the Feast of Pentecost, when the Renewal of the Covenant was celebrated, was the solemn occasion when the community welcomed new members into the New Covenant, members who were cleansed from their sins by the spirit of holiness and truth. And in this spirit they were instructed to walk 'until the time of His visitation'. (1 QS 3)

The Qumran scrolls show that the celebration of Pentecost as the Feast of the Renewal of the Covenant was practised long before the destruction of the Temple in 70 A.D. Schweizer has noted:

> If even before 70 Pentecost was regarded as the end of the passover which celebrates the exodus from Egypt, and if already in Deut. 4:10, 9:10, 18:16 LXX the day of the giving of the Law is called *he hemera tes ekklesia*s (the day of the assembly), such an interpretation is natural.[10]

The adoption of this Jewish feast is ideal for Luke's theological purposes: he presents the coming of the Spirit fifty days after the exodus of Jesus; the group which is assembled all together in one place (cf. 1:15; 2:1) will become the nucleus of the new Israel; they will receive new members, all of them Jews, who share the promise of the Holy Spirit that was made first 'for you and your children' (2:39); after Peter's instructions many will become new members through baptism: 'That very day about three thousand were added to their number'. (2:41)

The outpouring of the Spirit on the day of Pentecost is told in terms similar to the account of God's visit on Mount Sinai where God descended 'in the form of fire' and spoke 'with peals of thunder' (Ex 19:18.19). The link between the Pentecost scene and the Sinai theophany is reinforced if, as Haenchen has noted, we read with Philo the interpretation that the tongues of fire on Sinai became tongues of speech:

Here we have another tradition still closer to Acts: when God

---

10. E. Schweizer, 'Pneuma', in *Theological Dictionary of the New Testament* VI, p. 411.

spoke on Sinai his word divided into seventy tongues – corresponding to the seventy nations of the world – so that each people could hear the Law in its own language (though of course only Israel accepted it!). If Luke, however, was – as we may assume - acquainted with this or a similar tradition, he did not adopt it mechanically, for he says nothing of a new law and the Spirit is represented as an individual gift to each Christian (not only the Twelve but the whole congregation receive it).[11]

But Luke seems to be doing more than depicting the Pentecost scene in a Sinai tradition: there is a marked similarity between his account and the Septuagint reading of the final judgement scene in Isaiah 66:5-24. In that theophany God comes in fire and whirlwind, and the children of the new Jerusalem experience salvation as all nations and tongues are assembled to see God's glory. This eschatological reference suits Luke's purpose of seeing the Spirit as a substitute for the *parousia*. Thus it is possible to see Luke's Pentecost scene as one which stands between two theophanies: the past visit of God on Mount Sinai when he came to form his own people, and the future visit of God at the end of time when he will come in salvation and in judgement.

Luke describes the descent of the Spirit first as a sound from heaven 'like a powerful wind' and then as a sight like 'tongues of fire' which separate and rest on each person present. The immediate effect of the Spirit's descent is shown in the Spirit's gift of new speech to the whole body of disciples who are now able to speak in foreign languages. This in turn makes for amazement when the Jews from every nation under heaven hear their own language spoken. What they hear from the disciples is the story of the mighty works of God. Unlike the Easter experiences in Luke 24 there is no gap now between event and meaning, between experience and interpretation, between what has happened and the disciples' understanding of what is going on.

The dialectic which dominated Luke's resurrection narrative is now resolved in the experience of the Spirit. In the power of the Spirit the disciples can now account for their new experience as they praise the

11. E. Haenchen, *The Acts of the Apostles*, p. 174

marvellous deeds of God. And this is dramatically highlighted in Peter's address to the crowds.

Through Peter's sermon Luke interprets the event of Pentecost. First there is the familiar Lucan argument from prophecy as Peter explains that the Spirit-filled preaching is not a result of drunkenness but of the eschatological outpouring of the Spirit, one which comes as an offer of salvation for all who call on the name of the Lord (2:14-21).

In vv. 22-24 the tone changes as we hear the basic affirmation about Jesus: how he was attested by God through the mighty works and wonders that God did through him; how Jesus was delivered up according to the determined plan of God; how the Jewish listeners are responsible for his death; how, in contrast, God raised Jesus because it was not possible for him to be held by the power of death – a resurrection statement that seeks scriptural corroboration in Psalm 16:8-11. In dramatic contrast to the two disciples of Emmaus who could not hold together their experience of Jesus as a prophet mighty in deed and word before God and all the people and his rejection and death (Lk 24:19-21), this Spirit-filled address by Peter can now reconcile that paradox using, like the risen Christ on the road to Emmaus, the argument from Scripture. Peter, with the other apostles, has been opened to the meaning of the Easter events through the interpretative word of the risen Christ; he has, with the Eleven, experienced the promise of the Father in the Pentecost of the Spirit. Therefore now, with the Eleven, he can stand before the crowds and interpret the saving significance of all that has happened. And he supports the apostolic experience with proof-texts from Scripture.

In favour of the interpretation that Psalm 16 speaks of Jesus, the argument is adduced that since David is dead and buried, and therefore his body underwent corruption, the patriarch could not have been referring to himself when he spoke of the holy one who would not see corruption. As a prophet he knew God's pledge that his messianic successor would sit on God's throne. Peter proposes that what David foretold was the resurrection of the Christ, a prophecy that is now fulfilled in Jesus. And what the Scripture foretold is something that has been witnessed by the Twelve: 'God raised this man Jesus to life' (3:2).

Thus Scripture and apostolic experience confirm the truth about Jesus of Nazareth.

The kerygma now moves on to proclaim that, raised to the heights of God's right hand, Jesus has received the Holy Spirit, the promise of the Father (3:33). In the Gospel Luke declared how Jesus was conceived through the power of the Spirit and was endowed with the Spirit for the ministry; now the emphasis in on the exalted Jesus receiving the Spirit for the purpose of endowing his followers for their new ministry, an understanding that may have its original source in in an early credal formula (cf. Rom 1:4; 1 Tim 3:16). Here the outpouring of the Spirit is understood as an action of the exalted Jesus and is registered in the prophetic activity of his followers: thus 'what you see and hear is the outpouring of that Spirit.' (3:33)

An appeal is made again to the prophetic words of David, this time to Psalm 110:1, to verify the exaltation of *kyrios* at the right hand of God: since David did not ascend to heaven he could not have been referring to himself as the exalted *kyrios*. Peter concludes that because of this 'the whole House of Israel can be certain that God has made this Jesus whom you crucified both Lord and Christ.' (3:36; cf. Rom 1:3-4)

Peter's argument has the effect of moving his hearers to ask him and the apostles how to respond to what they have heard. Peter's answer is a summons to repentance – an appeal that, as Dibelius has pointed out,[12] is a standard conclusion for Lucan sermons in Acts. The people are invited to be baptized in the name of Jesus Christ for the forgiveness of sins. If they do this, they too will receive the gift of the Holy Spirit.

Clearly this gift of the Spirit is not a unique possession of the original group of believers; it is offered to all those (presently Jews) who repent. Through the gift of the Holy Spirit the forgiving power of Christ continues to work in the community. The saving action of God that was evident in the deeds and words of Jesus is now being extended in the experience of the Spirit. Reinforcing his arguments, Peter continues to urge his listeners to salvation. When his word is received, the people are baptized. In the name of Jesus and in the power of the Holy Spirit the community of the Church begins to grow.

12. Cf. M. Dibelius, *Studies in the Acts of the Apostles* (London: SCM, 1956) p. 165

WITNESSING TO JESUS IN THE POWER OF THE SPIRIT

The Holy Spirit, 'the promise of the Father', is mediated through the exalted Jesus. As the Spirit conferred on Jesus at his baptism was the *dynamis* working for the accomplishment of Jesus' saving mission (Lk 4:1.14.18), so the Pentecost event is an outpouring of the Spirit to enable the new community to bring that salvation to others in the name of Jesus. For Jesus and for his Easter disciples, the Spirit is the creative power of God which works through them for the purpose of their prophetic mission. Jesus began his mission in the power of prophecy (Lk 4:24) as do the Easter disciples (Acts 2:17ff.). As Luke showed in his Gospel how Jesus re-enacted the pattern of prophetic witness in mighty deeds/words which led to his rejection, so he will show in Acts how the followers of Jesus will re-enact that prophetic pattern of mighty deeds/words and rejection.

The power of the Spirit will be shown in a mission carried out in the name of Jesus: 'For of all the names in the world given to men, this is the only one by which we can be saved.' (Acts 4:12). As Conzelmann noted: 'We can go so far as to say that to speak of the efficacy of the name is the specifically Lucan way of describing the presence of Christ.' [13] In that name salvation will eventually reach the pagans (9:16), a work that will necessarily involve suffering for the name (9:17).

The question presents itself: on what basis are people going to accept the name of Jesus as one which is inseparably tied to their salvation? What or who functions as a witness to the claims of Jesus? These questions are particularly problematic in Jerusalem. Jesus was taken by the whole assembly of the Sanhedrin to Pilate; they voiced their accusations against him (Lk 23:1ff.). Although Pilate found no case to answer he gave the verdict that their demand was to be granted. In Luke's view the Jews have already passed a verdict on Jesus: they condemned him to die. Why should they change that verdict? What is the new evidence about Jesus to justify reopening his trial? What new evidence could lead the Jewish people to change their judgement about Jesus?

For Luke that new evidence is the resurrection. The verdict the Jews

---

13. H. Conzelmann, *The Theology of Saint Luke*, p. 178

passed on Jesus was formed in ignorance (Acts 3:17; 13:27). Peter presents to them the new evidence: 'God, however, raised him from the dead, and to that fact we are the witnesses.' (3:15) God's act of raising Jesus from the dead is the king-pin of understanding who Jesus is. And that is why this new case will be supported by a witness that is focused on the resurrection (Lk 24:48; Acts 1:22; 2:32; 3:15: 4:33; 5:32; 10:41; 13:31).

In the preface to his Gospel Luke stated that his account was based on tradition handed down by those who from the beginning were eye-witnesses and ministers of the word. As Fitzmyer comments:

> The Greek of this phrase is not easily translated. Another, more literal translation of *hoi ap' arches autoptai kai hyperetai genomenoi tou logou* might be: 'the original eyewitness who became ministers of the word.' The problem lies in whether Luke is referring here to one or to two groups of persons who shaped the early tradition.[14]

Fitzmyer argues that Luke is referring to one group of people; in the light of Acts 1:21-22 and 10:37-39, such a group would seem to be the Twelve. Fitzmyer is surely right in arguing that the eye-witnesses and ministers of the word are one group of people – the story of Luke 24 and Acts 1-2 can be understood as the account of how the eye-witnesses become ministers of the word through the revealing word of Christ and the outpouring of the Spirit.

But I doubt that this group is limited in Luke's understanding to the Twelve. Certainly, Luke declares a special interest in apostolic witness; but as Acts 1:21-22 shows, experience of the earthly Jesus and the risen Christ is not confined to the apostles. As argued earlier, the function of the Twelve is principally to maintain the link between Israel and the new community of the Church; the function of witnesses to the resurrection, among whom the Twelve are numbered, is quite different. Luke's resurrection narrative carefully presented the wider circle of Jesus' followers – the Eleven and the others – at the conclusion of the tomb scene (24:9), the conclusion of the Emmaus story (24:33), and at the opening of the story of Jesus' appearance to the plenary group (24:36). It

14. J. Fitzmyer, *The Gospel According to Luke I-IX*, p. 294

is to this wider group that the risen Jesus addresses his understanding of Scripture and his mission mandate, which concludes: 'You are witnesses to this.' (24:48)

The mandate to witness is clearly not limited to the Twelve just as, from the point of view of mission, the mandate given to the seventy-two did not differ from the mandate to mission given to the Twelve (Lk 9:1-10; 10 1-20). So too at the beginning of Acts it is to the whole group Jesus addresses himself when he says, 'you will receive power when the Holy Spirit comes on you, and then you will be my witnesses not only in Jerusalem but throughout Judaea and Samaria, and indeed to the ends of the earth.' (1:8).

We have already commented on Acts 1:21-22; two other texts which seem to limit the idea of 'witness' to the apostles form part of Peter's speeches:

> Now I, and those with me, can witness to everything he did throughout the countryside of Judaea and in Jerusalem itself: and also to the fact that they killed him by hanging him on a tree, yet three days afterwards God raised him to life and allowed him to be seen not by the whole people but only by certain witnesses God had chosen beforehand. Now we are those witnesses – we have eaten and drunk with him after his resurrection from the dead and he has ordered us to proclaim this to the people and to tell them that God has appointed him to judge everyone, alive or dead. (Acts 10:39-42)

> But God raised him from the dead, and for many days he appeared to those who had accompanied him from Galilee to Jerusalem: and it is to these same companions of his who are now his witnesses before our people. (Acts 13:31)

If the risen Jesus appeared to those who had accompanied him from Galilee to Jerusalem (13:31a), and Luke tells the story of Jesus' appearance to the two disciples of Emmaus, the two disciples clearly fit the description of 'these same companions of his who are now his witnesses before all the people.' (13:31b) Further, if God allowed the risen Jesus to be seen 'not by the whole people but only by certain witnesses God had chosen beforehand' (10:41a), those who have eaten and drunk with him after the resurrection and were part of the mission mandate (10:41b), the two disciples are part of this group as Luke has shown them to be in the final chapter of his Gospel. Although this description of witness excludes Paul, the Emmaus disciples are part of the corps that constitutes the Lucan witness.

In Luke's understanding, a witness is someone who can testify not only to Jesus' ministry from Galilee to Jerusalem and his death and resurrection, but also to the significance of all that this means in the light of the decisive interpretation of the risen Jesus. As the story of Emmaus showed clearly, being an 'eyewitness' to the deeds and words of Jesus is not in itself a qualification for being a 'minister of the word': thrown back on their own resources the two disciples were manifestly incapable of making sense of what happened to Jesus. On their own they were foolish and slow of heart (Lk 24:25). Their confusion was shared by the Eleven and the others when all together they read their experience of the risen Jesus as a shared fright at seeing a ghost (24:37). The shared confusion and fright of the assembled disciples is changed only in the revealing word of the risen Jesus, who explained the meaning of his own words during the ministry and opened their minds to understanding the words of Scriptures (24:44-47). Dillon remarks:

> Considering the nature of their experiences, these Easter disciples qualify as 'witnesses' of the pure gift of God's revelation, not as specially competent vouchers for its empirical foundation or historical veracity.[15]

Luke's careful structure of chapter 24 of his Gospel in exploring the dialectic between the paschal events and the disciples' failure to understand them serves to show that the disciples as eye-witnesses will become witnesses only after they have received God's decisive revelation in the risen Jesus and the gift of the Holy Spirit. Through that double experience which happens to them, they are then qualified as witnesses to Jesus' resurrection, and in that light can testify to the saving significance of all that Jesus did and said during his earthly ministry.

The function of the witness is to testify to Jesus whose death and

---

15. R. Dillon, *From Eye-witnesses to Ministers of the Word* p. 292

resurrection gives significance to the deeds and words in the ministry, and whose paschal words, opening up the Scriptures, reveal the meaning of all this. This combination of paschal event and revealing word, developed so surely in the Emmaus narrative, forms the content of the witnesses' testimony, one which must continue to remain faithful to a tradition received from the risen Lord.

The testimony of the witnesses is needed precisely because the claims about Jesus are being contested in an atmosphere of opposition and hostility. A verdict has already been passed on Jesus, and Luke is concerned to vindicate Jesus through the appointed witnesses who can testify to what God has accomplished in him. In his study of the New Testament concept of witness, A. Trites has observed:

> Luke is concerned to offer legally acceptable evidence for Christ which will be admitted as valid in the wider law court of life itself. That this is in fact the case is attested by a striking formal characteristic of Acts. Again and again everything is established in accordance with the principle stated in Deuteronomy 19:15; this is the law of the two or three witnesses which is so important to Luke. He accepts the Old Testament principle that everything must be established at the mouth of two or three witnesses, and formulates his historical material in accordance with it.[16]

Thus the principle of twofoldness becomes important for testimony. Pairs of witnesses attest the case for Jesus in their preaching ministry: Peter and John (3:1; 4:13); Barnabas and Saul (11:26 12:25); Paul and Barnabas (13:43; 15:2); Judas and Silas (15:32); Barnabas and Mark (15:39); Paul and Silas (15:40; 16:19); Silas and Timothy (17:14;18:5). Above all, in Acts there is the complementary witness of Peter and Paul. Luke describes Paul as a 'minister of the word' and a 'witness' (22:15; 23:11; 26:16), and it has been noted how Luke presents the apostleship and witness of Paul in parallel with that of Peter.[17] That principle of

---

16. A. Trites, *The New Testament Concept of Witness*, (Cambridge: Cambridge University Press, 1977) p. 133.
17. Cf. J. Fenton, 'The Order of the Miracles Performed by Peter and Paul in Acts' in *Expository Times* 77 (1965-6), pp. 381-383.

double witness reflects a practice that Luke already followed in the Gospel – from the sending out of the disciples two by two (Lk 10:1ff) to the witness of the two angels and the two disciples of Emmaus. And as Trites notes further: 'when the apostles say "We are witnesses to these things, and so is the Holy Spirit" (Acts 5:32), one can fairly assume that Luke intends his readers to take these two sources of testimony as offering compelling evidence for the historical foundation of the Christian faith.'[18]

Luke summarises the content of this witness as 'the word of God' or simply as 'the word' (*ho logos* and *to rema*) - terms which, as we have already seen, are used by Luke in the Gospel to describe the message and work of Jesus. E. Haenchen has argued that the word of God is the fundamental link between the Gospel and Acts:

> It is this 'Word of God' which fills the time after Pentecost; this Word is furthermore the message concerning Jesus, belief in whom brings forgiveness of sins and deliverance in the judgement. Here, then, is the clamp which fastens the two eras together and justifies, indeed demands, the continuation of the first book (depicting the life of Jesus as a time of salvation) in a second; for the salvation which has appeared must be preached to all peoples, and the very portrayal of this mission will serve an awakening of belief, and hence the attainment of that salvation.[19]

The visit of salvation accomplished in Jesus is proclaimed as a liberating message first to the Jews and then to the Gentiles. The message that is proclaimed is literally 'the word of this salvation' (13:26). Just as Luke showed in the Gospel how the word spoken by Jesus was effective, a word/event, so he shows in Acts how the word is a force which cuts to the heart (2:37) and which spreads successfully and widely (6:7; 12:24; 19:20). The word of this salvation is not an empty word; it is *dabar*. It accomplishes what it is sent to do. Through that word the saving work of Jesus continues.

This is illustrated in Acts through the healing ministry of Peter and

18. A. Trites, *The New Testament Concept of Witness*, p. 135
19. E. Haenchen, *The Acts of the Apostles*, p. 98

Paul. When these two ministers of the word speak to the crippled there is healing through their authoritative word (3:6; 14:10). The continuation of the healing ministry of Jesus is carried out in the name of Jesus and in the power of his presence. Thus Peter says to the paralytic: 'Aeneas, Jesus Christ cures you' (9:34) – a healing which moves the inhabitants of Lydda and Sharon to be converted to the Lord. The authority of the salvific word is seen at its most dramatic when Peter and Paul, like Jesus in the ministry (Lk 7:11-17; 8:49-56), deliver individuals from death through the power of the word (Acts 9:40; 20:10). The work of salvation is seen to be extended through the effective word of those chosen to be witnesses. As Jesus' prophetic ministry was one mighty in deed and word before all the people, so the prophetic ministry of his witnesses is seen to follow the same pattern. Luke described the miracles of Jesus in the traditional language of signs (Lk 11:16,29; 23:8) and mighty works (Lk 10:13; 19:37); in the same way he describes the miracles wrought by his followers (Acts 2:43; 4:30; 5:12; 14:3.27; 15:12). As the historical Jesus was attested by God through the miracles and signs God worked in him (Acts 2:22) the same is true of those who witness to the risen Lord. Both their deeds and their words form the 'word of salvation' to the people.

The prophetic pattern in the lives of those who witness to what God has done in Jesus is demonstrated not only in the word of salvation but in the prophet's destiny which they share with Jesus. Prophecy and mission are united in the life of the witness. In the Gospel Luke presented Jesus as one who understood his own mission in the pattern of persecution experienced by Israel's prophets (Lk 13:33) and who warned his own followers that the disciples' experience of suffering and persecution would form an essential part of their testimony as witnesses (Lk 21:12-13). The tradition they are committed to keeping alive is not only a tradition about Jesus, it is a tradition of experiencing suffering in Jesus' name, one in which they will re-enact the journey of their Master (cf. Acts 10:39). In that light, Jesus' statements about his own passion and death are not limited to interpreting the significance of his own divinely appointed destiny; they disclose the meaning of what is going on in suffering of his followers. Dillon has commented:

This is the reason why instruction in the mystery of the passion, from the perspective of its Easter termination, was found to be the thematic bond uniting the three Easter pericopes into an integral literary statement. This was the revelation which prepared observers of the *triduum paschale* for their mission as 'witnesses,' inaugurating 'from Jerusalem' a Church history in which the gospel's propagation and the witnesses' suffering were to be essentially, necessarily interrelated.[20]

The understanding of Jesus' *exodos* becomes the principal interpretative key to understanding the violent persecution that will surely befall his witnesses.

When the Sanhedrin which condemned Jesus calls in Peter and John to warn them not to preach in the name of Jesus, the apostles reply that they cannot but preach about what they have seen and heard (4:18-20). In the light of this experience of threat, the whole community prays, recalling how the condemnation of Jesus whom God anointed was for the purpose of accomplishing the predetermined plan of God (4:23-31). Because they can now see the divine plan in the persecution Jesus suffered, they do not pray to avoid persecution themselves; their understanding of the value and necessity of Jesus' suffering illumines what will happen to them as his followers. They ask God to help them to preach boldly and to attest their word through miracles. Luke shows how their prayer is answered when the Holy Spirit fills them with the power to preach boldly (cf. Lk 21:14f.). And when all the apostles are arrested and appear before the Sanhedrin their boldness is evident in their response to the floggings and the warnings that they receive: 'they left the presence of the Sanhedrin glad to have had the honour of suffering humiliation for the sake of the name.' (5:41)

The third trial before the Sanhedrin ends in the sentence of death on Stephen and the active persecution and dispersal of the Christian community. The prophetic destiny of the witness who works wonders in Israel but experiences repudiation and violent death is seen clearly in the ministry and martyrdom of Stephen. Clearly Luke does not strictly limit the ministry of the word to the apostles (*pace* 6:4): both Stephen and

---

20. R. Dillon, *From Eye-witnesses to Ministers of the Word* p. 296

Philip, chosen to ensure the social welfare of the poor in the community, will be seen as active ministers of the word. Stephen 'was filled with grace and power and began to work miracles and great signs among the people.' (6:8) It is unclear from Luke's text why the Hellenistic Jews of the diaspora would take issue with Stephen; more important for Luke's purpose is the fact that Stephen's rejection is another illustration of the fate of the wonder-working prophet at the hands of Israel. Moses and Jesus were prophets mighty in deed and word (Acts 7:22; Lk 24:19) who suffered rejection at the hands of Israel (Acts 7:39ff) because 'you are always resisting the Holy Spirit, just as your ancestors used to do. Can you name a single prophet your ancestors never persecuted?' (7:52) Stephen's own rejection is in line with the rejection of Moses and the eschatological prophet like Moses. Israel's rejection of its prophets has remained unchanged, and Luke emphasises that further when he recounts the martyrdom of Stephen after the pattern of Jesus' own death (7:55-60).

Israel's consistent and defiant rejection of God's messengers is proved anew in the bitter persecution of the Church in Jerusalem (8:1ff). The occasion 'when the blood of your witness (*martus*) Stephen was being shed' (22:30) has direct consequences for the scope of the mission: the word of God is carried beyond the threshold of Israel. Persecution provides the first impetus for the missionary enterprise.

Although Luke preserves the formal transition to the Gentile mission to Peter's inspired decision (Acts 10) and presents Paul as the missionary to the Gentiles *par excellence*, there is little doubt that the missionary outreach from Jerusalem was more complex than this stylised presentation. Before Stephen's martyrdom there is already a Christian community at Damascus (cf. 9:19 ff), which is some two hundred miles from Jerusalem, and we know that Paul did not begin the Christian communities at Antioch, Ephesus or Rome. Philip goes to Samaria where he preaches Christ and works miracles: through his ministry the possessed are liberated and the paralytics and cripples are cured (5:4-8). He is the one who, like the risen Jesus on the road from Jerusalem, reveals the meaning of the passion through the exposition of the Scriptures (8:26ff). Unnamed Hellenist refugees from Jerusalem go to Phoenicia and

Cyprus and Antioch where their mission is largely devoted to the Jews. 'Some of them, however, who came from Cyprus and Cyrene, went to Antioch where they started preaching to the Greeks, proclaiming the Goods News of the Lord Jesus to them as well. The Lord helped them, and a great number believed and were converted to the Lord.' (11:20-21) This acceptance of Gentiles into the Christian community as a work of the Holy Spirit begins a dramatic new development in the history of the Church - one which involves the Church in Jerusalem, Barnabas, and eventually Paul himself (11:21-26).

The mission to Samaria is given formal apostolic approval when Peter and John lay hands on the Samaritans who then receive the Holy Spirit (8:14-17). Thus the second term of the geographical conspectus of witness is reached – 'not only in Jerusalem but throughout Judaea and Samaria' (1:8) – a stage that reflects Jesus' own journey and teaching (cf. Lk 9:51-56; 10:29-37; 17:11-19). So too the mission to the Gentiles is given formal apostolic approval through Peter's divinely inspired direction which receives the approval of the apostolic Church (10:1-11:18).

In the Gospel the centurion of Capernaum, a man of piety, communicates his belief in the authoritative word of Jesus through a delegation of Jewish elders; Jesus commends this Gentile because 'not even in Israel have I found faith like this.' (Lk 7:9) This story clearly foreshadows the acceptability of pious Gentiles in the eyes of God. In Acts the centurion Cornelius, whose piety is emphasised (10;2.4.22.30), receives instructions from God to send for Simon Peter. He immediately acts on this word. While the delegation is on its way Peter sees a vision which he finds difficult to interpret. When the delegation arrives Peter receives instructions from the Spirit to go with these men who are agents of the Spirit. The men tell Peter the source of their request: Cornelius received a visit from an angel (10:22; cf. 10:30; 11:13). It is the visit of God which has initiated this new development. As Haenchen has noted: 'By the end of the story the reader will no longer forget that it was God who brought about the whole of these events: and thereby instituted the mission to the Gentiles.'[21]

---

21. E. Haenchen, *The Acts of the Apostles*, p. 358

When Peter reaches his destination Cornelius has already gathered all his relatives and close friends. The apostle tells the centurion that 'it is forbidden for Jews to mix with people of another race and visit them, but God has made it clear to me that I must not call anyone profane or unclean.' (10:29) To this Cornelius simply tells the story of what happened to him and asks Peter for the message God has given him. Peter shares his new understanding that God does not have favourites, 'but that anybody of any nationality who fears God and does what is right is acceptable to him.' (10:35) And while he is still addressing the household the Spirit comes down on all of them in a miniature Pentecost (10:46). Given this act of God, Peter finds that he cannot refuse water-baptism to people who are already baptized in the Spirit: he gives orders for all to be baptized in the name of Jesus Christ.

However, on his return to Jerusalem Peter is criticised for visiting the uncircumcised and eating with them. In response he interprets his recent insight and actions as divinely inspired; and in that light the apostolic Church concedes and praises God who can 'grant even the pagans the repentance that leads to life.' (11:18) Thus the admission of the Gentiles receives the formal apostolic approval of the Church.

The account of Peter's conversion of the household of Cornelius has obvious programmatic significance for Acts: now the transition to the third and final stage of witness 'to the ends of earth' (1:8) is begun with the approval and validation of the Jerusalem Church.[22] Central to Luke's story is the portrayal of Peter and Cornelius as chosen instruments who are acted upon by the power of God. In developing the story through acts of divine intervention Luke's theological purpose is clear: the admission of the Gentiles is the choice of God who reveals his purpose through acting in history.

Luke underlines this forcefully when he tells the story of the apostolic council in Jerusalem which is called to settle the question of whether the Gentiles are obliged to be circumcised and keep the Law of Moses (15:1-29). Peter's speech emphasises how the admission of the Gentiles was God's choice which was made effective through his own ministry. When

22. Cf. M. Dibelius, 'The Conversion of Cornelius' in *Studies in the Acts of the Apostles*, pp. 109 ff.

James speaks he summarises the principal argument: 'Symeon has related how God first visited the Gentiles to take out of them a people for his name.' (15:14 RSV) The verb Luke uses, *episkeptesthai*, is the same as that used in the canticle of Zechariah to denote God's act of salvation in visiting his people (Lk 1:68.78). Now, through his saving visit, God has made known his choice of the Gentiles, a truth that was recognised in the Gospel by another Spirit-filled 'Simeon' (Lk 2:32). For Luke, the development of the mission is an elaboration of God's saving act in electing the Gentiles himself.

The man who symbolises the new act of God in choosing the Gentiles is the apostle Paul. In his three accounts of Paul's conversion (9:1ff; 22:1ff; 26:12ff.) Luke elaborates on his fundamental theme of God's decisive action in history: the risen Lord acts directly in choosing Paul as 'my chosen instrument to bring my name before pagans and pagan kings and before the people of Israel' (9:16). The Lord takes the initiative in personally appearing to Paul to appoint him as servant and witness (26:16). His election by the risen Lord is closely associated with suffering (9:17), and in this Paul will follow the prophetic pattern of Jesus' life as the wonder-worker who is rejected by Israel – even to the point where Paul goes up to Jerusalem willing to die for the name of the Lord Jesus (21:13). His authenticity as an apostle and a witness will be shown in re-enacting the journey of Jesus.

Paul adapts his missionary programme to the apostolic pattern of witnessing first to the Jews and then to the Gentiles, and this is expressed programmatically when Paul declares with Barnabas: 'We had to declare the word of God to you first, but since you have rejected it, since you do not think yourselves worthy of eternal life, we must turn to the pagans.' (13:46) Again rejection acts as the impetus for the missionary outreach. When Paul is stoned in Lystra at the instigation of Jews from Antioch and Iconium and left for dead, that experience clearly informs his axiomatic words to the disciples: 'We all have to experience many hardships..before we enter the kingdom of God.' (14:22) The necessity of suffering, one which was argued so forcefully on the road to Emmaus (Lk 24:26), is true of the Lord and the Lord's disciples. Luke shows how Paul does indeed suffer in the course of witnessing to the Lord and carrying his message to the ends of the earth in Rome.

Luke's last portrayal of Paul shows the apostle persuading the Jews in Rome about Jesus, using Moses and the prophets to confirm his own testimony. Aptly, the last thing Paul has to say, using the testimony of the Holy Spirit, is to proclaim the success of the Gentile mission: 'Understand, then, that this salvation of God has been sent to the pagans; they will listen to it.' (28:28)

From the prophetic note sounded by Simeon in the Lucan infancy narrative (2:32) to Paul's affirmation at the end of Acts, Luke develops his understanding of the universalism of the Gospel. The salvation of God, brought in the person of Jesus and first offered to Israel, will be extended to the Gentiles by the chosen witnesses of the Lord. The note of rejection which Simeon sounded (Lk 2:34) is seen to happen from the opening scene in Nazareth (Lk 4:28ff), through Jesus' ministry and death, to the suffering and rejection of his witnesses. This rejection is part of the divine plan: in the midst of it the word of forgiveness is proclaimed insistently as God's response to human frailty.

The process of rejection serves another purpose in the divine plan: it shows the gradual emergence of the word of salvation from its ancestry in the people of Israel to its extension to all peoples. Salvation is not the exclusive property of those who have inherited the tradition of Israel: 'Then there will be weeping and grinding of teeth, when you see Abraham and Isaac and Jacob and all the prophets in the kingdom of God, and yourselves turned outside. And men from east and west, from north and south, will come to take their places at the feast in the kingdom of God.' (Lk 13:28-29) Through what God has accomplished in Jesus, and through the effective word of salvation proclaimed in the lives of his witnesses, the ends of the earth can hear the Goods News that God has visited the peoples.

Conclusion

IN WRITING the story of Jesus and the story of the early Church, Luke traces the continuous development of salvation from its beginnings in Israel, through its fulfilment in the mission of Jesus, to its proclamation in the apostolic and post-apostolic Church. Through his historical perspective Luke gives a sense of continuity, showing that the God of Abraham, Isaac and Jacob, who spoke through Moses and the prophets, is the same God who raised up a prophet like Moses in his servant Jesus whom he glorified. This same God has revealed that the salvation accomplished through Jesus must be offered to the Gentiles.

This study has attempted to show how Luke's theological venture is supported by his adoption of two Old Testament concepts, the visit of God and the word of God, which prove to be fast links not only between the past of Israel and the present of Jesus' life and mission, but between the latter and the future spread of Jesus' message of salvation to the ends of the earth.

In the infancy narrative we saw how Luke carefully brings representative figures of Israel's tradition into the Gospel to recognise God's salvation in Jesus. These people, whose piety is centred on the Law and on the Temple in Jerusalem, are seen to have their ancient hopes answered: God has kept his promise and visited his people by raising up a power for salvation in the House of David. In Jesus God saves. Appropriately the name of Jesus will spell his total identification with salvation: he is the saviour, Christ the Lord. Jesus brings salvation to people in a ministry which is inseparable from himself: through what he does and says, through the new life he brings, the truth is proclaimed that God has visited his people.

Jesus' whole mission is one destined by God to lead to Jerusalem, the place of salvation and the place of judgement for those who refuse to recognise the time of the visit of God. But while he recounts Jesus indicting Jerusalem with the same vigour and language as the ancient prophets, Luke reserves the full revelation of salvation to the gift of the risen Jesus. And this is done for the first time on the road to Emmaus.

We saw too how Luke gives support to the continuity between the time of Israel and the time of Jesus by his development of the idea of the word of God. The Spirit of God which moved the prophets of Israel is again active from the infancy narrative to announce the new word of fulfilment: God's ancient purposes are to be accomplished in Jesus. In Mary the word of God becomes event through the power of the Spirit. Luke picks up a theme declared in the Priestly creation story, the revelation to Abraham and the prophetic witness: nothing said by God is impossible, for God's word is inherently active.

This theme is developed throughout Jesus' ministry when Luke illustrates how the word that Jesus speaks is the word that comes from God. In the authoritative word spoken by Jesus Luke brings the Hebraism of word-event, *dabar*, into the Gospel: the word of God which accomplishes what it was sent to do is evident in the word of Jesus which effects what it says. Jesus re-creates by saying. The power which invests Jesus with this authority is the Spirit, the *dynamis* of God which marks the beginning of Jesus' ministry.

From the first scene of Jesus' prophetic ministry in Nazareth Luke celebrates the fulfilment of ancient words and acknowledges Jesus as being in line with the tradition of the rejected prophets of Israel. Through Jesus' whole journey Luke recapitulates the career of the prophet Moses: Jesus is the eschatological prophet like Moses who will reveal God's word and face rejection; eventually he will have to suffer and die that the exodus can have its completion.

Thus when the risen Lord discloses the significance of his death it is a revelation which begins with Moses and all the prophets. To understand who Jesus is, necessarily means to understand him within the larger context of the experience of Israel. The whole mission of Jesus is a saving word of salvation; and the disciple is seen to first understand that word as saving when he is gifted with its disclosure of the way to Emmaus.

In the death of Jesus a central question emerges: is the connection between Israel and Jesus severed when Jesus is rejected by the chief priests and the leaders and handed over to be crucified? In what sense can God have visited his people in the death of Jesus? No matter how powerful in deed and word Jesus was during his ministry, how can his death be seen as the fulfilment of ancient promises? Does not the death of Jesus annul the claims that he would be the one to set Israel free? How can a word of salvation emerge from the debris of Calvary? What can discipleship mean any more after the death of the master? In all this there is the fundamental question: what purpose is there in the death of Jesus? Without the answer to that question there can be no proclamation of a message of salvation.

This question is asked and answered by Luke in his Emmaus account and, because of this, the story acts as a bridge between the death of the mighty prophet and the understanding of Christ's suffering and death as necessary for glory. Through the revelation of the risen Jesus, the disciples are able to move from their experience of Jesus as a mighty prophet to the messianic hope of Israel via the suffering and death of Jesus.

We discussed the story of Emmaus as an experience of divine revelation, an encounter with the risen Lord who interprets the recent happenings in Jerusalem through his interpretation of the Scriptures. Outside that revelation the death of Jesus remains a depressing enigma to the disciples, for its meaning is hidden from them. They cannot understand the death of Jesus unless the veil of its mystery is parted for them. To be part of what has taken place without knowing what was going on, to see and hear without perceiving and understanding – this forms the gulf between being an eye-witness of an event and being a witness of its meaning. For Luke the hiddenness of the passion's meaning serves to highlight the need for the revelation of salvation: the disciples must await the initiative of God if they are to move from bewilderment to understanding.

So, it is the mystery of the passion which is at the heart of the Emmaus dialogue. That mystery is revealed only by the risen Jesus, and when he uses the Scriptures as his source for enlightenment he places what has happened within the frame of fulfilment. Rather than sever the relationship between the hope of Israel and the person of Jesus, the passion confirms it; it was essential for the fulfilment of God's purposes revealed in Scripture. It was necessary for the Christ to suffer and so enter his glory – a truth that is already available through the witness of all the prophets. In the revelation of the risen Jesus Luke celebrates the end of the passion's concealment. That time is now over. We look to a new time when the significance of Jesus' death can be proclaimed by those who are witnesses to his resurrection.

As Emmaus is the central section of Luke's composite resurrection narrative we discussed the story as part of a chapter which is dominated by the conflict between paschal witness and human reaction, between Easter event and hiddenness of meaning.

The two disciples of Emmaus became part of the plenary group, which is visited by the risen Jesus and receives his final instructions. Luke shows again how the mystery of the passion remains concealed until the visitor opens the disciples' minds to understand how the whole corpus of Scripture has its fulfilment in the risen Jesus. In this, the link is again reinforced between the tradition of Israel and what has been accomplished in Jesus.

Further, in placing the mandate to preach repentance for the forgive-ness of sins to the Gentiles within the tradition of Israel's Scripture Luke declares the continuity between the word of God to Israel and the missionary activity of the apostolic and post-apostolic Church, a conti-nuity verified through the new word of the risen Jesus. However, Luke is insistent that the disciples will be able to follow the mandate of the risen Jesus only after they have been empowered to do so by the Holy Spirit.

We reflected how Luke structures the beginning of Acts to show the Easter community beginning with the risen Jesus, the Twelve, and the Holy Spirit. With the ascension the visit of God in Jesus comes to a close; he will come again in the same way on the last day. Instead of the Son of Man coming in an imminent parousia, the Spirit comes at Pentecost – the Feast of the Renewal of the Covenant. Again there is the link between this new act of God and what God has done in the past in Israel.

Luke holds that continuity secure. The God who appeared to Moses on Sinai to establish his covenant with Israel is the same God who comes in the Spirit to renew his covenant with Israel. Israel still remains the first chosen. And the word of salvation that is preached is first preached to Israel.

Finally, in our reflection on the identity and function of the Lucan witness we saw how in testifying to the resurrection the witnesses represent the case for Jesus to the Jews who have already passed their verdict on him. God has attested Jesus by raising him from the dead. This case, presented by witnesses of his resurrection, is supported by the testimony of Scripture, the Holy Spirit, and by the wonders done in the name of Jesus.

In keeping alive the tradition of Jesus the witnesses re-enact in their own lives the divinely destined mission of the wonder-working prophet rejected by Israel. This rejection is evident in the persecution of the Church in Jerusalem; persecution acts as an impetus for missionary activity.

Here Luke confronts a major theological problem: how do you justify the irreversible break between the Jewish Law and a Gentile Church while preserving your claim that the Christian community is still rooted in Judaism and is its natural successor?

Luke answers this by showing this dramatic shift as a divinely destined act rather than an unfortunate outcome of history through using the notions of the visit of God and the word of God. Peter and Cornelius are acted upon by God; what happens to them is a result of divine intervention. Thus when Peter and James state the case for the acceptance of Gentiles into the community without demanding circumcision, their case is framed by the argument that this decision is an outcome of the visit of God and is supported by the word of God in Israel's Scripture. So Luke maintains the link with the tradition of Israel while at the same time declaring that this new act is the work of the God of Abraham, Isaac and Jacob. The word of salvation proclaimed to the Gentiles and their acceptance into the community of believers is the work of God and the word of God.

In carefully maintaining the chain of continuity from God's promises to Israel, through the ministry and exaltation of Jesus, to the missionary activity of the apostolic and post-apostolic Church, Luke offers his readers a profound historical and theological perspective to God's

revelation and salvation in history. Awareness of the divine plan provides the followers of Jesus with deep religious roots in the past and gives
substance to their hope that God will continue to care for the community
in the future.

The Spirit which gave birth to the apostolic Church is still active in the
life of the community: that force enables the community to dare again
and to face rejection and loss in the overriding belief that God's purposes
are being worked out in history. This theological outlook is neither
triumphalistic nor fatalistic: it is based securely on the pattern of Jesus'
life, death and resurrection, which is given as the way to all his disciples.
This is the way that led to Emmaus and leads beyond it.